Madame Blavatsky

Madame Blavatsky

THE MOTHER OF MODERN SPIRITUALITY

GARY LACHMAN

JEREMY P. TARCHER/PENGUIN
a member of Penguin Group (USA) Inc.
New York

JEREMY P. TARCHER/PENGUIN
Published by the Penguin Group
Penguin Group (USA) Inc., 375 Hudson Street, New York, New York 10014, USA •
Penguin Group (Canada), 90 Eglinton Avenue East, Suite 700, Toronto, Ontario M4P 2Y3,
Canada (a division of Pearson Penguin Canada Inc.) • Penguin Books Ltd,
80 Strand, London WC2R 0RL, England • Penguin Ireland, 25 St Stephen's Green,
Dublin 2, Ireland (a division of Penguin Books Ltd) • Penguin Group (Australia),
707 Collins Street, Melbourne, Victoria 3008, Australia (a division of Pearson Australia
Group Pty Ltd) • Penguin Books India Pvt Ltd, 11 Community Centre, Panchsheel Park,
New Delhi–110 017, India • Penguin Group (NZ), 67 Apollo Drive, Rosedale, Auckland 0632,
New Zealand (a division of Pearson New Zealand Ltd) • Penguin Books, Rosebank Office Park,
181 Jan Smuts Avenue, Parktown North 2193, South Africa • Penguin China, B7 Jaiming Center,
27 East Third Ring Road North, Chaoyang District, Beijing 100020, China

Penguin Books Ltd, Registered Offices: 80 Strand, London WC2R 0RL, England

Most Tarcher/Penguin books are available at special quantity discounts for bulk purchase
for sales promotions, premiums, fund-raising, and educational needs. Special books
or book excerpts also can be created to fit specific needs. For details, write
Penguin Group (USA) Inc. Special Markets, 375 Hudson Street, New York, NY 10014.

Library of Congress Cataloging-in-Publication Data

Lachman, Gary, date.
Madame Blavatsky : the mother of modern spirituality / Gary Lachman.
p.   cm.
Includes bibliographical references and index.
ISBN 978-1-58542-863-2
1. Blavatsky, H. P. (Helena Petrovna), 1831–1891.   2. Theosophists—Biography.   I. Title.
BP585.B6L33   2012   2012026169
299'.934092—dc23
[B]

Printed in the United States of America
1 3 5 7 9 10 8 6 4 2

Book design by Meighan Cavanaugh

To the Masters,

whoever they are.

I was in search of the unknown . . .

—HELENA PETROVNA BLAVATSKY

Contents

WHO WAS MADAME BLAVATSKY?

O f all the names associated with modern spirituality, that of Madame Helena Petrovna Blavatsky—or HPB, as she preferred to be called—is surely one of the most controversial. Although she died more than a century ago, Blavatsky's name still turns up in serious discussions about "ancient wisdom," "secret teachings," and "inner knowledge," and it is generally agreed that her Theosophical Society (or TS, as it is often called), which she founded in New York in 1875, with her colleagues Henry Steel Olcott and William Quan Judge, was more or less the official starting point of the modern spiritual revival. By "modern spiritual revival," I mean our contemporary widespread interest in a direct, immediate knowledge and experience of spiritual reality, and in a more profound relationship to the cosmos than traditional religions and mainstream science can provide. Represented by a heterogeneous collection of different occult, esoteric, or spiritual pursuits, today this revival is popularly, if often mistakenly, associated with the "New Age." This grassroots hunger for a sense of meaning and purpose that the official organs can no longer supply can be traced to the nineteenth century—indeed, in this book I will look at some of the sources of it—and can be said, I believe, to have been inspired by Blavatsky. In fact, as early as 1970, in an article for *McCall's* magazine, the novelist Kurt Vonnegut dubbed Blavatsky "the Founding Mother of the Occult in America."[1]

But one doesn't need to be a Theosophist to have felt Blavatsky's considerable presence. Her contribution to modern spiritual thought, and to modern culture in general, is so great that it can easily be overlooked, in the way that some prominent feature of the landscape can be overlooked—that is to say, taken for granted. Yet if Blavatsky's offering to our modern spiritual consciousness was to be suddenly removed, it would drag along with it practically everything we associate with the very notion of modern spirituality. And those of us who had taken Blavatsky's contribution for granted would certainly notice the loss.

To press my point: Anyone who meditates, or considers himself a Buddhist, or is interested in reincarnation, or has thought about karma, or pursues "higher consciousness," or has wondered about Atlantis, or thinks the ancients might have known a few things that we don't, or reads about esotericism, or who frequents an "alternative" health center or food shop, would be aware of it if modern spirituality somehow became "HPB free." And this, of course, would include quite a few people who never heard of Blavatsky, or who have only the vaguest idea of what Theosophy is or of its place in the history of Western consciousness. Which is to say most people. If nothing else, our endless fascination with the "wisdom of the East" would not have arrived, or would have taken much longer to get here, if it were not for her efforts and those of her early followers. It's been said that all of modern

Russian literature emerged from Nikolai Gogol's short story "The Overcoat." It can equally be said that practically all modern occultism and esotericism emerged from the ample bosom of his younger countrywoman and contemporary, HPB.

Yet, although she was one of the most remarkable women of the nineteenth century, to the general public, Blavatsky is virtually unknown. When I've mentioned her in recent times—when asked what I was working on at the moment—more often than not the response was a shaking head and a baffled look, although a few acquaintances mustered some questions like "Wasn't she a psychic?" or a "fraud?" or a "charlatan?" Yet, those who are aware of her, and of her contribution to Western thought, have a different view. Like the historian of esotericism Christopher Bamford, they wonder why she is not, as Bamford believes she should be, counted with Marx, Nietzsche, and Freud as one of the "creators of the twentieth century"?[2]

We may think Bamford pitches Blavatsky's claims too high, but he does so for good reason. By the time of Blavatsky's death in London in 1891, the Theosophical movement had spread from New York to India, Europe, and beyond, and included among its devotees some important names, such as Thomas Edison and Mohandas Gandhi.[3] And by the early years of the twentieth century, it was a force, as the saying goes, to be reckoned with, informing major developments, not only in spirituality and esotericism, but in politics, art, religion, and much more. Some of the individuals who were influenced, positively or negatively, by the Madame include the poet T. S. Eliot, who lampooned her in *The Waste Land*, a seminal work in modern poetry[4]; the artist Wassily Kandinsky, whose abstract paintings are informed by Theosophical ideas[5]; L. Frank

Baum, the creator of *The Wizard of Oz*, who became a member of the Theosophical Society in 1892[6]; Abner Doubleday, Civil War hero and purported inventor of baseball, who became president of the American branch of the Theosophical Society in 1878; the composer Alexander Scriabin, whose lush, ecstatic work is rife with Theosophical motifs; and Jawaharlal Nehru, India's first prime minister, who was initiated into the Theosophical Society by Annie Besant, the socialist and freethinker who converted to Theosophy after meeting Blavatsky, and who, as president of the society, helped India win its independence.[7] Even Einstein is said to have kept a well-thumbed copy of Blavatsky's *magnum opus*, *The Secret Doctrine*, on his desk, and some Theosophists have gone as far as to infer that the inspiration for Einstein's famous formula, $E = mc^2$, came from that dense and weighty tome, a claim many perhaps will find too hard to swallow.[8]

We may not want to follow Blavatsky's supporters this far, yet one has to ask why, having had such a huge effect on modern culture, outside of the "esoteric community" Blavatsky's name is not more well known? Feminists alone, one would think, would have caught on to her long ago. Yet even to use the phrase "well known" at all in the context of HPB is something of a misnomer, even within the esoteric community, if by "well known" we mean "accurately known," and not merely famous—or infamous.

As anyone who has tried to write seriously about HPB discovers, the question "Who was Madame Blavatsky?" isn't easy to answer, not the least because of the considerable difficulties Blavatsky herself puts in its way. To say that HPB is a bundle of contradictions is not only an understatement, it is to repeat what practically everyone who has written about Blavatsky has said.

Blavatsky spoke about herself and her life frequently, with great panache and at great length. But as her biographer Peter Washington points out, she "rarely said exactly the same thing twice."[9] Rudolf Steiner, who borrowed more from Blavatsky than his followers would care to admit, tactfully remarked that she exhibited a "lack of consistency in her external behaviour," a trait which Steiner accounted for by her Russian soul.[10] It would be relatively easy for a resolute researcher to tally up the many discrepancies in her accounts of herself and declare that HPB had, at best, a flexible grasp of the idea of truth—notwithstanding the Theosophical motto that there was "no religion higher than truth." Yet, after a time, one begins to wonder—at least I did—whether there was some conscious purpose behind the Marx Brothers mayhem and double talk, and one understands how one HPB scholar, K. Paul Johnson, came to feel that she made "a deliberate effort . . . to appear untrustworthy and suspicious and to render the biographer's task impossible."[11]

Some, confronting this problem, have collapsed in exasperation. The historian of religion Maria Carlson, whose study of Theosophy in Russia repeats many of the myths and misconceptions about HPB, concludes that "an accurate and completely factual biography of this remarkable woman will never be written."[12] For James Santucci, a historian more amenable to HPB and Theosophy, Blavatsky "remains an enigma to any fair-minded investigator of her life and writings."[13] Johnson, perhaps the most controversial HPB scholar of recent times, remarks that in Blavatsky's case, "the scholar's efforts to unravel the truth are frustrated by the deliberate occultation of history."[14] Sylvia Cranston, whose enormous but not quite exhaustive account presents the most complete "pro-HPB" view, cautions: "After her departure from Russia, HPB's life is not easy to document."[15] The historian of esotericism, Nicholas Goodrick-Clarke, confirms that it is only after her appearance in New York in 1873, at the age of forty-two, that "her career admits of continuous documentation," and that Blavatsky's references to her "Masters" during what K. Paul Johnson calls her "veiled years" are "almost all retrospective from the later, Indian phase of her life."[16]

Even Blavatsky's first biographer, the Theosophist and journalist A. P. Sinnett, ran into quite a few walls when attempting to rehabilitate HPB's reputation following the initial accusations of fraud that followed her for the rest of her life, and continue to haunt her legacy to this day. "From seventeen to forty," she told him, "I took care during my travels to sweep away all traces of myself wherever I went . . . I never allowed people to know where I was or what I was doing."[17] She restated this approach to her past life some years later in a letter to some followers: "To even my best friends," she told her correspondents, "I have never given but fragmentary and superficial accounts of [my] travels, nor do I propose to gratify anyone's curiosity, least of all that of my enemies."[18]

BLAVATSKY'S DECONSTRUCTIVE ATTITUDE to her past may have been informed by a sentiment she expressed in one of her last pieces of writing. In *The Voice of the Silence*, a translation of selections from *The Book of the Golden Precepts*—a work of "esoteric

Tibetan Buddhism" that, like the "Stanzas of Dzyan" of her most famous book, *The Secret Doctrine*, more than one Tibetan scholar has argued never existed—she writes: "One single thought about the past that thou hast left behind will drag thee down and thou wilt have to start the climb anew. Kill in thyself all memory of past experiences. Look not behind or thou art lost."[19]

A critic might remark that this was a convenient philosophy for someone who had a past worth forgetting, and HPB's detractors all agree she certainly had. But it is also an approach to one's past life that other questionable gurus adopted. The Greek-Armenian-Russian G. I. Gurdjieff—aptly, his real nationality remains debatable—had much in common with HPB, and he also went out of his way to obscure his past and to create a legend. More recently, Carlos Castaneda took pains to eliminate all traces of his life prior to his emergence as a best-selling guru in the 1970s, and did his best to stay incognito until his death in 1998. He also instructed his followers to do the same, with debatable results.[20] Staying out of the limelight and rejecting one's past are not uncommon practices on the mystic path. The Neo-Platonic philosopher Plotinus, with whom Blavatsky felt much accord, famously refused to be painted or to disclose any information about his life, arguing that this "public" side of himself was unimportant, as his "true self" was his immaterial spirit, striving after the absolute. We can admire Plotinus's dedication, and too many centuries have passed between his time and ours for us to wonder if there was something he didn't want his contemporaries to know. But we generally don't give the same benefit of the doubt to more recent adherents of this belief, and when they go out of their way to let us know they've made things purposefully difficult for anyone wanting to trace their careers, eyebrows and alarms are raised.

BUT THE PROBLEM isn't with Blavatsky alone. If Blavatsky's life becomes subject to independent corroboration only after her arrival in New York in 1873, accounts of her life prior to this time by others are also equally suspect. Her sister, Vera Zhelihovsky, whose relationship with HPB was rocky at best, provided accounts of Blavatsky's early years but changed her tune almost as often as Blavatsky did herself. It may be germane that Vera was a successful author of children's stories. At one point, having turned against her sister, she supplied damaging ammunition to the Russian Vsevolod Solovyov, a writer of historical fiction and the author of a sensational, slandering, and highly doubtful tabloid "memoir" of his brief time with HPB in Paris in 1884.[21] Vera then wrote a scathing criticism of Solovyov and his book. Other early accounts—by Blavatsky's Aunt Nadya Fadeyev, for example—are equally suspect, and along with several other equally doubtful reports, her "reminiscences" contribute to what the esoteric historian Joscelyn Godwin calls "the host of unreliable witnesses without whom there could be no Theosophical history at all."[22]

Yet family and friends are not the only sources for the difficulty in pinning the Blavatsky story down. Practically from the beginning of her public career, HPB was the recipient of some pretty bad press, both from hostile journalists and from those eager to spice up an already recherché story. And with Blavatsky's eccentric character, practically anything they said about her seemed plausible. So a journalist for the *Commercial Gazette* of Cincinnati, visiting HPB in

London in 1889, informed his readers that "One is told she is five hundred years old and renews her age in the far east as often as it is necessary," and repeats a story that "crisp new bills are improvised by a moment's thought," while comparing an afternoon at Blavatsky's home in Holland Park to an audience with the pope, the ascent of Mount Blanc, and a pilgrimage to Mecca.[23] By this time, Blavatsky was no doubt tired of correcting these exaggerations and falsehoods, and in any case, on many occasions she did not bother, seeming to agree with the showbiz adage that there is no such thing as bad publicity, as long as they spell your name correctly. Yet such reports, and ones only slightly less fanciful, became the source material for more lasting accounts of her life and career, and form the basis of the Blavatsky legend. Colin Wilson once remarked about Rasputin, Blavatsky's countryman, that he seemed "to possess the peculiar quality of inducing shameless inaccuracy in everyone who writes about him."[24] The same could be said for Madame Blavatsky.

IT MAY BE assumed that tabloid journalists do not spend much time checking their facts, but surely serious scholars are another matter? Yet, even with decades of Theosophical history to draw on, this seems not to be the case. So, in his recent book *The Immortalization Commission: Science and the Strange Quest to Cheat Death*, the London School of Economics Emeritus Professor of European Thought, John Gray—considered one of the most important social and philosophical thinkers of our time—manages in a brief paragraph to repeat several inaccuracies about HPB and to present the sort of "facts" about her that simply thicken the layers of misinformation making up the standard anti-Blavatsky account.[25]

One wonders why, if respected academics, who are supposed to be the guardians of scholarly accuracy, can spread rumors and take thirdhand hearsay as fact, Blavatsky is lambasted by them for telling stories about herself? Especially as many of these "facts" have been exposed as inaccurate, and more reliable accounts are available for the reading? But the answer is clear: the stories are too good, and the picture of Blavatsky as a "fraudulent guru" is too ingrained in the collective consciousness for anyone to bother about it.[26] Except, of course, for Blavatsky supporters, whose efforts will naturally seem suspect to those experts, and "fair-minded investigators" who even trouble themselves to try to arrive at a balanced view.

THE CULTURAL HISTORIAN Jacques Barzun once remarked that part of his job was to trace the history of reputations. This meant showing how, say, the "crude, barbaric, ignorant" Shakespeare of the early seventeenth century, who, according to the diarist Samuel Pepys, wrote "the most insipid, ridiculous play I ever saw" (*A Midsummer Night's Dream*), became the "immortal genius" we know today, and what was involved in the transformation of the one into the other.[27] Entailed in this is showing how some reputations become one-sided and misrepresentative. It's not a question of obscurity, of taking a writer, thinker, or artist no one knows about and making them better known. On the contrary, it means peeling away the myths and misconceptions that have accreted around a figure everyone thinks they know very well, but are actually quite wrong about. The legends, hearsay, and lazy repetitions collect around the writer or artist like a shell until they are rarely, if ever, seen "in the flesh." As Barzun writes, "It is the fate of geniuses to engender a conventional view, a plausible simulacrum of the true figure, which the attentive biographer must destroy before he can attempt a faithful portrait. This preliminary labor entails many things, the reorientation of the common mind upon the evidence, and the straightening out of faulty logic." Yet, even with all this, there is still no guarantee that the old, mistaken picture will dissolve and a more accurate one arise. "Under the strain of taking all this in," Barzun writes, "the common mind tends to be suspicious and it soon snaps back into its old groove of belief. That is why conventional opinion persists in spite of scholarship and critical biography."[28] "To educate the educated," Barzun tells us, "is notoriously difficult," and once the public and especially the "experts" have made up their minds, it is often a Sisyphean task to change it.

To my mind, Barzun has done remarkably well with the reputations he has repaired, and I believe Blavatsky shares in the "fate of geniuses" mentioned above. But I don't believe Barzun ever had a subject who laid as many traps for her would-be rescuers as she did.

But my concern here is not to recount the many inaccuracies that crop up in "the Blavatsky story," like potholes on a poorly maintained road, nor to excuse myself for not providing the reader with the "truth" about HPB. There are Blavatsky and Theosophical websites dedicated to those pursuits, and along the way the interested reader can find out how to reach them. My job here is to try to tell "the Blavatsky story" as best I can, and these preliminary remarks are offered as a general acknowledgment at the start that the following account, taken from a variety of sources, may or may not be true. If this seems like a lame excuse for poor research and an inability to "nail Blavatsky down," so be it. My only defense is that I am not the only one to make it. As many have recognized, "the facts in the case of Madame Blavatsky" may indeed be doubtful, but without them, there would be practically no case at all.

The writer Henry Miller, a reader of Blavatsky, once said that we should "live life to the hilt." Blavatsky certainly did that, and more. To take her own word for it, throughout her career she was a woman on a mission. Sent into the West by mysterious Eastern adepts, she was charged with the task of bringing a new spirituality to a civilization perilously sliding into a blind and deadening materialism. Whether she succeeded or not is debatable, but I for one think we could do worse than to try to understand her message, and to see if it holds out any prospects for us today.

ONE

FROM RUSSIA WITH LOVE

I first came across a reference to Madame Blavatsky in 1975. I was living in New York, playing in a rock band, and had just become interested in magic, the paranormal, and what I later learned was called "esotericism," and was busy reading my way through Colin Wilson's *The Occult*. There, amid accounts of Gurdjieff, Nostradamus, Rasputin, Aleister Crowley, and the Hermetic Order of the Golden Dawn, appeared Blavatsky. But although Wilson was convinced of her importance, there was an ambivalence about his account of her that was lacking in his analysis of Gurdjieff or Crowley. He was convinced that she "could not have held so many disciples entirely by means of confidence trickery"—she had, about midway through her career, been accused of fraud and the tag had stuck—but he also compared her to the eighteenth-century Freemason, magician, and, by most mainstream accounts, charlatan Cagliostro, an identification Blavatsky herself would have approved of. She had "the same charisma, the same adventurousness, the same mixture of humour, roguery, and genuine psychic ability."[1] This uncertainty about

Blavatsky must have stayed with Wilson. Years later, in a book called *The Devil's Party: A History of Charlatan Messiahs*, she appears in the company of David Koresh, Jim Jones, and other doubtful characters, and Wilson remarks that "the question of how far Madame Blavatsky was a fraud must be left open." She was "part genuine, part fraud," but "unlike most messiahs, she never became paranoid, and always retained her sense of humor," a trait sadly lacking in many spiritual teachers.[2]

After reading *The Occult*, and practically every other book on magic I could get my hands on, I went on to study Gurdjieff, Crowley, and many of the other figures Wilson wrote about. But to be honest, I didn't take Blavatsky that seriously, although "Theosophy" did turn up in a song of mine written at the time.[3] After all, what was one to make of the tales of mysterious mahatmas in Tibet, of Blavatsky's own travels there at a time when it was nearly impossible for a white European male, let alone a woman, to enter that forbidden land, of letters, teacups, and other items strangely "materializing" out of thin air, of stories about ancient Atlantis and Lemuria plucked from the mystical Akashic Record, not to mention the off-putting Theosophical jargon and jaw-breaking Tibetan terminology? I was gripped by Wilson's account of the occult because he had linked it to philosophy, history, literature, and science, and Blavatsky's Tibetan Masters and frankly improbable stories didn't fit this frame. It also struck me that while, say, Gurdjieff had attracted several creative, well-accomplished individuals, who had already made a mark on society before they became his followers—the philosopher P. D. Ouspensky immediately comes to mind, as does the brilliant editor, A. R. Orage—there was something about the kind of people attracted to Theosophy that

smacked of grandmothers' shawls and tea cozies, of Sunday afternoon conversations about astral bodies and past lives, conducted
with the same nonchalance with which one spoke about the
weather. It was all very nice, harmless, and "spiritual," but it lacked
the hard edge that led Wilson to equate some of Gurdjieff's ideas
with existentialism. It wasn't until some time later that I discovered with some surprise that both Ouspensky and Orage had
started out as Theosophists.

And there were Blavatsky's books, the huge, towering piles of
Isis Unveiled and *The Secret Doctrine*. Their length alone didn't deter me, but when I peeked into them, reading bits here and there,
there was something about the avalanche of information falling
from each page that made my curiosity dissolve. Blavatsky seemed
incapable of simply stating her ideas. She had a hectoring, blustery
style that didn't want to convince the reader so much as to bowl
him over. I came away from them feeling more bullied than enlightened, and I felt justified in avoiding more study when I read that
Gurdjieff himself had complained of the time he had wasted on
The Secret Doctrine.

So while I understood that it was Blavatsky and the Theosophical Society that had got the modern occult movement rolling,
I felt I could give suitable deference to this, but save myself
the trouble of really grappling with the "root races," "planetary
rounds," "Manvantaras" and "Pralayas," that jammed the pages of
her gargantuan tomes.

Yet as the years went by and my studies grew, I discovered that
many of the paths I traced led back to Blavatsky. It seemed clear
that practically everyone I read about, and later went on to write
about, owed something to her. Recognizing this, I finally found

myself having to come to serious grips with a character and a
body of ideas I had successfully avoided for some time.

THERE ARE, it seems to me, at least three different Madame Blavatskys, although I'm sure this is a conservative estimate; as her
contemporary Walt Whitman said of himself, she contained "mul-
titudes." And Whitman, we know, was also untroubled by his contradictions. There is the official "encyclopedia" version of HPB,
the colorful rogue and breezy bohemian who pulled the wool over
many intelligent eyes, but in the end was found out as a foul-
mouthed, overweight, chain-smoking charlatan—although, as we
will see, the evidence for this accusation is itself pretty questionable. Then there is the "pro-Blavatsky" version: the saintly, holy
guru steadfastly following her destiny, who fills the pages of more
than one hagiography, and is embraced by her uncritical devotees
who believe that everything she said was the unalloyed truth, and
who maintain the strict letter of her law against any deviation.
These two separate camps carry on in their own way, having little
if any communication with each other, aside from the obligatory
brickbats they fling across the great divide between them. As you
might imagine, neither of these Blavatskys is completely satisfying, and neither does her, or those who would like to know more
about her, much good, although it has to be said that some of
the critical accounts are quite entertaining and readable (HPB
always provided excellent copy), while the hagiographic ones
start out on a note of uplift and soon drift off into increasingly
ethereal realms, quickly leaving the interested, but not entirely
converted, reader far behind.

Then there is the third Madame Blavatsky, the one I discovered as I investigated her life and times. This was a much more fascinating, exciting, surprising, and "real" character than I, and I suspect most people, thought, and one that deserves to be made better known. What follows is my attempt to try to do precisely that.

MADAME BLAVATSKY WAS born Helena Petrovna von Hahn on August 12, 1831, in Ekaterinoslav (now Dnipropetrovsk) in the Ukraine, which was then part of Russia. Although the area had been settled much earlier, the modern city was built less than a century before, "for the glory of Catherine the Great," the free-thinking monarch and friend of Voltaire who, readers of esoteric history may recall, refused to be initiated into the Egyptian Free-masonry of the Sicilian magician Cagliostro. Whether this has any bearing on HPB's later career is debatable.[4] In the old Julian calendar, August 12 was July 30, and legend had it that those born at this time would acquire a power over evil spirits. True or not, from the start Helena caused trouble, arriving prematurely during a cholera epidemic that had already taken its toll on her grandparents' household. So many had died so quickly that coffins had been left to pile up, waiting their turn to be buried. Helena's teenaged mother, Helena Andreyevna von Hahn (nee Fadeyev), never robust, had come down with the disease, and neither she, nor her child, who was born frail, were expected to survive. Blavatsky herself would be plagued with a variety of illnesses for much of her life, and more than once would find herself close to death. Her entry into this vale of tears seems to have set the tone for the rest of her career.

With the godparents and the household in attendance, a priest was called in to perform the baptism quickly, lest the child should die and her soul be forced to spend eternity in limbo. It may have some bearing on HPB's later attitude to the church that as the priest performed the sacrament, Blavatsky's child aunt, Nadya Andreyevna Fadeyev, a central figure in her story, accidentally set fire to his robes with a candle. The infant Helena would not have been aware of it, but I'm sure she would have appreciated that, from early on, she made her mark on the world as a firebrand.

When Helena was brought into the world, her father wasn't on hand, and he wouldn't meet his daughter until six months later (some accounts say a year). A captain in the Royal Horse Artillery (later a colonel), and a descendant of German nobility, Peter von Hahn was one of the many troops that Tsar Nicholas I had sent into Poland, then under Russian rule, to stop a nationalist rebellion. Known as the "gendarme of Europe," Nicholas I was perhaps the most reactionary of the Russian monarchs, and a few years earlier he had successfully put down the Decembrist Revolt of 1825, essentially his first act of office. The Polish uprising would be suppressed just as quickly and violently. Russia under Nicholas I was a repressive police state, rife with spies, censorship, and rigid control of education, publishing, and public life. He believed in the unlimited authority of the tsar and the centrality of the Orthodox Church, and his motto, "Orthodoxy, Autocracy, and Nationality," was a bulwark against any fantasies of modernizing— that is, Westernizing—Russia.

HPB seems to have taken this conservative credo and, as Karl Marx would soon do to the philosopher Hegel, stood it on its head. She would become in every way unorthodox, subversive, and cosmopolitan. For all her advocacy of an "ancient wisdom" and "lost tradition," HPB was very much for the modern world. The dissonance between the Slavophiles, who envisioned a holistic, "wholly Russian" Russia, steeped in tradition and bonded by a mystical sense of racial unity, and the modernizers, who looked to Western science and rationality as a path into the future, would increase as the century moved on, and finally explode during the chaos of World War I. In some ways Blavatsky's later mission—to bring the truth of ancient wisdom to the awareness of modern rational consciousness—paralleled the tension between past and future dominant at her birth.

To get an idea of Russia at this time, we should realize that its first railway wouldn't open until Helena was seven years old. It was a primitive, barbaric land, a feudal state still stuck in the Middle Ages, at least according to western Europeans. It was the Russia of *War and Peace* and *Dead Souls*, whose authors, Tolstoy and Gogol, were HPB's contemporaries, along with Pushkin, Turgenev, and Dostoyevsky. It was a Russia of serfs—the vast majority—and aristocrats, and Helena's family were of the minor nobility. Helena's mother was the daughter of Princess Helena Pavlovna Dolgorukov, who seems a remarkable character. At a time when women were denied education, Helena Dolgorukov taught herself enough Greek, classical literature, art, botany, and archaeology to be lauded by celebrated contemporaries such as Alexander von Humboldt, and to have Sir Roderick Murchison, one of the founders of the Royal Geographic Society, name a fossil after her.[5] HPB, too, wouldn't receive a formal education, and the stunning erudition and autodidactic powers she later displayed no doubt had their roots in her maternal grandmother's efforts at self-education.

Helena's mother, Helena Andreyevna, would also educate herself and produce highly regarded creative work. Not long after she gave birth to her first child at the age of seventeen, HPB's mother became a famous novelist, writing under the pen name "Zenaida R-va." Her work is said to explore the fate of women in unhappy marriages, as well as other social issues, and it could be argued that her fiction provided a foundation for a nascent "women's movement." Nicknamed the "Russian George Sand" by the literary critic Vissarion Belinsky, and acknowledged the equal of Lermontov, Helena von Hahn was a sensitive, poetic, artistic soul who seems to have chosen for a husband someone of a radically different temperament. HPB's father had a cutting, ironic sense of humor, and a no-nonsense attitude that regarded his wife's literary pretensions with amused scorn, standard procedure—one would imagine—among captains of the horse artillery. HPB, who, with her sister Vera, would inherit her mother's and grandmother's penchant for writing and learning, also seems to have followed her mother in choosing an unsuitable mate, as well as one who was much older than she. We will come to Helena's misalliance with her first husband, Nikifor Blavatsky, soon. Here I note that, as her daughter would, Helena Andreyevna had chosen an older man. Peter was twice her age, and although the fact that HPB also married a much older man is often commented on, that her mother did the same suggests that the practice wasn't unusual.

Reading stories of HPB's early life, one soon comes to feel that Helena Andreyevna would have liked to cut her ties and, as her daughter would, take off for points unknown. It may have only been her children and ill health that prevented her. A passage from one of her novels, *The World's Judgment*, gives some idea of her feelings about her marriage. "The fine, sharp, and fast mind of my husband, as a rule accompanied by a cutting irony, smashed every day one of my brightest, most innocent and pure aspirations and feelings . . . all that was sacred to my heart was either laughed at, or was shown me in the pitiless and cynical light of his cold and cruel reasoning."[6] Is it reading too much into HPB's later career, which championed a magical view of the world over that of a deadening rationalism, to suggest that with it she was in some way defending her mother's poetic, idealistic temperament against the dismissive, reductive cynicism of her father? And yet, her fearlessness, her pugnacity, her willingness to take up arms and engage in "mental fight," as well as her unpretentious camaraderie: Where could they have come from, except from her military father? As with many children, HPB was a strange and new combination of two very different worlds.

HPB's mother had other reasons for voicing literary regrets for her marriage. As a captain of the horse artillery, Peter von Hahn moved about frequently, sometimes over vast distances, and for the most part, this meant that Helena Andreyevna had to uproot herself too. The constant movement and loss of friends drained her already poor health, as did the barrack talk, filthy conditions, and boring company, and although, as all aristocratic families did, she had servants to help, she tended to much of her daughter's needs herself. Some biographers assume that, as a novelist, HPB's mother must have been a "career woman" who had little time for her daughter, and have suggested a distance between them. Other accounts suggest that mother and child had as close a relationship as was possible, given the circumstances. One would think that with a husband who "smashed her brightest, most innocent aspirations" daily, she would find more than some recompense in her daughter.

A year after her father returned from Poland, the family moved to Romankov, an army town not far from Ekaterinoslav. Their stay here was brief, and Peter was soon moved to other places in the Ukraine. HPB's maternal grandfather, a civil administrator, was also moved frequently, and as HPB and her mother sometimes lived with her maternal grandparents, this meant that they often moved with them as well. It is a cliché of biographical writing to see in some early experience a pattern that will be repeated in later life, yet it is impossible to read of Blavatsky's early years, when she was hauled across half of Russia, and not see portents of her wandering life to come. She grew up very much "on the road," and it isn't surprising that, when the need and opportunity arose, she took to it and rarely settled down in one place for any length of time.

Other pain, beside that of constant movement, visited HPB's mother. When her daughter was two, her second child, Sasha, HPB's first brother, became terribly ill. The family was living in another army town, and the spring rains had made the roads impassable. No medical help was available and Helena Andreyevna could do little more than watch the infant die. In Odessa, on the Black Sea, three and a half years later, HPB's sister Vera was born. The territory had recently passed into Russian hands and Helena Andreyevna's father had been appointed an administrator for the colonizers. HPB's mother had gone there for the birth, but she soon was back in another god-forsaken part of the Ukraine. Then Helena Andreyevna was thrilled to hear that Peter had been transferred to St. Petersburg, the most European city in Russia. The 900-mile journey was made in a horse and carriage and must have been grueling, but Helena Andreyevna would have made it on foot for an opportunity to escape dull army life and to enjoy a cultural paradise. In a letter to her sister Catherine, HPB's mother told of seeing Pushkin at an art gallery. She caught up on her reading, devouring works in German, Italian, and English—as her mother did, Helena Andreyevna had a knack for languages, something HPB would herself acquire—and she translated some works of the English novelist Edward Bulwer-Lytton for a literary magazine. Her work was exceptional and she was invited to contribute more. It was the start of her literary career, and Bulwer-Lytton would later prove an important influence on Helena's oldest daughter.

She knew her time in St. Petersburg was limited, and she dreaded where Peter's orders would take them next. When Peter finally announced that he was being sent back to the Ukraine, Helena Andreyevna rebelled. And so HPB's parents separated, at least for a time. It was a fateful decision, and showed the kind of willfulness HPB was later noted for. Around the same time, in 1837, when HPB was six, Andrey Fadeyev, HPB's maternal grandfather, was appointed a trustee for the nomadic Kalmuck Buddhist tribes of Astrakhan, a semi-Asiatic city at the mouth of the Volga, where the ancient river empties into the Caspian Sea. Andrey had been sent to St. Petersburg to receive his orders, and he arrived while his daughter and grandchildren were there. One wonders if Helena Andreyevna was tired of traveling, or of her husband, because she suddenly decided to take her children and accompany her father on the 1,000-mile journey to the tip of Central Asia. They stayed in Astrakhan for a year, and it was during this time that HPB had her first contact with Buddhism. The Kalmucks had migrated from China in the seventeenth century, and while the von Hahns were in Astrakhan, they visited the Kalmuck leader, Prince Tumen. Here the young HPB was exposed to the Mongolian lamaic system, and had her first taste of Tibetan Buddhism. Her mother, too, was inspired by the meeting and later wrote a novel about Kalmuck life, which was translated into French. The prince spent his days in prayer in a Buddhist temple he had built himself. The colors, the images, the incense, the strange words murmured in an unfamiliar language, must have made a deep impression on the six-year-old, who had already led a remarkably adventurous life. Blavatsky would later say that her interest in Tibet began at that time. Fate works in strange ways. If her parents got along better, if her father had stayed in St. Petersburg longer, if her grandfather had not been made a Kalmuck trustee, this introduction to the mysterious East might not have happened at all. It did, and HPB would never forget it, and some years later she would visit Prince Tumen again.

SOON ENOUGH HELENA and her family were traveling again, and reunited with Peter. But Helena Andreyevna's health was failing. After a time in Poltava, where a governess took over many of her mother's tasks, HPB and family moved back to Odessa, where her mother could take the mineral baths. Here she found a young British woman to teach her children English, of which HPB would later display a peculiar mastery. But Helena Andreyevna was not getting better. In fact, her condition worsened. She was tubercular and, because she was expecting another child, a doctor was called in to live with the family. In June 1840, when HPB was almost nine, her brother Leonid was born. During her pregnancy and increasing illness, HPB's mother continued to write, something HPB herself would do years later, when illness and other woes pressed on her.

The family moved to Poland, then the Ukraine again. Helena Andreyevna's condition grew still worse, and the doctor urged her to travel to Kharkov for treatment. Perhaps she knew this would be useless. She decided to go once again to Odessa, where she had friends, and where her family could visit her comfortably. On June 24, 1842, Helena Andreyevna von Hahn, otherwise known as Zenaida R-va, died of tuberculosis. She was twenty-eight. HPB was nearly eleven. The family was devastated, and the outside world shared their pain. The critic Belinsky wrote a moving epitaph, and the loss of the young writer was widely mourned. Medical treatment was primitive at best, and the repeated bloodlettings her doctors administered certainly couldn't have helped. She is said to have died in her own mother's arms, and her last words to her eldest daughter were that her life would not be that of other women, and that she would have much to suffer. Apocryphal, most likely, but they certainly sum up much of her daughter's later career.

HELENA ANDREYEVNA'S PARENTS had moved from Astrakhan to Saratov, a town on the Volga, and Grandfather Fadeyev had been appointed governor of the area. Two years before, the family had spent several months there—it was where her brother Leonid was born—and now HPB, Vera, and Leonid were sent there again, to live with their grandparents. It is from around this time that we start to get a "character profile" of the young HPB. Her mother had already despaired over her governesses—Helena Petrovna seemed to get the better of them early on—and for a time thought it best to send her to the Odessa Institute, but nothing came of that. She was, according to her sister Vera, "the strangest girl one has ever seen," with a "distinct dual nature." One side of her was "mischievous, combative, and obstinate," while another was "mystical and metaphysically inclined,"[7] characteristics that those who got to know the mature HPB would agree on. Her Aunt Nadya— just a few years older than HPB—tells us that from an early age she was sympathetic to the lower classes, and preferred to play with the servants' children rather than with those of her own class, and often made friends with "ragged street boys."[8] This solidarity with her social inferiors wasn't uniform, and she once had to apologize to an elderly servant whom she had slapped.[9] Given to schoolboy pranks, she was equally obsessed with books, and had the embarrassing habit of telling people what she thought of them right to their faces: all traits that would, in later life, be part of the Blavatsky legend. Always helpful to the needy and oppressed, she had no capacity for grudges, and any evils done to her would soon be forgotten. Again, the magnanimous, mature Madame Blavatsky.

It was also from around this time that we start to hear about another side of Helena Petrovna's personality. According to Vera's account, the house at Saratov was old and huge, full of underground tunnels, long-abandoned passages, unused turrets, and dozens of "weird nooks and corners," reminiscent of a ruined medieval castle.[10] HPB used to haunt these empty places, sometimes hiding in them to avoid her lessons; even the stories of an evil caretaker who had imprisoned serfs in the subterranean passages didn't deter her.

Sometimes she would be found there, or in other unusual places, sleepwalking, or talking to "invisible companions," or playing with unseen friends she called the "hunchbacks." She also told spooky stories to the other children, and would often scare herself. She also seemed to display some unusual powers, and was able to put pigeons to sleep using "Solomon's wisdom," whatever that might have been. She seems also to have had some odd feeling for the life and consciousness in inanimate objects, in pebbles, stones, and pieces of decaying wood. Often, lying on a sandy ancient riverbed and looking at fossils, she would tell stories about the life of these strange creatures and those in the Saratov museum, and forget herself in her visions of some dim, remote past. She also seems to have had a peculiar fascination with the dead, an interest shared by other esoteric thinkers. Jung, Gurdjieff, and Rudolf Steiner all showed an early obsession with death and the dead. There are stories of her "whispering to herself" and telling of wild adventures, "marvellous tales of travels in bright stars and other worlds," which her governess considered "profane gibberish"—much as her later critics would her mammoth books—all of which made her clearly "unlike any other person."[11]

HELENA PETROVNA WAS given the usual education for a girl of her rank, who was destined to play her role in the world of drawing rooms, social visits, and afternoon recitals, while preparing herself for the arduous task of finding a suitable husband. She was taught French—the *lingua franca* of the civilized world—and had lessons in art and music, decorative pastimes designed to enhance her desirability. In the days before television and the Internet, part of a wife's job description was to entertain her husband. Her mother had shown talent in painting and on the piano, and early on had given her daughter instruction in both. In later life, HPB herself would remain a talented artist and musician. Like her mother and grandmother, Helena Petrovna received no grounding in mathematics, history, science, or the classics, all of which were considered unsuitable for the feminine mind. She did receive some extracurricular input from her serf, Baranig Bouyak, an aged healer, holy man, and according to some accounts, magician who lived in Saratov. He knew the occult properties of plants and the "language of the bees," and passed these on to the young girl. Bouyak had a knack for reading the future, and predicted great things for Helena; confirming earlier suspicions, he told Vera that her sister was "quite different from all the rest of you."[12]

At Saratov, she had another taste of the mystic East. One holiday was spent in the summer camp of the Kalmuck Buddhists she had met while in Astrakhan. Prince Tumen welcomed his old friends, and here HPB had a glimpse of the life of the desert nomads, and a lesson in the use of the Tibetan prayer wheel. In the Ukraine she had learned how to ride a Cossack horse, and now she rode out to the Kirghiz Steppe, a vast stretch of flatland that eventually led to Tibet. Tartar nomads traveled through the area, and soon Helena Petrovna learned enough Tibetan to ask questions about their life. On another occasion, an uncle took her to Semipalatinsk, a mining town close to the Siberian and Mongolian border. Here she rode into the country of the Harrachin Lama, and heard a story about a murder in a cave, which years later would be transformed into her own short story "The Cave of Echoes."

It was around this time that certain strange experiences seemed to enter her life. She spoke of a "protector" whom she saw in her dreams, and this is generally considered the first appearance of Blavatsky's "Masters." She told A. P. Sinnett, her first biographer, that in her early visions, his features never changed, and that years later, when she met him "in the flesh," she instantly knew it was the same man. She felt she had known him all her life. Even early on, this protector, however, could assume a more palpable form, and at the most convenient times. Looking at portraits of the Dolgorukov family, the ancestors of her maternal grandmother, one in particular piqued her curiosity. It was hung high on a wall and covered with a curtain, and no one would tell her whom it was a portrait of. Determined to know, Helena Petrovna pushed a table against the wall, and began to stack other tables and chairs on top of it. Climbing this rickety heap, she managed to reach the painting and pulled back the curtain. Whatever she saw must have shocked her, for she lost consciousness, and the next thing she knew she was lying safely on the floor, the furniture was back in its place, and the curtain had been drawn across the mysterious portrait. She considered that it may have been a dream—after all she was known to sleepwalk—but when she saw her handprint on the dusty wall she knew it hadn't been. On another occasion, while she was on horseback, the animal bolted and she fell, with her foot caught in the stirrup. Most likely she would have been killed, her head smashed against the ground, except for some "strange sustaining power" that held her head up until the animal was stopped. She later said it was a "tall Indian in whole linen" who had appeared to save her, the same figure that she had seen in her dreams.[13]

While many might account for these strange visitations by chalking them up to their guardian angel and leaving it at that, young Helena developed a deep need to *understand* them. Unlike many people who accept this sort of thing as "weird" or "odd" and quickly forget about it, HPB *needed to know* what it meant. In a letter about this time to her friend Prince Alexander Dondoukov-Korsakov, written much later in life, she said, "I was in search of the unknown." At this point we can say that Helena's quest for the answers to life's mysteries began.[14]

THERE'S SOME CONTROVERSY about where exactly HPB was around the ages of thirteen and fourteen. Some accounts have her traveling from Saratov to London and Bath with her father in 1844–45. She was supposed to have received piano lessons from Ignaz Moscheles, a celebrated Bohemian composer, pianist, and music teacher who was based in London at the time; his most famous pupil was Felix Mendelssohn, whom he taught in Berlin. Colonel Olcott, who recounts the story in his *Old Diary Leaves*, claims that on this trip she performed with Clara Schumann, wife of the composer Robert Schumann. If so, this would have been a gratifying tribute to Helena Andreyevna's work on her daughter's musicianship. Most Blavatsky scholars doubt the journey. The trip isn't mentioned in Vera's memoirs, although if Vera wasn't taken along, she might well omit it out of spite, or for other reasons. One biographer suggests that Blavatsky fantasized it, to compensate for her father's lack of interest in her.[15] Sylvia Cranston believes HPB mixed up the chronology—"she was poor at remembering dates"— and that this trip took place in 1850.[16]

. . .

HPB's NEED TO understand the strange phenomena happening around her had an opportunity to be satisfied when she discovered the library of her great-grandfather Prince Pavel Dolgorukov. In the letter to Prince Alexander Dondoukov-Korsakov mentioned previously, she says that "my great-grandfather Prince Pavel Vasilyevitch Dolgorouki, had a strange library containing hundreds of books on alchemy, magic and other occult sciences," and she tells the prince that she had "read them with the keenest interest before the age of 15." "Soon neither Paracelsus, Kunrath, nor C. Agrippa would have anything to teach me," she boasted.[17]

Readers familiar with the Western occult tradition will know these names, and if HPB's dates are correct, then the library must have been of great importance to her grandmother, as she must have taken it with her for their stay in Saratov. By the time HPB was fifteen, her grandfather was being replaced as governor of Saratov and awaiting a new assignment.

HPB's great-grandfather appears to have been an interesting character. A military commander during the reign of Catherine the Great, he had been initiated into Rosicrucian Freemasonry toward the end of the 1770s, a time when the esoteric current in Europe was strong, and many secret societies, such as the notorious Bavarian Illuminati, were operating. Prince Pavel belonged to the Rite of Strict Observance, which was founded in Germany in the 1750s by Baron Karl Gottlieb von Hund.[18] "Strict Observance" got its name because the rite required a vow of absolute obedience to those whom von Hund called "unknown superiors." These were high-ranking secret Grand Masters of an extreme esoteric

Freemasonry that, von Hund claimed, had its roots in the Knights Templar of the Crusades.[19] In Russia, von Hund's rite grew to include higher esoteric degrees that involved the study of alchemy, magic, and Cabala, and it is possible that Prince Pavel met both Cagliostro and the mysterious Comte de Saint-Germain, the eighteenth-century alchemist, diplomat, and wit, believed to have secured the secret of immortality.

In a footnote to what she called her "first Occult shot," which we will look at more closely further on, Blavatsky mentions a manuscript given to her great-grandfather by Saint-Germain. This purportedly "predicted in every detail" "the thorough metamorphosis of nearly the whole of the European map, beginning with the French Revolution of '93," and which she claimed was "now in the possession of the descendants of the Russian nobleman to whom he gave it." The "Russian nobleman," it is assumed, was her great-grandfather, and, according to Colonel Olcott, who refers to this mysterious document in his *Old Diary Leaves*, the "descendants" were HPB's Aunt Nadya Fadeyev.

The notion of "unknown superiors" became particularly important in Russian Freemasonry through the work of Nikolai Novikov, a writer, freethinker, and satirist who is often considered Russia's first journalist. Prince Pavel joined Novikov's Lodge Latone in Moscow, and it is possible that he belonged to an inner, secret group called the Harmonia Lodge, formed by Novikov in 1780, the aim of which was the "inner perfection and union of all masons." This secret group consisted of only eight or nine members who were known as "The Brothers of the Inner Order." As with von Hund's Strict Observance, members were sworn to secrecy and to absolute obedience to the "unknown" Head of the

Order. There were nine "Heads" in all, leading nine Orders, and according to a mysterious document ("The Rosy Cross in Russia," published in *The Theosophical Review* in 1906), they lived in Egypt, Cyprus, Palestine, Mexico, Italy, Persia, Germany, India, and England: all places that would later turn up on HPB's world itinerary.

In 1792, alarmed by the French Revolution and the belief that Freemasonry and other secret societies were behind it—perhaps justified, given the "thorough metamorphosis of nearly the whole of the European map" that the document given to Prince Pavel by the Comte de Saint-Germain spoke of—Catherine the Great had Nikolai Novikov and other high-ranking Masons imprisoned. The fact that Novikov's newspaper satirized the Russian aristocracy was surely a factor too. Prince Pavel wasn't arrested, but that his library contained works on alchemy, magic, and Cabala suggests that he was involved in some of the higher degrees of Novikov's order. When Catherine died in 1796, Novikov was released, but he was so shaken by his imprisonment that he resumed neither his Masonic nor satiric careers.[20]

"The Rosy Cross in Russia," which provides information on Novikov's Inner Order, also refers to another mysterious manuscript. Dated 1784, which was not a good year for Freemasonry—fearing an Illuminati conspiracy, the Bavarian government outlawed all secret societies then—it states that "true Masonry will arise once more in Tibet," a notion that HPB was apparently aware of. In her introduction to *The Secret Doctrine*, she speaks portentously of "several documents in the St. Petersburg Imperial Libraries" which show that "in the days when Freemasonry and Secret Societies flourished unimpeded in Russia . . . more than one Russian mystic travelled to Tibet . . . in search of knowledge and

initiation *in the unknown crypts of Central Asia*."[21] Yet the idea that
fleeing a dangerous Europe, Freemasonry sought refuge in the
mystic East, didn't originate with Blavatsky, nor with the unknown
author of "The Rosy Cross in Russia." The idea first came from
Heinrich Neuhaus, a Rosicrucian pamphleteer who is thought to
have collaborated with Johann Valentin Andreae on the original
Rosicrucian manifestos.

The "Rosicrucian furor" began in 1614, when a strange docu-
ment announcing the existence of the Brotherhood of the Rosy
Cross appeared in Kassel, Germany. The Brotherhood proclaimed
the coming religious, scientific, social, and political reformation of
Europe, couched in strange Hermetic and alchemical language,
and called on those who heeded its message to join it in its work.
In an immediate sense, this meant liberation from Catholic and
Hapsburg rule, an aim which, as readers of Frances Yates's classic
The Rosicrucian Enlightenment know, was soundly trounced at the
Battle of White Mountain in 1620, at the start of the Thirty Years'
War. Many wished to join the Brotherhood, but try as they may,
they could not, because the mysterious Rosicrucians could not be
found. Even the philosopher Descartes, father of modern, rational
thought, tried to find the brethren, but couldn't. This led to their
being given the nickname "the Invisibles." For some, this meant
that the whole thing was a hoax. For others, it meant that the
Brotherhood only made themselves known to the worthy. Yet after a time, when the name "Rosicrucian" became a synonym for
charlatan, some of their defenders offered a different explanation,
and Heinrich Neuhaus claimed that the reason the Rosicrucians
couldn't be found was that they had left Europe and gone to Tibet.

The notion of "invisible" Rosicrucian adepts and Masonic

"unknown superiors" is not that far from that of "Hidden Masters," and the idea that some of them traveled to Tibet makes the connection with HPB's later philosophy all the more secure. Having devoured her great-grandfather's library, the young HPB now had a framework in which to understand the strange experiences that had colored her last few years. And learning of her great-grandfather's involvement with esoteric groups led by "unknown superiors," that combined spiritual aims with political ones, she was filled with the conviction that somewhere in the world there were men and women who had the knowledge she sought, and who might share her own sense of solidarity with the oppressed classes. For all its modern character as an "old boys" club, Freemasonry began as an expression of universal brotherhood and egalitarianism, two ideals that were at the foundation of Theosophy. The truth was *out there*, and Helena Petrovna was determined to find it. She was indeed "in search of the unknown," and now, having absorbed her great-grandfather's library, she had some idea of where to look for it.

TWO

AROUND THE WORLD IN EIGHTY WAYS

There's something in the Russian soul, especially when touching on religious, occult, and mystical matters, that's unlike any other national temperament. The English corner the market on ghosts. The Irish are known for second sight. The French have a long, and still active, alchemical tradition. The Germans have produced many astrologers, and Americans, always good on "know-how," invented the New Age. But Russia tends to produce what Colin Wilson calls "mages—men or women who impress by their spiritual authority."[1]

We can think of Tolstoy and Dostoyevsky, but also of Rasputin and Gurdjieff. In Russian Orthodoxy there is the tradition of the *staretz*, elders of the church who are seen as spiritual advisers and teachers, charismatic figures who enjoy no authority other than their own personal *gravitas*. Readers of *The Brothers Karamazov* will remember Dostoyevsky's portrayal of the *staretz* Father Zosima. Many of these holy men took to the high roads and, like itinerant Buddhist monks, carried their message throughout the land. Often they were believed to have the power to heal and to prophesize.

Perhaps it was this tradition of "holy wanderers" that informed the kind of quest that Gurdjieff, Ouspensky, and other Russian seekers embarked on. Rasputin, the "holy devil," once *walked* from his home in Pokrovskoe, Siberia, to the monastery of Mount Athos, in Greece. On the same trip he also took in Jerusalem. It's not surprising that one of the classics of Russian spirituality is the anonymous *Way of a Pilgrim*.

There is an obsession here with things of the spirit unlike that of any other people. The Russian existential philosopher Nikolai Berdyaev wrote that "Russia has always been full of mystical and prophetic sects and among them there has always been a thirst for the transfiguration of life."[2] Berdyaev himself was a deeply religious seeker, and he tells a story that characterizes the intensity of the Russian spirit. On one occasion, in the early hours of the morning, after a long, drawn-out religious argument, the proprietor of a café wanted to close up shop. Immediately the men clustered around the table shouted out, "We can't go home yet! We haven't decided whether God exists or not!" and carried on.

Berdyaev came from the generation of Russian intelligentsia known as the "God-seekers." In the years prior to the Bolshevik Revolution—in what is known as Russia's "Silver Age"—they were a powerful spiritual force.[3] All were informed with the peculiarly antinomian character of Russian spirituality, the drive to go "beyond good and evil." Talk of Rasputin as a "holy devil" encapsulates the idea, and in an important essay on Dostoyevsky, Hermann Hesse expanded on it. Writing about *The Brothers Karamazov*, Hesse speaks of what he calls "Russian Man." For Hesse, "Russian Man" is a hysteric, a drunkard, a criminal, a poet, and a holy man, all wrapped up in one.[4] He is a "primeval, occult, Asiatic ideal," at once "murderer and judge, ruffian and sensitive soul . . . complete egoist and a hero of total self-sacrifice." Or, perhaps more appropriate for our context, a guru or a fraud.

HPB had a good share of both of these Russian traits—an intense devotion to spiritual truth, combined with a profoundly contradictory character—and both grew as she began her own quest for knowledge. But to the two fundamental traits of Russian spirituality mentioned above, I would add a third. Berdyaev speaks of what he calls *yurodstvo*, "being a fool for Christ's sake." This meant "accepting humiliations at the hands of other people" and "acquiescing in the mockery of the world, and thereby throwing out a challenge to it," what in the Sufi tradition is known as "the way of blame."[5] As we follow Blavatsky in her own wanderings, we will, I believe, see each one of these deeply Russian characteristics come into play.

WHEN GRANDFATHER ANDREY was replaced as governor of Saratov, he found a new appointment as director of state lands in the Transcaucasus. Before HPB and her siblings joined their grandparents in Tiflis (now Tbilisi), the capital of Georgia, they spent a year with their aunt Catherine Andreyevna Witte, mother of HPB's cousin, Count Sergei Witte. Years later Count Witte, a friend of Rasputin and Russia's prime minister before the Bolshevik Revolution, provided an account of his celebrated cousin in his memoirs, published posthumously in 1920 (Witte died in 1915). They are less than accurate; among other mistakes, he states that she founded the Theosophical Society in England, and settled and died in Paris. According to most HPB scholars, they are most likely doctored and in any case suggest a spiteful temper and a taste for low gossip.[6]

After a time in a small town across the Volga, they made the long trip to the Caucasus, the mountainous setting of Lermontov's Romantic novel, *A Hero of Our Time*. It was at this time, at the age of sixteen, that Blavatsky says she began to live a "double life," which was "mysterious" and "incomprehensible," even to herself, until she "met for the second time my still more mysterious Indian." Even by fourteen, she claimed, she lived by day in her physical body, but at night her astral form took over.[7] In a more public form, this dichotomy presented itself as a loss of interest in the social life she had earlier enjoyed. A friend of the family, Madame Yermolov, wife of the governor of Tiflis, remembered HPB as a bright, fun-loving, delightful young lady, as many young socialites no doubt saw her. But as she became more and more absorbed with the ideas she had discovered in her great-grandfather's library, a more serious cast of mind came over her, and a life of endless parties and social gatherings began to pale. One friend who helped the young HPB prioritize her interests was Prince Alexander Golitsyn, a frequent visitor at her new home. With him and with precious few others, Helena Petrovna felt she could talk about the ideas that obsessed her.

According to most accounts, Alexander was a Freemason, mystic, and magician who had traveled in Greece, India, Iran, and Egypt, seeking out sacred places and meeting men and women like himself, with a passion for the spiritual and the occult. His grandfather, another Alexander Golitsyn, Minister for Religious Affairs and Education under his friend Tsar Alexander I, had predicted that Russia would be the birthplace of a new universal church, expressing the messianic strain that Nikolai Berdyaev argues is a constant in the Russian psyche. The first Alexander Golitsyn also seems to have embodied the contradictory, unpredictable character of the Russian soul. He spent his youth in debauchery, until a reading of the Bible led to a spiritual transformation; this later gave birth to the influential Bible Society.

He was also influenced by a friend, A. Koshelev, who was an intimate of many of the influential Masonic and spiritual minds of Europe, figures like the "unknown philosopher" Louis-Claude de Saint Martin and the Christian mystic Karl von Eckartshausen, whose mystical classic *The Cloud upon the Sanctuary* ironically inspired the career of the notorious dark magician, Aleister Crowley.[8] That Eckartshausen wrote of a secret "Interior Church," and that Saint Martin signed his books as "the unknown philosopher" should suggest a fairly obvious link to "invisible" Rosicrucians and Masonic "unknown superiors." (Later, with typical humor, for some of her articles in her magazine *Lucifer*, Blavatsky's byline was the "unpopular philosopher.")

Golitsyn's friend Koshelev promoted Russian Freemasonry, and as Berdyaev tells us, this had a powerful influence on Russian politics at the time; the Decembrist revolt, crushed by Nicholas I, was informed by much Masonic thought. Under the influence of Golitsyn and Koshelev, Tsar Alexander I, Nicholas's predecessor, studied both the writings of Saint Martin and Eckartshausen, and also the enigmatic metaphysical teachings of the seventeenth-century Silesian cobbler and mystic, Jacob Boehme, with whom the term "theosophy" is also associated, and underwent a religious crisis and conversion himself. As Maria Carlson remarked, Alexander I "surrounded himself with intimates who were in-

volved with Swedenborgians, Freemasons, mystical sectarians."[9]
Koshelev was believed to have had contact with Swedenborg, or at
least with the Swedenborg groups that grew up after the Swedish
sage's death in 1772.[10] And the elder Prince Golitsyn was known to
have invited the German esoteric philosopher Franz von Baader
to Russia.[11]

Not much is known about the younger Prince Golitsyn, except
that he is supposed to have encouraged HPB to travel "in search
of the unknown," and one rumor is that he had suggested the two
of them join forces and run off together. Soon after this, it's said, he
left Tiflis and it is unclear if the two ever saw each other again. No
doubt the prospect of running off with a young prince as interested in the occult and esoteric as she was piqued HPB's fancy,
but it must have set off alarm bells among her chaperones. Although by the time of her public career HPB had put on weight
and photographs of her show a stout, massive frame—her face,
however, retained a certain beauty—in her early years she was considered attractive. She had already run away once from her Aunt
Catherine, and was most likely kept on a short rein. But the real
trigger for her wanderlust came in a very different form indeed.

Exactly why the seventeen-year-old Helena decided to marry
the forty-something Nikifor Blavatsky, vice governor of the prov-
ince of Erivan, is unclear. One story is that she did so to spite her
governess, who said that no man would have so unruly, ill-
tempered, and unpredictable a woman for a wife, not even the old
gentleman she had recently taunted and laughed at so much. Faced
with such a challenge, the teenaged HPB cast her spell, and her
"plumeless raven" was quickly netted. Another story is that hearing of the plan to run away with Prince Golitsyn, the family felt

duty-bound to protect her honor, and its own, and hastily shang-haied the old (by their standards) Nikifor into making an honest woman of her. A third possibility is that she married Nikifor out of anger at her father, who had recently remarried, to a Countess von Lange.[12]

Yet Blavatsky herself tells a different story. Prince Golitsyn, it seems, wasn't the only one who took her mystical passion seriously. In the letter to her friend Prince Alexander Dondoukov-Korsakov, mentioned earlier, she wrote: "Do you know why I married old Bla-vatsky? Because whereas all the young men laughed at my 'magi-cal' superstitions, he believed in them!" She explains that her suitor had "so often talked to me about the sorcerers of Erivan, of the mysterious science of the Kourds and the Persians, that I took him in order to use him as a latch key to the latter."[13] This suggests a fairly calculating sensibility for a seventeen-year-old, and a keenly opportunistic one. Blavatsky is eager to make clear, however, that Nikifor did not make out in the bargain. "But," she tells the prince, "I *never was his wife.*" Nor was she ever anyone else's. "Never have I been anyone's wife, as evil tongues have pretended," meaning that neither this marriage, nor any other, was ever consummated. This is a point that will come up more than once in HPB's later career, and she uses a colorful metaphor to make her meaning clear. "Never," she says, "physically speaking, has there ever existed a girl or woman colder than I. I had a volcano in constant eruption in my brain, and—a glacier at the foot of the mountain."

Readers familiar with the Indian esoteric system of chakras—nodes of spiritual energy believed to be located in the physical body—may note that Blavatsky may be referring here to the link between the Muladhara chakra, located in the sexual organs, and the Sahasrara, found at the top of the head. In Kundalini yoga, the idea is to awaken the energy in the lower chakras, and transmute it into a finer, more subtle form that will, with persistence, explode in the brain in a sudden illumination, as the sexual orgasm does lower down. As HPB refers to a "glacier at the foot of the mountain," this suggests that it was not an area of great stimulation for her—nor, apparently, for her husband. One suspects, then, that unless he was as uninterested in sex as HPB was, young Prince Golitsyn may have had an unhappy surprise if he and Helena Petrovna had rode off into the sunset together.

In her letter HPB speaks mysteriously about "the marriage of the Red *Virgin*, with the astral mineral," and "the marriage of the Red Virgin with the Hierophant," a crucial operation in the alchemical union of the opposites, talk of which she had found in her great-grandfather's library. And she makes clear that whatever was needed in the masculine half of the equation for a successful operation, Nikifor Blavatsky simply didn't have it. This could not have been mere potency, because although old by HPB's and her contemporaries' standards, Nikifor, in his forties, would not have been impotent, not necessarily at least. But as she admits the fact that she was "cold," it wasn't sex per se that she was searching for. But one gets the impression she was *saving herself* for something, and depending on whom you believe, she remained celibate throughout her life. Later in her career she will even produce a gynecological report proving it.

But whatever she was saving herself for, it was not the honeymoon with Nikifor. She seems to have had second thoughts about the marriage and tried to get her family to call it off. She even asked Nikifor to let her out of it. He was, she told him, making a great mistake in marrying her, a truth with which he would soon agree. Perhaps Nikifor's other prospects were not that good, or perhaps he really was besotted with her; either way, he didn't relent. She ran away for a few days; where, no one knows, but a romantic escape with Prince Golitsyn was suspected. Then she returned to make the best of it, reflecting that as a married woman she would at least be beyond the control of her family. On July 7, 1849, they were married; Helena was just short of eighteen. The story is that when the priest said "Thou shalt honor and obey thy husband," she muttered "I surely shall *not!*," as Galileo did when signing the recantation of the Copernican system forced on him by the Church. (Galileo is said to have muttered under his breath "It moves anyway," meaning the earth around the sun.)

No sooner had the knot been tied than Helena tried to cut it. On the day of the wedding, which was a big affair, with Kurdish horsemen riding in to honor the bride of their vice governor, HPB planned an escape. On the way to Daichichag, the summer residence of Erivan officials and where the couple would spend their honeymoon, Helena conspired with one of the Kurds to ride off to the Iranian border. The Kurd informed Nikifor, and after that Helena was put under guard. For the next three months, in Daichichag and Erivan, Nikifor tried to enjoy his marital rights, but Helena refused. In Erivan, they lived in the sumptuous Palace of Sardar, home to the territory's earlier Turkish rulers, and with Mount Ararat looming in the distance, Helena concentrated on her great escape, crossing the Turkish border more than once on chaperoned journeys into the countryside. Eventually, the frustrated Nikifor let down his guard, and an exultant Helena galloped off to Tiflis alone.

Helena swore that she would rather die than return to "old Bla-vatsky," and after many arguments, the family decided that she should be sent to her father in St. Petersburg. They arranged for her to meet him in Odessa. But again, HPB had other plans. With an elderly servant and a maid, she was sent to Poti, on the Black Sea, where she would board a steamer. Helena made sure they missed that boat. She persuaded the captain of an English vessel, the *Commodore*, to go along with her plans, and for a hefty gratuity he agreed. Boarding with her servants, they sailed to Kerch, in the Sea of Azof, en route to Constantinople (Istanbul). She told the servants that at Kerch they would get back on the road to Odessa, and sent them ashore to secure lodging, arranging to meet them in the morning. That night she sailed away. At one point the harbor police came on board, and in order to avoid being caught, Bla-vatsky disguised herself as a cabin boy. Trouble with the captain arose and when they reached the Bosporus, HPB secretly fled ashore in a *caïque*.

IF THE READER feels this sounds like something out of Alexander Dumas and *The Count of Monte Cristo*, I'm not surprised. HPB's "journey into the unknown" had begun, and at this point her life becomes a series of adventures, much like those her contemporary Jules Verne would pack into the pages of his novels. *Around the World in Eighty Days* was published in 1873, the year that Blavatsky surfaces in New York, and it made Verne an international success. But between 1849, when she escaped her crestfallen husband, and that year, HPB embarked on a voyage that even Phileas Fogg would have found impressive. For the next nine years, aside from her father, who sent her money when he could, no one in her family heard from her. She thought that if they did, they would help her "plumeless raven" track her down. Some accounts say that Nikifor himself sent her money, so perhaps by this time he agreed with her warning that marrying her would be a mistake, and bade her well on her *Wanderjahre*.

HER FIRST STOP was Constantinople. It was here that her cousin Count Witte claimed she became a "circus equestrienne," and later speculation had it that her celibacy was the result of an injury she received while riding bareback. There's little evidence for either claim, although later HPB would have a near fatal fall from a horse. She did have some traveler's luck though, and met the Countess Kisselev, whom she knew from earlier days. The countess took her under her wing and they traveled together for a while in Egypt, Greece, and eastern Europe. Helena was soon to meet more exciting and adventurous companions, although the countess herself seemed to have some peculiar tastes. HPB told A. P. Sinnett that the countess liked her to dress as "a gentleman student." We've already seen Helena disguise herself as a cabin boy, and she also told Sinnett that in India she wore men's clothes too, and that at that time she was "very thin," difficult as that may be to believe. For European women to dress as men in Eastern lands is not unheard of. Perhaps the most well-known example is that of Isabelle Eberhardt, the Swiss writer and traveler who, dressed as a man, moved unmolested among the Sufis and Muslims of North Africa in the early twentieth century. Yet this fetish of Countess Kisselev's—HPB does not explain why she asked her to cross-dress—combined with Blavatsky's lack of interest in men, led to suspicions that she was a lesbian and a transvestite, although it's doubtful if her glacier was melted by women either. (Aleister Crowley was one source of this rumor, but then he also claimed that she was Jack the Ripper.[14])

We have some idea of what HPB was up to in Constantinople from her article "The Luminous Circle" about the "Wonderful Powers of the Divining Girl of Damascus," originally published in *The Sun* (New York) of January 2, 1876. In Pera, the European quarter of the city, the Mevlevi dervishes, followers of the thirteenth century Sufi master Rumi, had a lodge, or *tekke*.[15] In her account, HPB visits a dervish there in search of a lost dog. The dervish induces clairvoyance in HPB and she finds the dog.[16] HPB was in search of more significant knowledge than how to find a missing pet, but the idea of seeking out *those who know* comes through. Another more dramatic discovery also happened in Pera. There, Blavatsky would come upon someone who would weave in and out of her life mysteriously during what K. Paul Johnson calls her "veiled years." While returning home one evening, HPB was walking through Pera when she suddenly stumbled upon "the apparently dead corpse" of the Italian-Hungarian opera singer Agardi Metrovitch. He had been stabbed several times by a gang of Maltese and Corsican "ruffians," three in all, who, she said, were in the service of the Jesuits. A policeman, for a price, offered to push the body into a ditch, and when she saw him eyeing her jewelry, she flashed her pistol at him. She said she then stood over Metrovitch for hours, until she finally arranged for him to be taken to a Greek hotel where he was known and could be cared for. It is unclear if Metrovitch had any esoteric interests (although he may have been a Mason) but his friendship with HPB, which lasted until his death in 1872 in Ramleh (an Arab city now in Israel) after being poisoned by the Maltese in Alexandria—by HPB's account, at least; the doctors said it was typhoid—links her to several subversive political movements of the time. Agardi was, by Blavatsky's account, a "Carbonaro, a revolutionist of the worst kind, a fanatical rebel," who had insulted the pope, and who hated the priests, especially the Jesuits, and who escaped being hung by them in Austria only through the services of herself and Countess Kisselev.

Mention of "ruffians" in HPB's account of her first encounter with Agardi Metrovitch leads the Masonically minded to the foundation myth of Freemasonry, the story of Hiram Abif and his murder by three "ruffians" when he refused to reveal to them the secret "Mason's word." And for what it's worth, the Jesuits were the main target of the most radical Masonic offshoot, the Bavarian Illuminati. (The Jesuits themselves had no love for any form of Freemasonry.) "Ruffian" is an antiquated word, but was still in use in HPB's time, and she had a peculiar command of the English language. But given Agardi's political links, one wonders if in telling the tale Blavatsky chose the name and number of his attackers on purpose, to communicate, to those who might get the reference, Agardi's and her own spiritual-political affiliations? Coincidence, perhaps. But given the strange world that HPB was moving through, it's not entirely unreasonable to wonder.

METROVITCH COMES INTO HPB's life at different junctures, none of them with any definitive clarity. According to Count Witte, HPB left Constantinople with Metrovitch for "one of the

European capitals," from which he sent letters to her grandfather, claiming they were married. Their paths parted and he later turns up in Tiflis, where HPB has returned for a brief time to her husband. Now on the decline, Metrovitch is a singer at the Tiflis Opera House and he demands of HPB *his* marital rights. Scandal forces them to Kiev, from which they flee after poems written by HPB about her friend Prince Dondoukov-Korsakov, at the time the city's governor general, appear throughout the city apparently alluding to some past liaison. They then turn up in Odessa, where HPB gives séances, and tries her hand at an artificial flower factory and the manufacture of ink (like Gurdjieff, HPB seems to have had a knack for "hands-on" work). Then the couple head to Cairo. En route their ship explodes. HPB survives. Alas, Metrovitch does not. . . .

We are getting ahead of our story, but Metrovitch's most controversial contribution to "the Blavatsky story" is that he allowed her ward, Yuri, who died in 1867 at the age of five, to be buried with his last name. Exactly what Yuri's relationship to HPB was has been a matter of much debate. Some have said he was her love child by way of the Estonian Baron Meyendorff. Blavatsky herself said that she took the child in because neither the father, Baron Meyendorff, nor the mother, Nathalie Blavatsky, her sister-in-law, wanted it, as it was illegitimate. Again, we are getting ahead of our story, but during the brief reconciliation with Nikifor—lasting, depending on your sources, either a few days or a few years—HPB agreed to adopt the child. A passport issued to HPB mentions her "infant ward, Youri," and the gynecological report mentioned above suggest that the child wasn't Blavatsky's. The report, issued in 1885, states that she "has never bourne a child."[17] Anti-HPB biographers, such as Marion Meade, think otherwise, and argue that the boy was the product of an adulterous relationship between HPB and Metrovitch.[18] Baron Meyendorff and Nathalie Blavatsky will reappear further on, when we come to examine HPB's relationship—or lack thereof—with the Victorian medium Daniel Dunglas Home.

AFTER CONSTANTINOPLE, HPB went to Greece, and from there Cairo. Although in later years her mystic compass will point toward India and Tibet, in her early days, all occult roads led to Egypt, and we can say that here her esoteric quest truly begins. She was in good company. Legend has it that Pythagoras, Plato, Moses, and other Western greats went to school in the land of the pyramids, and Christian Rosencreutz himself, mythical founder of the Rosicrucians, went there too. In her travels, HPB would echo the legendary journeys of earlier seekers. Paracelsus, the Swiss alchemist and sixteenth-century father of alternative medicine, met shamans in Russia, visited tin mines in Cornwall, studied alchemy in Cairo and the Cabala in Spain, and was a military surgeon in Italy. Later seekers such as Cagliostro and the Comte de Saint-Germain gave rise to the theme of the "Noble Traveller," whose "wanderings," according to the mystical poet O. V. de Lubicz Milosz, "though apparently haphazard, rigorously coincided with the adept's most secret aspirations and gifts."[19] As chroniclers of HPB's adventures soon realize, her itinerary coincided with quite a few interesting things.

One character she met in Cairo was the American artist, scholar, and traveler Albert Rawson. Like HPB herself, Rawson is one of these dizzyingly accomplished nineteenth-century figures, who no longer seem to be made in our time. He was born in Chester, Vermont, in 1828, so was only a few years older than Helena when they met. He had studied theology and medicine, and had published his first book, *The Divine Origin of the Holy Bible*, at seventeen, and went on to write many more, on themes ranging from religious history to Eastern geography and language, Freemasonry and occultism. He also wrote fiction, and made some three thousand engravings. He was a much sought-after illustrator—his most famous subjects were Queen Victoria, Louis Napoléon, and the Empress Eugenie. He received doctorates in Divinity from Oxford and in medicine from the Sorbonne, studied law and archaeology, and in his spare time traveled, mostly to the Orient. At one point, as the explorer Richard Burton did, he journeyed to Mecca disguised as a Muslim; in fact, his visit preceded Burton's.[20] Another of his interests were secret societies and the shadowy world of "fringe Masonry." He was "adopted" by the Aduan Bedouins of Moab, and accepted by the Lebanese Druze, and either joined or initiated several Masonic groups.[21] He was also a freethinker and an early member of the Theosophical Society. In K. Paul Johnson's controversial work on the identity of Blavatsky's "Masters," Rawson plays an important role as one of the "seekers of truth"—in Gurdjieff's phrase—with whom HPB associated during her "veiled years," before surfacing in New York at the start of her "mission."

Rawson described his meeting with HPB in an article he wrote for an English magazine, *The Spiritualist*, in 1878, following the success of *Isis Unveiled*. He wrote another similar account years later, after her death. He records that he met HPB and Countess Kisselev at Shepherd's Hotel, a four-star accommodation, which suggests that Blavatsky's road trip was being financed, either by her father or by Nikifor. Two items of his account are worth noting. One is that HPB used hashish. This is something that will be repeated a great deal (I'm guilty of it myself) and, in the 1960s and '70s (as well as today) made HPB more "relevant" to youthful seekers, who found Theosophy so much more interesting with the thought of its founder enjoying a joint.

The only other reference to HPB using hashish comes in an article by Hannah Wolff, written during Blavatsky's early days in New York. This is little more than an exercise in character assassination; conveniently, it was only published after her death. In it, HPB is also addicted to opium, her complexion is "torpid," "grimy," and "pasty," her nose a "catastrophe," her hair "wooly, like a negro's," and she is a "very stupid and unprepossessing woman," who would "go to any length to dupe."[22] Hannah Wolff was the wife of John B. Wolff, president of the First Spiritual Society of Washington, D.C., and at the time, and throughout her career, HPB was Public Enemy No. 1 to devout spiritualists, for reasons which will become clear shortly.

There are dozens of references to HPB rolling and smoking her own cigarettes; it is a set piece in accounts of her, with numerous reports of her "delicate fingers" deftly rolling one cigarette after another. But there are no reports—aside from those of Rawson and Wolff—of her ever adding hashish to her tobacco. And if she did use hashish, at that time it was usually eaten, not smoked, which meant its effects were much more powerful.[23] This would certainly have been the case in Cairo circa 1851, or New York in 1873. She could not, as some have suggested, have written while under its influence, or at least written anything worth reading. Faithful adherents deny that HPB ever touched the stuff, and Blavatsky herself warned against the use of drugs and alcohol—which, of course, does not mean that she never used them.²⁴ Some writers have suggested she may have, early on, and then dropped it. I don't know, but I'm inclined to think not, just because of the lack of any other references besides those of Rawson and Wolff. Although slightly disreputable, use of hashish and other drugs did not become a sign of moral depravity until the early twentieth century, and given HPB's other eccentricities, one would imagine most journalists would have thrown it into their stories. I'm also inclined to wonder if Rawson did, precisely because it made for good copy, and it was what was expected of someone steeped in "Eastern mystery." But of course, HPB may have tried it, and where else to do so but in Cairo? (It was, in fact, from Egypt that the use of hashish spread to Europe, when Napoléon's troops brought the practice back to France.) Some of the occult schools that she came into contact with did employ drugs, so in that context it would not be unusual for her to use them also.

The other item of note is that she and Rawson visited a Coptic "magician," Paulos Metamon, whose address HPB may have got from Prince Golitsyn. Disguising themselves as young Muslim men in order to move through Cairo undisturbed, they visited Metamon, who quickly saw through their disguise. They explained that they had come in order to learn from him. Metamon was happy to oblige, for a price, and showed them his books of magic and astrology. Rawson remarks that they tried to form "a society for occult research" sometime after the visit but that it was unsuccessful, and Metamon suggested they wait until a better moment. K. Paul Johnson suggests that Metamon may have been involved

in the unsuccessful *société spirite* that HPB started in Cairo twenty
years later, in 1871, an idea first suggested by the Traditionalist philosopher René Guénon, no friend of Theosophy, in 1921.[25] Johnson
suggests that Metamon may be the original of Serapis, one of the
earliest of HPB's Masters to make an appearance, at least to her
and Colonel Olcott. Joscelyn Godwin suggests he may be the original of "M," which is usually taken to be the sign of Master Morya,
the mysterious Indian of her dreams whom she will soon meet in
the flesh. As HPB's early occult references tend to be Hermetic
and Egyptian, the "M" that she refers to in 1875, when she once
again tried to launch an "occult society," may have been Metamon.[26]
Called "the Miracle Club," this attempt also failed. Apparently in
the world of occult societies "three strikes and you're out" doesn't
apply; as we will see, it wasn't until her fourth attempt that she was
successful.

FROM CAIRO, in 1851 HPB crossed Europe and headed to Paris,
bringing the knowledge she had learned about magic, occultism,
Freemasonry, and related subjects from Rawson, Metamon, and
possibly others, with her. In Paris, she is supposed to have "aston-
ished the Freemasons," at least according to some accounts. One
person whom she impressed was the mesmerist and spiritualist
Victor Michal. Michal was familiar with astral projection and
crystal-gazing, and used hashish in his work—a possible link to
HPB's own disputed use—and he is said to have found HPB a
wonderful trance subject. He said that while in trance she would
become a completely different character, but that on returning to
her "self," she would be subject to fits of anger. This seems an echo

of HPB's remark about leading a "double life," and when we come to the writing of *Isis Unveiled* and other works, we will look at the idea that Blavatsky exhibited some form of multiple personality. Michal wanted to keep HPB in his employ, and she was in contact with other spiritualists while in Paris, but, again, she had other plans, and we will return to HPB's controversial relationship to Spiritualism further on.

From Paris, Blavatsky headed to England, where, as the cliché goes, she met her destiny. HPB's first meeting in the flesh with her Master Morya is perhaps the most important moment of her life—although if the accounts of her being saved from her early fall from a horse are true, she had met him to some extent already. Yet, as with practically everything else in her story, there is no one definitive version of this fateful meeting. It is supposed to have occurred in London in 1851, the year of the Great Exhibition, while she was there as a companion to her godmother, Princess Bagration-Murransky, although some accounts have her there with her father on their disputed London journey. HPB and Princess Bagration were staying at Mivarts Hotel, which is now Claridge's, again, not a budget accommodation. In one version, perhaps the most well known, she sees the "tall Indian" of her dreams in a crowd and he tells her to meet him later in Hyde Park; he was there, she said, as part of "the first Nepal Embassy." She told A. P. Sinnett "I *cannot*, I *must not* speak of this. I would not publish it for the world." In another version, told to C. W. Leadbeater, who would become a high-ranking Theosophist after Blavatsky's death, she meets him at the Great Exhibition, which was held in Hyde Park, and he was there with a delegation of Indian princes. But in a letter to Prince Dondoukov-Korsakov, she says that the Master saved her when, in a fit of depression, she considered jumping into the Thames from Waterloo Bridge.[27] And in another version, recorded in an old notebook sent to her companion Countess Wachtmeister by her Aunt Nadya, while the countess and HPB were staying in Würzburg, Germany, HPB says that the meeting took place in Ramsgate, an English seaside town popular in the nineteenth century on, of all days, her twentieth birthday. When asked why she had recorded the meeting at Ramsgate rather than London, HPB told the countess that Ramsgate was a "blind," a false clue.[28]

Whichever of these is the "real" account—if indeed there is one—the upshot was that Morya had sought her out purposefully, for he had a special mission in mind for her, which suggests that he somehow knew she would be in London. If she accepted it, it would require special preparation. She would, he told her, have to spend three years in Tibet. HPB had no intention of turning this offer down. Who Morya was, what HPB's mission was, and how she got to Tibet—if she ever did—will be looked at in the next chapter. Right now, HPB decided that the best way to get to India—in order to get to Tibet—would be to follow Columbus's route. So she steered west, and headed to America.

BY THE AUTUMN OF 1851, HPB was en route to Canada. She was a fan of James Fenimore Cooper, and his descriptions of Native American Indians—although neither Cooper nor anyone else called them that at the time—led her to want to meet some real-life examples. In Quebec, she was introduced to some Indians whom she hoped would share their knowledge of the medicine men with her. Instead, they stole her boots and other possessions. In *Isis*

Unveiled, she later explained their actions as a result of the work of Christian missionaries, whose effect on other Indians—those of the subcontinent—she would also find reprehensible. Around this time she is supposed to have received a legacy from Princess Bagration; exactly how much is unclear, and she is said to have used some of it to buy land, to which she lost the deed. But she had enough left to travel. She then thought to investigate the Mormons, but as their first city, Nauvoo, in Illinois, had just been decimated by a mob, leaving the survivors homeless, she changed her plans. Mexico piqued her interest, but she would pass through New Orleans first on the way, in order to study voodoo. In a dream, Morya warned her about this dark practice, and she moved on. Passing through Texas, she reached Mexico, and then headed further south, to Central and South America, where she explored the ruins of ancient Incan temples and believed she had found the location of a lost treasure, which, sadly, she was unable to retrieve at the time. (It was allegedly a ransom that an Incan queen had offered to Pizarro in return for her husband's life.)

In 1852, it was time to head to India. An Englishman she had met in Germany two years earlier was, she knew, on a similar quest, so she wrote to him and suggested they meet in the West Indies, and from there travel East together. They were joined by a Hindu she had met in Honduras, a *chela*, or student, of the Masters (by now there were more than one), and the three headed for Ceylon via the Cape of Good Hope. From Ceylon they reached Bombay (today Mumbai), where they separated. Blavatsky told Prince Dondoukov-Korsakov that she stayed in India for two years, receiving monthly payments from some unknown benefactor and following an itinerary set out for her. Morya sent her letters, but during this time she didn't meet him. It was during this visit that she made her first attempt to reach Tibet, sometime in 1853.

After her first attempt on Tibet, HPB returned to England via Java. (There is some debate over the chronology here; I follow that of Sylvia Cranston and Boris de Zirkoff, editor of the *Collected Writings*, which seems the most widely accepted.) She left India on board the *Gwalior*, which she says was "wrecked near the Cape," but that she survived with twenty others. By the time she got to England, in 1854, the Crimean War had broken out and she was a hostile alien. She remained in England for some time under contract as a concert musician and member of the Philharmonic Society.[29] She also had another meeting with the Master, this time "in the house of stranger." He was in the company of a "dethroned native prince," whom most accounts suggest was Dalip Singh, the recently deposed maharaja of Lahore. HPB and the Master spoke, but, strangely, when recounting this meeting later, Blavatsky forgot what they spoke about. After this, HPB headed to America again, this time New York, where she again met Albert Rawson. His description of her at this time, "supple, muscular and well rounded," suggests she hadn't yet started to put on the weight of her later years. After New York, she headed to Chicago, and from there she made a journey to the West, crossing the Rockies in a covered wagon. She stayed in Salt Lake City with a Mrs. Emmeline Wells, a Mormon, who noted that HPB was wearing men's shoes in preparation for travel over hard country.[30] Wells thought she was heading to Mexico. It's unclear if on this trip Blavatsky did go south of the border again, but she did make it to San Francisco, en route to the Orient, specifically India, which she reached via Japan.

On this trip to India, it seems HPB may have made contact

with the Master, unlike during her first journey. In *Isis Unveiled*, she speaks of coming into contact with "certain men, endowed with such mysterious powers and such profound knowledge that we may truly designate them as the sages of the Orient." Some account of her adventures during this time may be found in her book *From the Caves and Jungles of Hindustan*, which was originally serialized in the *Moscow Chronicle* under the pseudonym "Radda Bai" from 1878 to 1886. Her editor, M. N. Katkov, later reprinted her accounts in the *Russian Messenger*, and they appeared in book form in English in 1892. For most of HPB's career, she was known in her homeland as the author of these semifictional tales of adventures in the mysterious East, and they remain very readable "ripping yarns" today, in many ways setting the mold for later tales of similar journeys. In HPB's stories, the Master appears as "Gulab Singh." This Indian journey, which included another attempt on Tibet and travels in Kashmir, Ladakh, and Burma, ended in 1857—just before the Sepoy Mutiny, which posed a major challenge to British rule. Receiving "orders" from the Master, HPB left Madras (today Chennai) for Java, and headed again to Europe.

ON CHRISTMAS NIGHT, 1858, the doorbell rang at a house in Pskov, not far from St. Petersburg. A wedding party was going on, and HPB's sister, Vera, one of the guests, answered the door. It was HPB. They had not seen each other for nearly a decade. As a wedding had started HPB's long adventure, it seems appropriate that one should be at the end of it—or at least at its temporary end. En route to Russia, HPB had spent some months in France and Germany, and had already been in touch with Aunt Nadya, whom she had asked to keep her return a secret. She was afraid that Nikifor would try to assert his rights again, but he had assured Nadya that those days were over. When Vera asked about her years of travel, HPB was strangely noncommittal, merely mentioning that she had seen Europe, America, and Asia. It was of this time that she later spoke when she said she had "swept away" all traces of her travels, and did not let people know where she had been or what she had been doing. Her reason was that if her relatives knew she had been studying occultism, they would have been horrified, as though she had sold her soul to Satan. It would have been preferable, she said, had she spent the last decade as a prostitute. Yet the HPB who had returned to them had strange powers that suggested a knowledge of the dark arts.

"Things" started happening around her. "Raps" were heard on the walls, windows, and floors, and furniture moved of its own accord. HPB tried to avoid responsibility for these phenomena but eventually she admitted that she was causing them unintentionally, although she could, if she exerted herself, to some degree control them. At one point, trying to convince her father and her brother Leonid, now a university student and typical skeptic of the time, of her abilities, she said she could make an object too heavy to lift. Leonid challenged her. She asked him to lift a small chess table that stood before them. He did so easily. Then she concentrated and looked at it, focusing her gaze intently. She asked Leonid to lift it again. He couldn't, nor could a friend who got below the table and tried to lift it with his shoulders. When she "let it go," the table shot up with such force Leonid's arm was almost dislocated.

On another occasion, in St. Petersburg, the family met a friend.

Intrigued by reports of Helena's powers, at his home he suggested that Colonel Hahn leave the room and write down a word, and that Helena should try to spell it out with her raps, using the code one rap for "A," two for "B," etc. HPB's raps spelled out "Zaitchik." When her father returned, he was stunned. He had written down a question: the name of his favorite horse during his first Turkish campaign. It was Zaitchik. At Rougodevo, in a house owned by Vera's late husband, a piano played by itself, without opening. While there, a mysterious wound under the heart that HPB had sustained in her travels opened, and when a doctor tried to treat it, a strange brown hand appeared, preventing him—perhaps it was the same hand that saved her from the bolted horse as a child? The open wound triggered a strange illness, which lasted several days and involved convulsions and a "deathlike trance," the first of a series of near fatal attacks that would visit HPB throughout her career.

During a visit with Vera to the Metropolitan Isidore in Zadonsk (equivalent to an archbishop), more "phenomena" occurred. Furniture moved, walls creaked and cracked, raps sounded, and the chandelier seemed to take on a life of its own. The Metropolitan asked HPB if her "friends" could answer a question for him; they did. The Metropolitan was not shocked by these things, and said he believed Helena could use her powers for good. Vera relates many other occurrences and also mentions that on some occasions, when HPB was pressed to "produce," nothing happened at all. Blavatsky later said this was because of her disgust "with the ever growing thirst for phenomena," a recognition of their essential unimportance that would increase as her career moved on.

The sisters journeyed to Tiflis to visit their grandmother, who died while they were there. On this trip, which happened in 1860, HPB is said to have met another Master, Hilarion Smerdis, a Greek, who will reappear later on in our story; Sylvia Cranston has their first meeting at a later date.[31] It was also on this trip that Metrovitch and his wife, Teresina, also an opera singer, came to Tiflis to work in the opera house; in HPB's notebook, there is a sketch of them as Mephistopheles and Gretchen from Gounod's *Faust*. Not long after this, in 1862, came HPB's reconciliation with Nikifor, and their adoption of Yuri. How long she and Nikifor lived together is unclear. During this time she supported herself in a variety of ways, through needlework and by rafting logs for the production of spunk, a porous white substance which is highly inflammable and is used as a touchwood for fires. She noticed that the fungus, which turns wood into spunk, covered many trees in her neighborhood, and she had the brainstorm of floating the logs downriver for export.

She had acquired a reputation in Tiflis and other places as a magician, a seer, and what we would today call a "psychic" and healer. By this time, she had given up answering questions by raps, which was tiring and time consuming, and taken up giving spoken or written replies. She later told A. P. Sinnett how she could read people's thoughts by seeing them emerge from their heads as a kind of spiral of "luminous smoke" that formed pictures and images around them, and she remarked that often these thoughts find a home in the consciousness of other people. She had, it seems, begun to learn how to *control* the strange phenomena happening around her.

In 1864, in Mingrelia, on the shore of the Black Sea, HPB was thrown from her horse. She fractured her spine and entered a

coma that lasted for months. She wasted away, and it was feared she
would die. She could respond to questions, but most of the time she
was, she later said, in a kind of dream in which she was somewhere
else *as* someone else, another example of the strange "double life"
she had entered years ago. She said that while in this state, she had
no idea who Helena Blavatsky was and that she seemed to travel
in a far-off country as a "totally different individuality."[32] Back in
Tiflis, she recovered, and along with her health she received something else. She had gained complete control of her powers. Like
many other esoteric figures—Steiner, Jung, Gurdjieff, Swedenborg—
HPB had passed through what the historian of psychology Henri
Ellenberger calls a "creative illness," and had come out a changed
person.

Following her "creative illness," HPB hit the road again, traveling in Italy, Transylvania, and Serbia. Colonel Olcott claimed that
during this time she toured France and Italy giving music recitals
as "Madame Clara," and this is also the time that Count Witte
said she managed the Royal Choir of King Milan of Serbia—except
that King Milan wasn't king yet, and so the choir could not have
been his. It is unlikely, too, that Metrovitch, whose wife had
recently died, would have accompanied her, and his work with the
opera house no doubt obliged him to stay in Tiflis. Tiflis, although
a cultural center, began to bore Blavatsky, and the hunger for more
knowledge and experience drove her out of it again. Her sketchy
travel diary speaks of Odessa, Syria, Lebanon, Jerusalem, Egypt,
Greece. She may have studied Cabala with a learned rabbi at some
point during these travels; Sylvia Cranston records that she corre-
sponded with him until his death, and that his picture was one of
her treasures. In 1867, she was in the Balkans, Hungary, Venice,

Florence, and Mentana, where on November 3 she was wounded while fighting against the French and the papal army on the side of Garibaldi. She later impressed Colonel Olcott with the musket balls still embedded in her leg and shoulder, and showed him where a saber had broken her left arm in two places. She was left for dead in a ditch—the battle was a rout and Garibaldi himself was captured—and, as with her earlier "creative illnesses," this near-death episode, too, helped her gain greater control of her powers. From Mentana she returned to the Balkans, where word came from the Master to head to Constantinople; from here she proceeded for the third time to India and Tibet.

Let us take a look, then, at her time in the land of the eternal snows.

THREE

SEVEN YEARS IN TIBET?

Given the itinerary followed in the last chapter, that HPB claimed that in her travels she also took in the "roof of the world," may not seem so unusual. Yet, if all she did was to journey to the land of the eternal snows, that alone would make her one of the greatest travelers of the nineteenth century. At that time, no place was more inaccessible than Tibet, and it was not until the British expedition of Sir Francis Younghusband in 1903—which burst open Tibet's closed borders with military force—that the West had any kind of untrammeled access to this mysterious land. This was the time of the "Great Game" between Russia and Britain over dominance in Asia, and fearing the Russians were gaining undue influence in Lhasa, capital of the forbidden kingdom, the British Lord Curzon, the viceroy of India, sent Younghusband in as a kind of preemptive strike. Although the "White Tsar" Nicholas II did have designs on a "Russian Asia," Curzon, it turned out, was wrong, but this did not become known until more than a thousand Tibetans lost their lives and the thirteenth Dalai Lama had fled to Mongolia, in the company of his tutor, the

mysterious Buriat Russian, Agwan Dordjieff.[1] Before Younghusband crashed Tibet's locked gates, any travelers who attempted to
enter the forbidden land were turned back, when they were not
murdered by bandits, defeated by the cold, unforgiving landscape,
or lost on difficult, confusing trails.

Surprisingly, many who did try to breach Tibet's defenses were
women, and leaving aside HPB's disputed attempts, in the late
nineteenth century at least three other female travelers took their
chances on crossing the highly guarded border. In 1892, Annie
Royal Taylor, a Christian missionary, tried to reach Lhasa in order
to spread the gospel to the Dali Lama. On horseback and in disguise, she got within three days of her goal before she was discovered and turned back by the border guards. In 1895, Mrs. St. George
Littledale—as well as her husband, her nephew, and her dog—got
within forty-nine miles of the holy city before they were forcibly
expelled. And in 1898, the Canadian missionary and doctor Susie
Rijnhart lost her first child and her husband attempting to reach
Lhasa. Rijnhart remarried and soon made a second attempt, only
to die on the borderlands, just three weeks after giving birth to her
second child.

Yet, even after Younghusband's invasion, entry and travel to the
"roof of the world" was not easy. Accounts by Alexandra David-
Neel, who, in 1923, became the first European woman to enter the
forbidden city of Lhasa, make clear how arduous the trek must
have been. Like many who made the perilous journey, David-Neel
had to travel in disguise, well armed against bandits and corrupt
officials, with maps hidden from covetous eyes and often going for
days without food and spending many freezing nights without
shelter.

David-Neel journeyed to this unearthly realm, where she endured constant threat and physical hardship, because she was driven by a need to understand the mysteries of Tibetan Buddhism.[2] And most of those who made earlier attempts to reach Tibet, before the British unceremoniously opened its borders, were also driven by either religious or scholarly concerns. In 1667, the Hermetic philosopher, polymath, father of Egyptology, and sinologist Athanasius Kircher produced his *China Illustrata*, which featured illustrations of the Dalai Lama and Lhasa's Potala Palace, based on reports by Jesuit missionaries. In 1811, Thomas Manning, a scholar and medical doctor who had traveled to China and India, became the first Englishman to enter Lhasa, having arrived there with Chinese troops after curing some of the soldiers of illness; he was also the first Englishman to have an audience with the Dalai Lama. In 1823, the Hungarian linguist Alexander Csoma de Kőrös, reached neighboring Ladakh—often called "Little Tibet"—having more or less walked there from eastern Europe; his journey had started some three years earlier. In 1824, at the Zangla Monastery in Zanskar, Csoma de Kőrös wrote the first English-Tibetan dictionary, and in 1831 in Calcutta, he added a Tibetan grammar to it. Csoma de Kőrös reportedly was fluent in seventeen languages, and is known as the "father of Tibetology." In 1842, he planned to journey to Lhasa, but contracted malaria in Darjeeling, where he died.

The French Abbé Évariste Régis Huc entered Lhasa in January 1846, having already endured a treacherous journey across the Ordos Desert, and having spent several months studying the Tibetan language and Buddhist literature at the ancient Kumbum Lamasery in China. Because of political developments, Huc and his fellow traveler, Abbé Joseph Gabet, were forced to leave Lhasa in October that same year. Huc's picturesque account of his travels in Tibet, China, and Tartary (what we now know as Siberia, Turkestan, Mongolia, and Manchuria) appeared in 1850; it was extremely popular and was soon translated into several languages. Huc's sympathy with Tibetan and Chinese culture, and his belief that Catholic and Buddhist ceremony had much in common, led to his delightful work being placed on the Vatican's index of prohibited books, and later critics took argument with what they saw as his sensationalism—which meant that his work was read and enjoyed by the general public. Alexandra David-Neel writes that Abbés Huc and Gabet both reported that on the leaves and trunk of the "miraculous tree of Tsong Khapa"—the fourteenth-century founder of the Gelugpa school of Tibetan Buddhism—which they saw in the Kumbum Monastery, they could read the words "Aum Mani Padme Hum," a Buddhist mantra of compassion commonly translated as "O jewel in the lotus."[3] On hearing of this miraculous "Tree of Great Merit," believed to have sprung from the blood of the newborn Tsong Khapa, the French priests were understandably skeptical; but their suspicion soon turned to astonishment when their close inspection discovered no possibility of fraud. Perhaps it was accounts like this that led some to question both their religious affiliations and their veracity.

Although HPB's "Buddhism" was *sui generis*, the Gelugpa school, which demands strict celibacy, is the form of Tibetan Buddhism with which her own practice is most often related, and on one occasion, a Buddhist scholar is said to have remarked that HPB was a reincarnation of Tsong Khapa himself.

The main reason why Blavatsky's critics doubt that she ever got anywhere near Tibet is that there is no record of her doing so, except, of course, her own. Some, like her biographer Marion Meade, argue that in the decade between abandoning Nikifor Blavatsky and ringing that doorbell in Pskov on Christmas night, she never reached India, let alone Tibet, and that her tales of traveling in Asia, North and South America, and other points were fabrications, designed to hide the fact that she was really leading a immoral, dissolute life among the demimonde of Europe's capitals.[4] For these critics, Blavatsky's account is at best on a par with the implausible tales of Tibetan adventures found in the best-selling books by T. Lobsang Rampa. Rampa, whose real name was Cyril Henry Hoskins, was an Englishman from Devon and was never in Tibet, but claimed that he had lived there in a previous life as a lama and that his present body was the "host" of his previous incarnation. *The Third Eye*, Rampa's first book, sold millions of copies and is still very popular. He went on to write nineteen more, one of which, *Living with the Lama*, was dictated to him by his cat. In the late 1950s, Heinrich Harrer, author of the classic *Seven Years in Tibet*, hired a private investigator to look into Rampa's claims. Subsequent accusations of fraud led Hoskins to move to Canada, where he died in 1981. Ironically, in 1997, revelations about Harrer's own youthful membership in the Nazi party marred the debut of Jean-Jacques Annaud's film *Seven Years in Tibet*, based on Harrer's memoir.

While it is true that some, perhaps most, of HPB's travelogue sounds like unabashed tall tales, we have to admit that the idea of her slinking through the nightlife of Paris, Vienna, or other European cities as someone's mistress is equally unbelievable, perhaps even more so, and the only evidence for this suspicion is itself fairly suspect. Yet while there is some independent support for some of HPB's travels—in a letter published in 1878, Albert Rawson provided names of people who knew Blavatsky in India prior to her relocating there in 1879—there is very little corroborating her journeys to Tibet.[5] And although the records of Annie Royal Taylor, Mrs. St. George Littledale, Susie Rijnhart, and Alexandra David-Neel make clear that it was possible for women to travel in the forbidden land, we know that it was because others saw them there and recorded their attempts. No one saw Blavatsky there, or at least that is what her critics say.

And she would, they also say, be hard to miss. Peter Washington, author of the very readable but often inaccurate *Madame Blavatsky's Baboon*, voiced this reservation succinctly. At a time when "Tibet remained closed to all but a very few travellers," and when "Chinese, Russian, and British missions"—not to mention the Tibetans themselves—patrolled the borders "alert to the presence of military spies," the idea that HPB could slip through unseen seems very doubtful. As Washington writes: "the thought of the breathless, tactless and massively stout Blavatsky managing to climb steep mountains in brutal weather while concealing herself from trained observers is just too difficult to imagine."[6] No doubt it is, but the thought also raises a few questions. Blavatsky herself, if she is to be believed, remarked that during her first trip to India, she was "very thin." If she was, it is less difficult to imagine her scampering up the Tibetan trail. But if she wasn't, then it is equally—again, perhaps even more—difficult to imagine a "breathless, tactless and massively stout Blavatsky" being the belle of the ball or enjoying herself in Europe's fleshpots. We can't have it both ways.

· · ·

BUT WASHINGTON HIMSELF offers some evidence in HPB's favor. Blavatsky told A. P. Sinnett that her first attempt to reach Tibet failed because she was turned back by the British border guards. Washington remarks that two British Army officers serving in Tibet testified after HPB's death that they "had seen or heard of a white woman travelling alone in the Tibetan mountains in 1854 and 1867." One officer in question, Major-General Charles Murray, met Colonel Olcott in March 1893 on a train between Nalhati and Calcutta. During conversation, Murray told Olcott that while in command at Darjeeling as a junior officer, he had been told of a white woman at Punkabaree, near the Darjeeling hills, who was trying to pass through Nepal to get to Tibet. She was there, she said, doing research for a book. Murray had orders not to let any Europeans cross the border, for fear they would be slaughtered by bandits. Only recently, two French missionaries had been murdered and Murray did not want another dead European on his hands. Murray detained Blavatsky and she wound up staying as his guest for a month. When she accepted that he would not let her cross the border, she changed her plans and left, according to Jean Overton Fuller, for Lahore. Olcott wrote Murray's account in his notebook, and asked him to sign it. Murray did, and in April 1893, it appeared in an issue of *The Theosophist*. Murray specifically named Madame Blavatsky as the "white woman" in question—a point Marion Meade leaves out when referring to the story—and the anecdote came up because in conversation Olcott had mentioned his work for the Theosophical Society. Sylvia Cranston remarks that Murray had ample opportunity to correct the account or to ask Olcott to withdraw it; that he did neither suggests that it was accurate, unless we want to argue that for some obscure reason, he lied about it. The only thing missing is a description of the "white woman," telling us whether she was thin or "massively stout."[7]

Other critics argue that in order to travel to Tibet at that time, one would have had to carry a considerable amount of equipment, which Blavatsky, on her own, couldn't have done. Gertrude Marvin Williams, a hostile biographer, argues that as there would be no possibility of getting provisions along the way, a traveler would have to bring along a pack team, interpreters, tents, bedding, food, water, and other rations, a stove and fuel, as well as servants to carry these things, not to mention everything necessary for the return journey, an argument made against HPB's Tibetan adventures as early as 1895.[8] Critics also speak of an "impassable" terrain. Jean Overton Fuller, whose mother and grandfather made the journey themselves, argues that there are markets in Tibet where one can get what one needs along the way, and that unlike the British, who were there scouting for secret and unknown paths through which the Russians might descend on them, HPB would most likely take the easiest, most well-traveled route—which would be the one, indeed, where there would be markets, used by other travelers. We also know that HPB could ride a horse—even if she wasn't a "circus equestrienne"—and that she is thought to have learned enough Tibetan from the Tartar nomads she met during her stay at Saratov to ask questions, buy supplies, and get directions.

Yet if Major-General Murray's account above can be taken as proof that HPB made an attempt at getting into Tibet, it is also evidence that, at least on this occasion, she wasn't successful. On her second try, though, she says she was. This happened in 1856 and her point of entry was through Kashmir, in the northwestern part of India; like Ladakh, Kashmir is also sometimes called "Little Tibet." The story is that while in Lahore, she met a friend of her father, a German ex-Lutheran minister by the name of Kühlwein, who may have been a relative of one of her governesses. Hearing that his friend was planning an expedition to Tibet with two other travelers, HPB's father asked Kühlwein to look out for his daughter, as he assumed she would be attempting the same thing. HPB and Kühlwein's group joined forces, and among their guides was a Tartar shaman, who had left his home in Siberia many years ago and now wanted to return. The idea was that as a Russian, HPB would be able to help him to do this.

At Leh—once the capital of Ladakh, now a district in the Indian regions of Jammu and Kashmir—Kühlwein came down with fever and had to abandon the journey. The others carried on, but soon Kühlwein's companions also dropped out—either turned back by the border guards or for some other reason—and HPB was left alone with the shaman. HPB's features have been described as "Kalmuck" and "Mongolian," and Sylvia Cranston suggests that it was because of this that she and the shaman were allowed to continue past the frontier. Something happened though and they lost their bearings. It's possible that the shaman, who wanted to get to Siberia, not Tibet, finding himself off his route, tried to get back on it and in the process got lost. Eventually they found themselves in a Tartar camp, and the shaman arranged for them to stay and share their provisions. The Tartars, however, had no idea where they were nor how they could get back on route, and there is some reason to think that they had meandered to the fringes of the Gobi Desert. HPB speaks of the peculiar silence of the region, a reflection that Sir Francis Younghusband himself made when traveling in the Gobi years later.[9]

It was during their stay here that HPB witnessed the shaman in action, an account of which appears in *Isis Unveiled*. HPB had noticed that the shaman kept a strange stone under his left armpit. When she asked why he did, he refused to tell her, but now she discovered its purpose. Outside their tent, the shaman stuck a wooden peg in the ground, and on top of this he placed a goat's head. This, he told her, was a sign that he was about to perform magic and that no one should disturb him. He then took the stone and put it in his mouth. Almost immediately, he fell into a trance; his body became as stiff as a corpse, and a deep voice seemed to rise up from the ground, asking what they wanted. HPB realized that his astral body was now free, and she took the opportunity to get help. She asked the shaman to send his soul to the Kutchi of Lhasa, whom she knew—a Kutchi is a kind of influential Kashmiri merchant— and that he should be made aware of their situation. He did, and a few hours later, some horsemen arrived. They were friends of the Kutchi. They took HPB to the border and sent her on her way back to India. What became of the shaman is unknown. Many years later, Colonel Olcott received some independent confirmation of this second attempt on Tibet. When traveling with HPB in northern India in 1879, they passed through the city of Bareilly, in the state of Uttar Pradesh. There Olcott met a "Hindu gentleman" who said he recognized Blavatsky as the European woman who stayed with him many years before, when she was trying to enter Tibet through Kashmir.[10]

. . .

ON NEITHER OF these attempts did Blavatsky achieve her goal, to reach the secret school in eastern Tibet where, she believed, the Master and his fellow initiates often stayed and where she too could be initiated. On her third attempt, she says, she was successful.

In 1867, HPB was in the Balkans, where she got word from the Master to proceed to Constantinople; from here she would strike out once again for Tibet. Jean Overton Fuller suggests that she met Master Morya there, and with him took the "short, direct, but terrible overland route" across Turkey, Persia, Afghanistan, India, and the Kashmir.[11] Just to get to Tibet itself must have been grueling. The "short, direct" route from Constantinople to Shigatse, where they were headed and where the Tibetan Buddhist monastery of Tashilhunpo is located, is just over three thousand miles. It is short when compared to the sea route, which would have had HPB heading west again, to Marseilles, where she would have boarded a ship that would have taken her round the Cape of Good Hope to India. Fuller suggests they could have made twenty miles a day on horseback. At that speed it would have taken them some five months to reach their destination.

Once in Tibet, the demands on the travelers would have increased. A later traveler in Tibet, the Lama Anagarika Govinda, writes of his own trek across the roof of the world:

Imagine . . . toiling for some 200–300 miles over endless mountain ranges, through steaming hot valleys and over cold, cloud-covered passes, fording wild mountain streams, where a slip of the foot means certain death, or crossing the thunderous abyss

of a torrential river, clinging precariously to a shaky reed-rope
of uncertain age. . . . Imagine . . . travelling through gorges,
where stones are falling from invisible heights and where
waterfalls seem to rush down straight from the clouds. . . .
Imagine . . . negotiating overhanging cliffs on narrow mountain paths and sharp-edged rock ledges which cut into . . .
sore and tired feet.[12]

The idea of a thin Madame Blavatsky, let alone a "massively stout"
one, making this journey is enough to raise questions about it. But
then we remember Rasputin walking from Siberia to Mount Athos,
and the Hungarian Csoma de Kőrös reaching Ladakh from eastern
Europe, mostly on foot, and we realize it *would* have been possible,
even if, as HPB's critics believe, highly unlikely.

Although forbidden to most outsiders, Tibet's borders, it seems,
were open to people of neighboring lands, and traders and pilgrims
from Ladakh, India, Bhutan, China, and Mongolia often entered
undisturbed.[13] HPB's "Mongolian" features would have helped in
this case. And while HPB's critics often refer to her Masters as
Tibetans, the truth is that they were not. Master Morya was from
the beginning her "tall, mysterious Indian," and another Master,
whom she would meet and stay with on this journey, was, at least
according to some researchers, of Sikh and Punjabi extraction. In
To Lhasa in Disguise, the adventurer and anthropologist William
McGovern—often said to be the inspiration for the filmmaker Ste-
ven Spielberg's character Indiana Jones—reported that Kashmiris
and Nepalese are generally allowed to settle in Tibet, so the presence of two northern Indians in Shigatse would not have been
unusual. Although it is typically ignored, HPB repeatedly said that

the school near the Tashilhunpo monastery, where she said she received her initiation and training, was *not* the central headquarters of the circle of adepts whose agent she had become, and that they had similar locations in other parts of the world, in South America, Japan, Syria, even China. Egypt, too, was another important spot for this mysterious brotherhood.

Blavatsky describes being taken to the home of Master Morya's friend and colleague, Master Koot Hoomi—his name is spelled in different ways, but for convenience's sake I will use this version. At the house he shared with his widowed sister, which was situated in a ravine, near a stream with towering mountains in the background, KH (as he is often called) taught *chelas*, or students, of the Gelugpa, or "Yellow Hat" sect of Tibetan Buddhism. This was founded, as mentioned earlier, by the teacher Tsong Khapa in the fifteenth century. In Tsong Khapa's time, the Buddhist teaching had deteriorated and become decadent under the influence of the primitive Bön-po religion, indigenous to the region, and had resorted to dark magical practices and animal sacrifice. Neither Koot Hoomi nor Morya were monks of the monastery nor Tibetan Buddhists proper. But they were closely associated with the monastery, and the monks at Tashilhunpo sent them any students whom they thought would be good candidates for their own special instruction. One such *chela* was the fifteen-year-old Djwal Khool (again, spellings of his name differ), who later became the alleged source for the thousands of pages of "channeled" material taken down by the neo-Theosophist Alice Bailey—I say "neo-Theosophist" because most mainstream Theosophists considered Bailey's work unreliable.[14] Djwal Khool later made a silk illustration of the house where he, HPB, KH, and M lived. Jean Overton Fuller argues that the architecture depicted in Djwal Khool's picture is Nepalese, and that this suggests that Master Morya was from Nepal, and we remember that in one version of his initial meeting with HPB, he is in the company of "the first Nepal embassy." The furnishings for the house were spare, if there were any at all—rugs and cushions on the hard floor seem the only concessions to comfort—and a sunken chamber was said to house the Master's library and museum. Djwal Khool depicts a stream, and HPB remarked that she would follow this to a lake, where she bathed. Fuller remarks that HPB must have taken only short dips as the water would have been freezing and "she was not a swimmer," which raises questions about how HPB managed to survive two sea disasters.

KH himself was a highly cultured, highly educated individual. He had traveled to London, attended classes in Leipzig, spoke fluent French, and his English was better than Master M's. Both he and Master M were vegetarians—unlike Blavatsky—yet Master M himself enjoyed some pleasures, such as smoking a hookah pipe. Blavatsky herself, we know, enjoyed tobacco; whether she did while in Tibet is unclear. Critics trying to discredit her account point out that smoking was banned in Tibet, a practice seemingly well in advance of our own health and safety concerns. Supporters, however, point out that the ban was only nominal and never enforced—as, say, the law against crossing a street against the light isn't in many major cities. And in any case, as a Master and ascetic, Morya would have been able to indulge in it if he liked, a liberality of behavior enjoyed, we know, by many gurus.

Critics argue that the descriptions HPB gives of Shigatse, Tashilhunpo, and neighboring locations, of local customs and manners, and of her life in general there, were cribbed from Abbé

Huc's account. But as the good Abbé did not visit Shigatse or Tashilhunpo, it is difficult to see how she could have used him as a source for her descriptions of these places, although she could have relied on his and other accounts to supply some basic information. Abbé Huc, we know, did go to Lhasa, and did describe it in his book, and HPB would have had better luck palming off some retouched account of his as her own observations of the forbidden city than in making up descriptions of Shigatse and Tashilhunpo out of thin air. But even though both her sister and her biographer Sylvia Cranston suggest that she did visit Lhasa, HPB never said she did. Yet, if she was trying to impress and mystify people with accounts of make-believe travel—as her critics say she was—wouldn't she have "gone the whole hog," as Gurdjieff says, and thrown in Lhasa, too? After all, Lhasa is less than a hundred and fifty miles from Shigatse, there was Abbé Huc's account to crib from, and she may as well have been hung for a sheep as for a lamb—if she was going to lie, why not tell a big one?

It is possible, though, that she did travel near Lhasa. In 1927, a Major Cross, who had been manager of the tea estates of the Dalai Lama in the early years of the last century, gave a talk to the Toronto Theosophical Society. He is one of the two British officers mentioned earlier who provided sightings of Blavatsky in India. Cross related that while in his capacity as the Dalai Lama's agent, he became interested in stories told by some of the oldest workers on the estates of a "white woman" who, while journeying to a lamasery in the far north, had passed through their lands, some ten years after the Sepoy Mutiny—that is, in 1867 to 1868, when Blavatsky would have been there. Cross believed the woman to have been Blavatsky. To be sure, this is not an actual sighting, as

Major-General Murray's is, and is little more than hearsay, but it does add some weight to the possibility that HPB had passed through this territory.[15]

SOME OF THE other evidence in support of HPB's being in Tibet will be examined when we come to look at her most "Buddhist" piece of work, *The Voice of the Silence*. But along with the question of her being in Tibet comes another directly related to it, namely, what she did while she was there. Master M had told her nearly twenty years earlier that he had a mission in mind for her, and that in order to fulfill it she would have to spend three years in Tibet. Now she was there. What was the mysterious "preparation" for her task that he had spoken about? It could not have been only the study of Tibetan Buddhism, as important and worthy a pursuit as this undoubtedly is. Otherwise, why would the monastery send some of its most promising *chelas* here, to the special school of Koot Hoomi? It must have been something else. Blavatsky does speak of visiting the monastery but of not being allowed to enter. She was told, however, that on its altar were curious cube-shaped tablets, on which verses in an unknown language, Senzar, were inscribed. She speaks of "thin, oblong squares," and "discs or plates" containing these verses, which were preserved "on the altars of the temples attached to centres where the so-called 'contemplative' or Mahayana (Yogacharya) schools are established."[16] Mahayana, or "Great Vehicle," is the form of Buddhism that by most accounts appeared around the time of Christ, and includes the notion of the bodhisattva, an enlightened individual who rejects his own salvation, or passing into Nirvana, until that of all sentient beings is accomplished. The verses inscribed on the "oblong squares" were recited to her; she memorized them, and some of them would later be translated by her and appear as *The Voice of the Silence*. The mysterious "Stanzas of Dzyan," on which her *magnum opus*, *The Secret Doctrine* is an enormous commentary, were also inscribed in the same strange tongue.

Part of Blavatsky's work while in Tibet included learning this mysterious language which, perhaps needless to say, no one before her had ever mentioned, let alone spoke. Senzar was not the only unknown language to appear in a mysterious location in the mystic East. In the late 1890s, the French occultist Alexandre Saint-Yves d'Alveydre met the enigmatic Haji Sharif, who, along with teaching him Sanskrit, also relayed to him the hitherto unknown language of Vattan, which, he told him, was the official language of the "Great Agarthian School." Agartha, like its sister Shambhala (with which it is often confused), was a vast sunken city located somewhere beneath the Gobi Desert, and was the home of the King of the World, a somewhat sinister variant on Blavatsky's Masters. While the idea of Shambhala is based in Buddhist legend and is associated with the Vajrayana and Kalachakra teachings—Blavatsky herself speaks of it—Agartha seems a Western creation, linked to fabled Asgard, home of the Norse gods. In 1871, in his *Dialogues et Fragments Philosophiques,* the French theologian Ernest Renan wrote of "Asgaard" being located in Central Asia. In *Les Fils de Dieu* (*The Sons of God*), the French writer and traveler Louis Jacolliot wrote of "Asgartha," a 15,000-year-old city in Central Asia that was the source of the Aryan race (the Aryans were the "noble" northern Indians, so named by the nineteenth-century philologist Max Müller). Jacolliot heard the story from Indian Brahmins while serving as a magistrate in Chandernagore, and his work would be a major influence on Blavatsky's own.

Emma Hardinge Britten, a one-time friend of HPB and an early member of the Theosophical Society, does not mention Agartha in her book *Ghost Land* (1876), which Blavatsky knew, and which we will look at further on, but does draw on the legend of the subterranean city hidden beneath the sands. This theme, of a "hollow earth," would find mass dissemination in Jules Verne's classic tale *A Journey to the Center of the Earth* (1867) which, along with being a masterpiece of adventure, is also full of esoteric hints—the popular film version leaves out all of Verne's references to alchemy, a central thread running through the novel. And the "hollow earth" and "hidden civilization" themes would be combined in the early science-fantasy novel *The Coming Race* (1871) by Edward Bulwer-Lytton, an author whose work, we've seen, would be a powerful influence on Blavatsky.

HPB's talk of a sacred, primeval language was also very much in line with scholarly research into language and its roots at the time, with Sanskrit being the most likely candidate for some ur-tongue from which all others descended. Other, more eccentric ideas about a single, primeval language were popular in occult and eso- teric circles going back to the late eighteenth century, and were linked to a similar notion of some single, primal, sacred revelation, the *prisca theologia* or "perennial philosophy" associated with the mythic sage and founder of all knowledge, Hermes Trismegistus.[17] Blavatsky herself speaks of Senzar as "the mystic name for the secret sacerdotal language . . . the mystery speech of the initiated adepts all over the world."

This theme of a primordial revelation at the dawn of man is one that Blavatsky herself would revive in her monumental works *Isis Unveiled* and *The Secret Doctrine*. It is curious, though, that along with Senzar, HPB's syllabus in Tibet also included English, something she was supposed to have been taught already by her Yorkshire governess Augusta Jeffries as a child in Odessa.[18] She had already been in England and had traveled across the Midwest, where, one assumes, she had put Ms. Jeffries's lessons to good use. But perhaps there are mystic mysteries hidden in the English tongue as well?

BUT ALONG WITH learning Senzar and English, while in Tibet HPB engaged in a perhaps even more difficult study: the development and control of her psychic powers. The Masters Morya, Koot Hoomi, and others of their school were adepts, men—and one assumes also women—who possessed remarkable abilities. They could communicate at a distance through "thought transference"— the term "telepathy" would not be in use until the psychical investigator Frederick Myers coined it in 1882. They could also read minds. They could project their astral bodies, or "bilocate," as the phenomenon came to be called, and seemingly appear to be in two or more places at once. They could "de-materialize" and "re-materialize" objects, and transport them over distances, rather like *Star Trek*'s "transporter." They could enter and dominate another's consciousness, what in contemporary New Age speak is known as "walk-ins." They were clairvoyant and clairaudient. They could perceive and command occult entities, or "elementals," the salamanders, undines, sylphs, and gnomes related to ancient elements of fire, water, air, and earth.[19] They could see "etheric" auras and read the history of objects through the power of psychometry. They were precognitive and had other powers as well.

If her being in Tibet is difficult enough for Blavatsky's critics to swallow, the idea that while there she was trained in the use of these remarkable abilities is, to put it mildly, absolutely unbelievable. Whether she was in Tibet, Tanganyika, or Timbuktu, this sort of thing, they say, is simply impossible. It should be pointed out, however, that other travelers in the forbidden land also encountered individuals with some unusual talents. Although Alexandra David-Neel found no traces of Blavatsky's Masters, she encountered enough magic in Tibet to write a book about it. Tibet, she said "seems to offer peculiarly favourable conditions for telepathy—as well as for psychic phenomena in general." [20]

Lama Anagarika Govinda confirms Alexandra David-Neel's remarks, commenting on "the frequency of telepathic phenomena among the inhabitants of Tibet," an observation also made by the Swedish explorer Sven Hedin, who had no Theosophical bias. [21] Govinda gives an example of his guru knowing his thoughts at the very second they came to him. [22] Govinda also saw evidence of psychometry, or the ability to mentally "read" the history of an object, and of the power of a Tibetan hermit to "take possession" of his consciousness. This is known as creating a *"tulku,"* and may be related to HPB's experiences of leading a "double life," and the strange duo-consciousness she experienced during her "creative illness" in Mingrelia. Govinda relates that while staying the night in a rest house near the hermitage of Gomchen, he felt that he had "no more control over my thoughts, but that somebody else was thinking them," and that he was losing his identity. Govinda believed that the hermit was doing this unintentionally, simply by directing his powerfully focused attention on him, while he drifted off into sleep. Significantly, Govinda says that he was "hovering between the waking and sleeping state" at the time. This is known as the "hypnagogic state," and there is a huge amount of evidence suggesting that it is a condition of consciousness strongly linked to paranormal or "occult" phenomena.[23] It can also be seen as a form of Blavatsky's "duo-consciousness."

Another strange phenomenon found in Tibet is that of "*lunggom*," or "trance walking," a method of seemingly "walking on air," of moving across the terrain at great speed and with "the elasticity of a ball." This may be how HPB managed to cover great distances during her sojourn, but the idea of a "massively stout" Blavatsky bobbing up and down across mountain trails is somehow too comical.

But perhaps the most remarkable "power" travelers found in Tibet is that of the "*tulpa*," a mental or imaginary image or form that takes on a concrete and *living* character. These may happen involuntarily, when one's own image appears elsewhere and interacts with others, as one would in everyday life; only later is it realized it was a "phantom" and not the "real" person that was seen. More remarkable is the conscious creation of a "thought form," which is "tangible and endowed with all the faculties and qualities naturally pertaining to the beings or things of which they have the appearance."[24] David-Neel writes that "when he fled from Shigatze, the Tashi Lama left in his stead, a phantom perfectly resembling him who played his part so thoroughly and naturally that everyone who saw him was deceived."[25] (This was in 1924, following a dispute with the Thirteenth Dalai Lama; the Tashi or Panchen Lama is Tibet's "second-in-command.")

David-Neel herself had problems with a *tulpa* of her own. She relates how, after performing the "prescribed concentration of thought and other rites," she created a *tulpa* of a monk. It took her a few months, but eventually his form became "fixed" and he became "a kind of guest, living in my apartment." The form was mostly visual, she said, but she could also feel "as if a robe was slightly rubbing against me." Once she felt his hand touch her shoulder. After a time, the *tulpa* became an unwanted guest, and it took David-Neel six months to "de-materialize" him.[26] In 1912, the Thirteenth Dalai Lama, Thubten Gyatso, told David-Neel that

> A bodhisattva is the basis of countless magic forms. By the power generated in a state of perfect concentration of mind he may, at one and the same time, show a phantom of himself in thousands of millions of worlds. He may create not only human forms, but any forms he chooses, even those of inanimate objects, such as hills, enclosures, houses, forests, roads, bridges, etc. He may produce atmospheric phenomena as well as the thirst-quenching beverage of immortality . . . there is no limit to his power of phantom creation.[27]

When we remember that "the philosophers of the Mahayana"— the form of Buddhism that the Tibetan variant is based on—"liken the universe to a magical display, a mirage, a flash of lightning, or the ripples of waves on the sea," then we may not find it difficult to accept the idea that "Gods, demons, the whole universe, are but a mirage which exists in the mind."[28] And we may also accept that when the mind is focused powerfully, and achieves full concentration, it can accomplish extraordinary things. It was this concentration of the mind that Blavatsky learned, she tells us, during her time in Tibet.

IF BY NOW the reader feels that, for all our reflections, he is no nearer to knowing whether or not Madame Blavatsky was in Tibet, I cannot blame him. In all honesty, I do not know myself. Blavatsky claimed that, all in all, she spent seven years there. In a rebuttal to criticisms by the spiritualist Arthur Lillie, published in *Light*, a spiritual magazine, in 1884, she said, "I have lived at different periods in Little Tibet as well as in Great Tibet, and that the combined periods form more than seven years." She never said that she had passed "seven consecutive years in a convent." "What I have said . . . is that I stopped in Lamaistic convents, that I visited Tzi-gadze, the Teshi Hlumpo territory and its neighbourhood, and that I have been further into, and have visited such places of Tibet as have never been visited by other Europeans." And as to visiting the Master Koot Hoomi at his house in the ravine, she writes, "I have better proof in store—when I believe it needed."[29] What that proof was is unclear, but that later on in her career she sorely needed it, will become painfully apparent.

FOUR

A HAUNTING IN CHITTENDEN

In the curious world of HPB chronology, a letter often sited as the first from the pen of the Masters was received by Blavatsky's Aunt Nadya in Odessa in 1870. It would only be first reported, however, in 1884, when Nadya wrote about it in a letter to Colonel Olcott. It was later published in 1885 in a report of the General Council of the Theosophical Society. The letter was written in French in what became known as Koot Hoomi's handwriting, and it informed Nadya that her niece was safe and that she would return to her family shortly. "The noble relatives of Mad. H. Blavatsky," it said, "have no cause whatsoever for grief." Although Madame Blavatsky had been ill, it went on, she was now well, owing to the protection of "the Lord Sangyas"—the Tibetan name for the Buddha—and to the devotion of friends. The letter ended by assuring Nadya that "before 18 new moons shall have risen"—18 months—HPB "will have returned to her family."

Although receiving a letter from Tibet, hand-delivered by "a messenger of Asiatic appearance," was strange enough, the messenger's manner of departure was stranger still. According to Aunt

Nadya, he "disappeared before my very eyes." One would think that such an unusual event would have prompted Aunt Nadya to speak about it straightaway, yet it wasn't until fourteen years later that she remembered it and mentioned it to Colonel Olcott. In her letter to Olcott, she remarks that it is "difficult, not to say impossible for me, to comprehend how there can exist people so stupid as to believe that either my niece or yourself have invented the men whom you call the Mahatmas," and she goes on to say that HPB spoke to her about the Masters "at great length, years ago." As more than one commentator has pointed out, this seems to contradict some remarks by Vera that none of the family knew anything about the Masters until well into Blavatsky's "ministry" and were baffled when they heard her talk about them. This suggests that Aunt Nadya may have been doing some creative backtracking in order to support her niece, but it could also mean that her memory was poor, or that she interpreted the young Helena's remarks about the strange "Indian" visitor in her dreams in light of later developments. And although one would think that having someone—let alone a mysterious Asian—disappear before your eyes would warrant a comment or two, perhaps the experience was so strange that she thought no one would believe her, or, being a devout Christian—as her letter to Olcott affirms—that it was a trick of the devil's. Yet if it was, it brought welcome news about her wayward niece, about whom there had been no word for some time.[1]

Not long after Nadya received this letter, which arrived, she said, in early November, HPB left Tibet—or wherever she had been—and headed out to accomplish her mission. This, along with learning Senzar and mastering her occult powers, was what she had

learned during her time with Koot Hoomi. Her mission, it turned
out, was to prove the *reality* of the spiritualist phenomena that had
become a craze on both sides of the Atlantic—but also to show that
people were mistaken about their alleged source, the dead. This
was not true. In other words, psychic phenomena were real and
offered incontrovertible proof of a spiritual reality, against the rising dominance of scientific materialism. But they were *not* caused
by the spirits of the dead, or at least not by the dead that the many
who participated in séances in Europe and America believed they
were contacting. This seems like rather an abstruse point on which
to focus, and we will examine it in more detail further on. But for
HPB and her Masters, it was absolutely crucial.

Before arriving back in Odessa, and thus proving Aunt Nadya's
mysterious letter correct, HPB embarked on another tour of eastern Europe. Passing through the newly built Suez Canal, she
reached Greece. While she was away, a lot had happened; for one
thing, Germany had defeated France in the Franco-Prussian War,
a development that brought the French occultist Eliphas Lévi to
despair. In Greece, or possibly Cyprus, she met Master Hilarion
again, who was part of one of the Masters' groups in that part of
the world. After learning what she could from Hilarion at Piraeus,
the port of Athens, HPB boarded the S.S. *Eumonia*, heading for
Cairo. On July 4, 1871, not far from the island of Spetsai, the *Eumonia* blew up; gunpowder it carried in case of a pirate attack was the
cause. Out of four hundred passengers, only sixteen survived,
among them HPB. All her money and luggage were lost, and she
spoke of seeing "limbs, heads, and trunks all falling around me."[2]
As she was not a swimmer, one assumes she was quickly hauled out
of the water, although if she was by this time "massively stout," this

must have been a challenge. She was taken to Greek land and later accepted passage on another ship to Alexandria. Here she apparently played roulette with some of the money the Greek government had given her for immediate expenses. She came up lucky, and with her winnings moved on to Cairo.[3]

At the Hotel d'Orient, where she stayed—when she had the money, HPB liked to treat herself to some comfort—she met a woman who would later prove a key player in her downfall. Miss Emma Cutting worked at the hotel, and she would later say that at the time she lent HPB some money, indeed, had taken her in after her shipwreck, although if Blavatsky had been lucky at roulette and was staying at the hotel, why she needed the money is unclear. Nevertheless, they got to know each other, and Emma became involved in an idea HPB had in mind. She wanted to start a *société spirite*, much like the one she and Albert Rawson had tried to start twenty years earlier. She again met Paulos Metamon, and may have also studied with Louis-Maximilian Bimstein, also known as Max Théon, an eccentric Polish-Jewish Kabbalist associated with the mysterious Hermetic Brotherhood of Luxor. Both Metamon and Théon were possibly involved in the new *société*, which would be based on the ideas of Allan Kardec, a successful French spiritualist who died in 1869. Kardec (whose real name was Hippolyte-Léon Denizard Rivail; the spirits had given him his new one) was an educationalist who had been converted to Spiritualism—or "Spiritism" as he called it—at a séance at which he saw tables and chairs dance around a room of their own accord, or, more precisely, that of the spirits who controlled them. Although there are more subtle differences between Kardec's Spiritism and Spiritualism—they can be found in his classic work, *The Spirits' Book*, published in

1856—the central one is that Kardec believed in reincarnation, something that spiritualists and their close kin, the Swedenborgians, rejected. After Kardec's death, what we might call "mainstream Spiritualism" came to dominate. Oddly, Kardec's version went on to become widely popular in Brazil, where it remains one of the country's major religions.

In mainstream Spiritualism, after spending time on earth, the soul resides for eternity in the spiritual realm. For Kardec, on the death of the physical body, the soul enters the spiritual worlds but then after a time, it returns to earth in order to continue work on its perfection. In fact, the soul can choose the life in which it reincarnates, in order to have the best chance of development, leading to the reflection that we should never complain about our lot in life, as we chose it before we were born. Blavatsky's relation to both reincarnation and Spiritualism will be more than a little ambiguous, but this vision of a kind of cosmic evolution found in Kardec is one with which she would be in accord.

HPB's second try at a *société spirite*, however, was as unsuccessful as the first. Even more so, actually, as some of the mediums involved were caught cheating. Not surprisingly, there's more than one account of this fiasco. According to a report given some years later by Emma Cutting—by this time Emma Coulomb—Blavatsky used a "long glove stuffed with cotton" as a materialized "spirit hand," and this clumsy device was soon found out.[4] Yet, as will be seen, Emma Coulomb's trustworthiness as a witness is itself highly questionable. Blavatsky's own account has it that although she was against the idea of contacting the dead, she would allow the mediums to perform—Emma Coulomb (née Cutting) was apparently one of these—and then explain to the audience the truth behind the phenomena. What Blavatsky wanted to show was the difference between a *passive* medium—that is, someone who was merely the *means* by which phenomena could occur—and what she called an "active *doer*," someone who could produce and *control* the phenomena, and not, as with mediums, be controlled by them. In other words, a magician. This, in essence, is what she learned in Tibet— or wherever she was.

Yet HPB seemed to be a poor judge of character, at least at this time. Or perhaps her generous nature was taken advantage of, something that will prove to be the case down the line. In any case, while she was away, the mediums—amateurs, according to her account—decided to try to fleece the members of the society by staging fake séances. They also drank a great deal, something HPB was decidedly against. When she returned and discovered what had happened, she closed the society down—not, however, before a Greek "madman," "who had been present at the only two public séances we held," tried to shoot her. She thought he must have been possessed by some "vile spook." Although the society lasted only two weeks, the attempt on her life—if it was not an exaggeration— in a way proved her point. What her mediums were contacting were not the souls of the dear departed, but a species of astral hobo, psychic tramps with nothing better to do than hover near the borderland between the living and the dead, looking for some mischief. It was this insight that would lead to the lifelong feud between HPB and the major spiritualists of her time.[5]

Although Blavatsky was away when her mediums tried to pull a fast one, because it was her society she received the blame for the affair and was branded a fraud. Yet a letter from a fellow Russian who was in Cairo at the time—a Mr. G. Yakovlef—that her sister

Vera claimed to possess, argues for HPB's authenticity. In it he speaks of Blavatsky being able to tell him whose portrait and whose lock of hair it was that he kept in a locket, which he had possessed for only a short time and which no one knew about. He also tells a story about how she "magically" caused a glass and a tumbler to shatter.[6]

Yet, even if Mr. Yakovlef was a satisfied customer, the situation in Egypt was unsatisfactory. HPB decided to leave Cairo and once again travel. Before she did, however, she met the famous French Egyptologist Gaston Maspero at the Boulak Museum, and also a Coptic adept, Serapis Bey, one of the Masters. Later, in New York, Colonel Olcott would receive mysterious letters from Serapis Bey, but now he seems to have been involved with furthering Blavatsky's occult knowledge. She tells the story of how once, while camping in the desert, she expressed the wish for a *café au lait*, made in the fashion of the Café de la Paix in Paris. Serapis Bey (or, possibly, his "son," Tuitit Bey, another Master) drew some water from their supply and handed the cup to HPB. It was a steaming hot *café*, just as she ordered it. Amazed, she began to drink, but as she did, it became mere water. Serapis Bey explained that he had created the illusion of hot coffee.

By some accounts, Serapis Bey is Paulos Metamon; Tuitit Bey is sometimes thought to have been Max Théon. K. Paul Johnson suggests that, while in Cairo, HPB also came into the orbit of two individuals who combined an interest in Freemasonry and esotericism with radical politics, the Sufi and Islamic modernist Jamal ad-Din al-Afghani, and the Jewish-Egyptian playwright James Sanua, whom Johnson casts in the role of two of HPB's "Masters." Johnson's exhaustive research places Blavatsky as a "fellow traveller" with the Islamic reformer "al-Afghani," as he was known, on at least five occasions, and although direct contact between the two is still a matter of speculation, the fact that they were both in India, Tiflis, Cairo, India again, and Paris, at the same time—early 1850s and 1860s, 1871, 1879, and 1884, respectively—and had very similar agendas, is strongly suggestive of some connection. Johnson also speculates that the mysterious "Chaldean Book of Numbers," which Blavatsky claimed was the source of what she called the "Oriental Cabala" and which, like her *Book of Dzyan*, is unknown to scholars, may have come to her through al-Afghani. Blavatsky claimed that this ancient text was "in the possession of some Persian Sufis," a description that would fit him. A few years later, when Blavatsky begins to talk about a mysterious "Brotherhood of Luxor," it is more than likely, as Joscelyn Godwin suggests, that she is speaking about the loose group of esoteric "fellow travellers" she knew during this time.[7] One of these, Agardi Metrovitch, we know, died during her time in Egypt, either from typhoid fever, or from poison administered by the Maltese agents of the Jesuits. Blavatsky claimed that the Master Hilarion had warned her of his peril, and according to some accounts, Metrovitch was in Cairo searching for her, as her family was concerned, having heard of her near fatal adventure on the S. S. *Eumonia*. (He was, it seems, in Odessa when word came, and as he was going to Egypt anyway on business, the family asked him to track her down.) As no church would bury him, she had to do it herself, and with another pupil of Hilarion, she dug a grave near the sea and laid him to rest.

Leaving Cairo, HPB traveled in Syria, Palestine, and Lebanon, where she came into contact with the Druze, the highly secret Middle Eastern religious sect into which her friend Albert Rawson had been initiated. It may have been through Rawson's contacts that she became intimate with the Druze. It was also at this time that she met the writer and traveler Lydia Pashkov, a little known but very accomplished character who was, among other things, a correspondent for *Le Figaro* and "the first woman to make travel literature her profession."[8] While on caravan near Baalbek, Pashkov met HPB's party, and the two decided to travel together. Pashkov tells the story of how Blavatsky raised the spirit of a strange monument in the sand, and the description she gives of the event makes HPB seem like some magician of old. At night, after drawing a circle around herself and uttering many spells, Blavatsky "pointed with her wand at the monument." A great ball of fire flashed. Jackals howled in the darkness, incense burned, and Blavatsky commanded the spirit of the person to whom the monument was dedicated to appear. An old, bearded man materialized and told them that the monument was the altar of an ancient temple of a forgotten god. HPB commanded the spirit to show them how the temple was in its glory. Suddenly they saw a vast, colossal structure and a magnificent city, then all vanished. Like Rawson and a few others, Pashkov would later testify to the authenticity of HPB's travels.

After her adventure in Baalbek, HPB turned toward home. Again, she arrived unannounced, turning up in Odessa in July 1872, roughly keeping to Koot Hoomi's schedule. Her stay was short, though, and by April 1873, she was on the road again. She went to Bucharest, and then Paris, where she stayed with a relative on the Hahn side of the family. Here, she spent her time writing and painting, although later critics claimed that she was once again trawling through the fleshpots and leading a wild life. These

claims seemed punctured by a letter from a friend of the time, a
Dr. Lydia Marquette, who told Colonel Olcott that HPB's behavior in Paris was "unexceptional," and that she considered her "one
of the most estimable and interesting ladies I ever met."[9] But her
stay here, too, was cut short. Out of the blue a message came from
Master M, along with a huge roll of French bank notes—at least
according to one account. She was to head to America, *tout de suite*.
    And so the next day she did.

AT LE HAVRE, Blavatsky booked a first-class passage on a
steamer to New York. Just as she was about to board, she noticed
a woman and two children sitting on the pier. The woman was
in tears, and when Blavatsky asked her what was wrong, she told
her that the tickets she had bought in Hamburg for the voyage had
turned out to be fake, and they were not allowed to board. She had
spent all the money her husband had sent her from America on the
useless tickets—she and the children were to join him there—and
now they were penniless. Blavatsky told the woman to come with
her. At the ticket office, Blavatsky exchanged her first-class ticket
for four in steerage, and they all boarded. For the next two weeks
HPB huddled with the masses in the overcrowded, rank, and filthy
conditions below decks, en route to the new world. Having already
survived the *Eumonia* and the *Gwalior*, to get on board itself was
a sign of bravery. To exchange the comfort of a first-class cabin
for steerage misery in order to help another was the act of a
bodhisattva.

    HPB landed in New York on July 7, 1873. She was forty-two
years old and had last passed through some twenty years earlier.

She was there on a mission from the Master, but exactly what to do next was not clear. As Ellis Island had yet to be established as a center for immigration control, she would have been processed at the Castle Garden Immigration Depot at what is now Fort Clinton in Battery Park, and would later submit her naturalization papers. Before leaving France, HPB had written to her father, asking him to send money ahead to the Russian consulate. Even if she had kept her first-class ticket, she would have arrived practically empty-handed, having the equivalent of only a few dollars left after booking her passage. (Apparently she had no intention of using any of the bank notes given to her by the Master. These she was later instructed to deliver to someone in Buffalo. Who that was or why she was giving him the money is unclear.) When she reached the consulate, she was disappointed; nothing was waiting for her. HPB found herself in the situation of many of the immigrants she had traveled with, and in many ways her adventures in the next few years are a kind of American success story, in which a penniless foreigner arrives in the new world and, through courage, persistence, and determination, makes good.

But first she had to find a place to live and a way to make a few dollars to tide her over until help from Russia arrived. An article by Elizabeth Holt, a schoolteacher and one of the first people to meet HPB on this journey, published in *The Theosophist* many years later, gives us an idea of what New York was like in those days. Readers familiar with Martin Scorsese's film adaption of Edith Wharton's novel *The Age of Innocence* may recognize the milieu. No skyscrapers, of course, and travel was by horse-drawn carriages. The north end of Manhattan was mostly granite cliffs, "even as far down as Fortieth Street." "A solid boulder" occupied what is now the space between Second and Third avenues, and on it squatters set up shanty towns. The East River lapped over parts of what is now First and Second avenues, although Broadway and Fifth Avenue were well traveled. The main attraction that year was the opening of Central Park, which drew some ten million visitors. The boulders and rocky outcrops that children in the park delight in climbing on today give us a sense of what early New Yorkers had to contend with.

A woman traveling alone then was usually turned away from respectable boarding houses, and in any case HPB's lack of funds—not to mention her exotic appearance—would make most of these off-limits to her. Someone mentioned a new and, for the time, unique development that at least temporarily provided a solution. A group of forty or so working women who couldn't afford the more "respectable" rents banded together and established a housing co-operative in Manhattan's Lower East Side. HPB headed to 222 Madison Street, not far from the East River, and soon her powerful personality made her a dominant figure in the place. It must have been a comedown for a countess—her cousin, we remember, was a count and her grandmother was a princess—but as usual, HPB made the best of it, and her openness and upfront manner led to her becoming a kind of "den mother" for the other residents, who came to her for advice about their problems. She had found some work, sewing for a local Jewish shop that sold "fancy" items—nearby Orchard Street today remains a haven for discount clothing stores and tailoring shops—and later spoke well of her employer. She also did leatherwork, and designed and made advertising cards for some of the local businesses, along with other piecework. Again, like Gurdjieff, Blavatsky showed impressive resourcefulness in

dealing with what he called "the problem of roubles." She also
began to gain a reputation as a psychic, much as she did years earlier in Tiflis. She spoke of being under the guidance of "unseen
powers," which her neighbors understandably took to mean "spirits," and told her new acquaintances about the *diaki*, or elementals.
One woman was stunned when Blavatsky told her things about her
life that no one, outside of herself and some deceased relatives,
knew. But when she asked HPB to make contact with her mother,
who had died some years before, Blavatsky explained that she
couldn't, as her mother was now occupied with much more important things and was in any case outside her reach. Blavatsky also
impressed her fellow residents with tales of her exotic past. Miss
Holt was surprised when she casually described how she had decorated the Empress Eugénie's private apartments.

Another person to meet HPB in those days was the journalist
Anna Ballard, who worked for the New York *Sun*. Ballard had been
assigned to write an article on a Russian theme, and a friend had
mentioned that she had met an extraordinary Russian woman
recently. About a week after she arrived, Blavatsky was interviewed
by Ballard. One imagines they met in the common room of the
women's co-operative, which HPB used as a kind of office, and
where she sat daily, smoking endless cigarettes. Elizabeth Holt
speaks of HPB's "conspicuous tobacco pouch, the head of some
fur-bearing animal, which she wore around her neck," a fashion
accessory today's animal rights advocates and health and wellness
experts might disapprove of. HPB's tobacco intake was apparently phenomenal, although the "pound a day," that Hannah Wolff
claimed she inhaled is exaggerated.[10] Her habit also served an additional purpose. One evening, one of the women came running

into the office breathless and distressed, and explained that a man had been following her; the neighborhood, already rough, seemed to be getting worse. Blavatsky reached into her capacious dress and produced her tobacco-cutting knife, explaining that if any man tried to molest her, she had *that* ready for him.[11]

Blavatsky told Ballard that she had no intention of leaving Paris for America until the day before she left. That, to be sure, was surprising enough, but then HPB added, with special emphasis, "I have been in Tibet." Ballard wondered why, after telling her about her travels in Egypt, India, and other exotic lands, HPB thought her time in Tibet especially important. We may have some insight into this that Ballard, who became friends with HPB, lacked at the time. But what is important about these remarks is that they seem to be HPB's first public announcement about her travels to the forbidden land. Blavatsky may have been, as Peter Washington writes, a woman "who was to court publicity without understanding how to manage it," but she certainly lost no time in nailing her colors to the mast.[12] An article about her in *The Sun*—which had counted Edgar Allan Poe among its contributors—telling of her adventures in the mysterious East certainly wouldn't hurt her mission, whatever that might turn out to be.[13]

By October 1874, Blavatsky had moved to another women's cooperative, this time on Elizabeth Street near the Bowery, at that time a place of down-market music halls, brothels, beer gardens, flophouses, and pawn shops, and home to the infamous Bowery Boys, one of New York's earliest street gangs. Here Blavatsky received word that her father had died, and that her share in his legacy would soon be sent to her.[14] When it arrived, it turned out to be a considerable sum.[15] Hannah Wolff writes that she used the money to move to a hotel on Fourth Avenue and 23rd Street, where she lived lavishly.[16] Other accounts have her meeting a Countess Gerebko, whom she had known in Russia, who persuaded her to invest a large part of her inheritance in land in Long Island. This would be used as a chicken farm and a market garden. Here she could live, work the land, and sell her goods. As HPB had made money as a logger in Tiflis, to profit from chickens in Long Island doesn't seem too fantastic, but it turned out that the land was not as she expected and her trusting soul—or poor business sense—led to legal action to retrieve her investment. But her unfortunate encounter with Countess Gerebko was soon overshadowed by what was probably the most important meeting of her life, aside, perhaps, for the one with Master Morya.

BLAVATSKY KEPT HERSELF apprised of all the latest spiritualist and occult news, and in those days there was quite a bit. We tend to think that popular interest in the occult, the esoteric, and the spiritual started sometime in the 1960s, during that decade's occult revival.[17] Yet a look at history shows this isn't true. By the time of HPB's arrival in New York, Spiritualism had been popular in both America and Europe for decades. Although its roots can be traced back to earlier movements such as Mesmerism and the teachings of Swedenborg, the nineteenth-century spiritualist "craze" began in 1848, in Hydesville, upstate New York, in an area known as the "Burned-Over District," because of the many religious revival movements that had erupted there. In March 1848, the Fox family became troubled by weird "knocks" and "raps" that sounded around their farmhouse; they seemed to come from nowhere. Although they searched for a source, none could be found. One evening, hearing the noises, as a joke Kate Fox, one of the young daughters, called out "Mr. Splitfoot, do as I do!"—Mr. Splitfoot being a name they gave to who or whatever was making the strange sounds. She snapped her fingers, and immediately heard a snapping sound in reply. Margaretta, her sister, joined in, as did their mother. In order to "test" Mr. Splitfoot, Mrs. Fox asked "him" to tap out her children's ages. Mr. Splitfoot obliged, even throwing in the age of a child who had died young. To make it official, Mrs. Fox said, "If you are spirit, then tap twice." Two loud bangs rattled the walls. Eventually it turned out that Mr. Splitfoot was the spirit of a man who had been murdered in the house before the Foxes lived there. Excavation in the cellar eventually revealed human hair and bones buried in quicklime.[18] The living could speak with the dead, it seemed, and soon others discovered this fact as well.

By the time Blavatsky was mystifying reporters and residents of the Lower East Side with tales of her adventures, Spiritualism, as this apparent contact with the dead came to be called, was a major movement. It had even gotten into politics. In 1872, the year before HPB arrived, Victoria Woodhull, a medium, magnetic healer, and advocate of "free love," became the first woman to run for the U.S. presidency; her Equal Rights Party, a motley coalition of feminists, workers, spiritualists, communists—she was responsible for publishing the first English translation of *The Communist Manifesto*—and "free lovers," challenged Ulysses S. Grant and Horace Greeley for the office. Needless to say, she didn't win, and such was the outrage against "Mrs. Satan," as the tabloid press of the day named her, that she spent Election Day in jail. I haven't come across any references to Woodhull and Blavatsky ever meeting, but she seems exactly the kind of person HPB would have liked to have known. A scandal involving the highly successful preacher Henry Ward Beecher—brother of Harriet Beecher Stowe, author of *Uncle Tom's Cabin*—led to Woodhull's downfall, and she left the United States for England in 1876.[19]

Blavatsky had been following the newspaper accounts of even more impressive phenomena than had amazed the residents of Hydesville. These centered around a farmhouse in Chittenden, Vermont. The first reports had appeared in *The Sun*, and soon after, a rival newspaper, *The Daily Graphic*, had begun a series of articles on the strange events in Chittenden. The illustrations of the weird manifestations—spirits of all sorts—by the artist August Kappes had captured her attention, and just about that of everyone else in New York. So popular was this biweekly "on the spot" coverage, that copies of the *Graphic* were going for a dollar an issue, which, at the time, was a lot of money. Blavatsky read with growing excitement and then had an idea. She would go to Chittenden herself and meet the man responsible for these articles.

BLAVATSKY'S FATEFUL ENCOUNTER with Colonel Henry Steel Olcott, author of the original *Sun* article and the ongoing series in the *Graphic,* was, like the very similar first encounter between Gurdjieff and his most influential follower, P. D. Ouspensky, an act of premeditation. Certainly, she trusted in fate and above all in the Masters, but when she had a good idea, she went for it. She already had a taste for notoriety and knew what one well-placed article in a newspaper could do. If she wanted an audience to whom she could announce herself and get going with her mission, here was one ready and waiting.

WHEN HPB ARRIVED in Chittenden on October 14, 1874, accompanied by her friend, Mrs. Magnon, a French-Canadian woman with whom she stayed briefly, she had, it is safe to say, an impressive past behind her. But the man she was purposefully going out of her way to meet and bring over to her cause—whatever that might turn out to be—was no slacker either. Henry Steel Olcott was born in Orange, New Jersey, on August 2, 1832, which made him roughly a year younger than Blavatsky. In his younger years he had been deeply interested in clairvoyance and had some success as a mesmerist, having cured one cousin of inflammatory rheumatism and another of toothache through magnetic passes. But his interest in Spiritualism had only recently been revived, and the last few months had seen him rise to national notoriety through his articles on the Chittenden "haunting."

Before this, Olcott had a string of accomplishments that anyone would be proud to possess. His family roots went back to settlers who arrived not too long after the *Mayflower*. An early passion for agriculture, which had him farming in Ohio in his late teens, led to his establishing an agricultural school in Mount Vernon, New York, and a medal of honor from the U.S. Agricultural Society. A model farm in Newark, New Jersey, that he worked on was so successful that the Greek government offered him a chair in "scientific agriculture" in Athens, an appointment he declined. After studying farming techniques in England, he became the

associate agricultural editor for the *New York Tribune*. Before he
was thirty, he published two highly respected books on farming;
and in 1859, he covered the hanging of John Brown, the abolition-
ist, in Charlestown, Virginia, also for the *Tribune*. He fought for
the North as a signals officer in the Civil War, but was invalided
out with malaria, and then acted as a war correspondent. This led
to his being commissioned to investigate corruption and profiteer-
ing in the army. His rank of colonel and special commissioner of
the War Department was conferred on him through this, and
because of his success, he continued his investigations for the
navy. In August 1865, Olcott was one of three men commissioned
to investigate the assassination of Abraham Lincoln; he uncovered
at least one conspirator, who was arrested after a raid Olcott had
organized. He received special commendations from the Secretary
of War and the Judge Advocate General, and in 1868, after being
admitted to the New York Bar, he practiced law, specializing in
insurance and customs cases. His clients included the Treasury of
the City of New York, the New York Stock Exchange, the Gold
Exchange Bank, the Panama Railway Companies, several insurance companies, as well as steel and heavy goods manufacturers.

I relate Olcott's résumé at some length because in accounts of
his life with Blavatsky, he is often portrayed as a gullible, earnest
dimwit, taken in by the crafty Russian adventuress and his own
incorrigible credulity. Yet overly credulous and gullible dupes do
not, as a matter of course, get appointed to investigate the assas-
sinations of U.S. presidents, nor do they receive medals of honor
or requests to head departments of agriculture by the Greek government.

A few months before Olcott started covering the haunting in

Chittenden, he found himself sitting in his law office on Beekman Street, when the thought came to him that of late he had paid very little attention to Spiritualism. Later, Olcott would wonder whether this thought was really his, or if it had come from somewhere or *someone* else. But then it led to his rushing out and buying a copy of the *Banner of Light*, a popular spiritualist magazine. In it he read about the strange doings in Vermont, in which "phantom forms" were said to become "solidified." The Eddy brothers, whose family had a history of second sight—a Scottish great-great-great-grandmother was said to have been a witch—were displaying remarkable abilities at their farmhouse. They were known to levitate, which was remarkable enough, but the most incredible display was by William Eddy. If the reports were accurate, he could manifest a whole host of spirits. Red Indians, deceased men, women, and children, who sang, danced, played music, and even fought duels with etheric swords: All were "materialized" while William, and sometimes his brother Horatio, sat within a closed cabinet on a makeshift stage in a room the locals called "the ghost shop."

Olcott was struck. If this was true, he thought, and the people there could "see, even touch and converse with deceased relatives who had found the means to reconstruct their bodies, and clothing so as to be temporarily solid, visible, and tangible," then it was "the most important fact in modern physical science."[20] He decided to find out for himself. He did, and wrote about his observations in *The Sun* in an article entitled "The World of Spirits, Astounding Wonders that Stagger Belief," which was published on September 5, 1874. Soon after this, the *Graphic* commissioned him to supply articles every other week about what was happening in Chittenden, and sent an artist along with him to capture the scenes.

One reason Olcott's interest in Spiritualism had declined and then revived may have been because his wife, the daughter of an Episcopalian rector, whom he had married in 1860, had no interest in it at all, and more than likely thought it devilish. At the time of his reawakening he was living at the Lotus Club—then located at Fifth Avenue and 21st Street—and awaiting divorce papers. It is often claimed that Blavatsky "lured" Olcott away from his wife and family—he had two teenaged sons—but this isn't true. The marriage had long ago failed, and Olcott, "a man of clubs, drinking parties, and mistresses," had recently arranged for a visit to a brothel in order to provide his wife with the required grounds for divorce; whether he made the best of a necessary evil is unknown.[21] At forty-two, he had already achieved success in several fields and had reached the time of life when the psychologist Carl Jung argued that men begin to think of a more meaningful, spiritual fulfillment. Earlier interests, such as Freemasonry, Mesmerism, and spiritual healing again began to occupy Olcott's mind, and the attraction of corporate law and customs cases no doubt began to pale. The situation is again remarkably similar to that of P. D. Ouspensky who, like Olcott, was a journalist who found himself increasingly detached from the "real" world around him—in Ouspensky's case it was current events like the Hague Conference of 1906—and drawn to the strange world of the occult, an attraction that eventually led to his meeting with Gurdjieff, as Olcott's did with HPB.[22] On the eve of meeting Blavatsky, Olcott may have "lost all sense of direction in his dreary life," as Peter Washington writes, but this suggests a desperate, confused character, seeking anything to fill an empty existence.[23] Perhaps his inspiration had more purpose behind it? Perhaps his sudden return to the spiritual world was the result of some inner prompting, a psychic compass Olcott had lost track of and which had just started working again, pointing him to true north? Whatever the cause, that sudden urge to rush out of his office and get the latest spiritualist news certainly led to some remarkable developments.

WHEN HPB ARRIVED in Chittenden, she knew exactly why she was there. She also knew how to make an appearance. When Olcott saw her sitting at the communal table at lunchtime—the family played host to dozens of spectators and charged a small fee for the show—the first thing he noticed was her red Garibaldi shirt, a military tunic in blazing scarlet that had been the height of haute couture for a season or two and was not yet out of fashion. Amid the sober dress of Vermont farmers it must have been a sight, as must have been the Mongolian features that may have helped her in her Tibetan forays. After the shirt, Olcott next noticed her hair, "a thick blond mop" that "stood out from her head, silken-soft and crinkled to the roots, like the fleece of a Cotswold ewe." Then the "massive Calmuck face," full of "power, culture, and imperiousness," that contrasted sharply with the dour looks of the other guests. This caught his eye, as must have the fur tobacco pouch, the many rings that adorned her delicate fingers and, perhaps lastly but most effectively, her eyes, sometimes said to be blue, sometimes blue-gray or azure, but always "magnetic." Olcott whispered his amazement to Kappes, and then made a beeline for a seat opposite her, to make a careful, detailed study.

Olcott overheard HPB and her friend speaking in French, and following lunch, when the two stepped outside to have the inevitable cigarette, Olcott broke the ice with a less than original line. "*Permettez-moi*," he said, striking a match for her. They started talking, and Blavatsky told him of her travels and search for occult knowledge—but not before disingenuously admitting that she hoped that the man responsible for those articles in the *Daily Graphic* wasn't there, as she was afraid he might write about her. Since she had arrived in New York, so many journalists had. Clearly this bit of reverse psychology was not lost on the Colonel, and he admitted that he was indeed the man in question. Ah, well then, it must be fate. But then she admitted that she had come to Chittenden precisely because of his articles.

SOON OLCOTT REALIZED that here was no run-of-the-mill medium, but a woman of *power*, who apparently had the denizens of the other world at her beck and call. HPB soon gave evidence of this on the spot. While she was there, the "red" Indians, Americans, and Europeans who had been called up from the other side on a regular basis by the Eddys faded away and in their place more foreign "spooks" turned up, all of them hailing from HPB's own homeland. There was Michalko Guegidze, a Georgian HPB had known in her childhood and who had died a few years back. After exchanging greetings, he obligingly strummed the *Lezginka*, a Georgian national tune, on a guitar. A Muslim merchant from Tiflis appeared, along with a Russian peasant girl, and a Kurdish cavalryman, complete with scimitar and lance. One figure, that of a gentleman wearing the cross and collar of St. Anne, turned out to be HPB's uncle.

On another occasion, the materialization of a silver buckle

from which a military decoration hung, and which was allegedly buried with her father, led to some controversy. It will take us a bit ahead of our story, but a digression here may help clear up at least two ambiguous issues in HPB's career: her relationship with the medium Daniel Dunglas Home, and that of her ward, Yuri.

Olcott reported the appearance of these strange etheric figures, and HPB's ability to conjure them at will, in his book *People from the Other World*, published in 1875. The medium Daniel Dunglas Home, then the reigning king of the afterlife on both sides of the Atlantic, read his account and took some offense. In a letter to a Dr. G. E. Bloede of Brooklyn, Home pointed out that the Russians do not bury military decorations with the dead, but return them to the government, basing his assertion on the remarks of his friend Baron Meyendorff, whom we met in Chapter 2 as the possible father of Blavatsky's ward.[24] HPB therefore, according to Home, could not possibly have materialized the decoration from the grave, and was then a fraud. And anyway, Home added, she had already tried the same kind of tricks in Paris in 1858.

Although the controversy, as well as the decoration, hung on the buckle, that was the easiest point to clarify. In reply, HPB stringently pointed out that it was only the buckle, and not the decoration—which, indeed, was returned to the Russian government—that had materialized. But the business with Home ran deeper than this. Home's remarks appeared in an article by Dr. Bloede published in the *Sunday Herald*, a Boston newspaper, on March 5, 1876. On different occasions Blavatsky said that she had and that she hadn't met Home. In an interview published in Olcott's paper, the *Graphic*, in November 1874, she claims that in Paris she "made the acquaintance of Daniel Home, the spiritualist," and that he converted her to Spiritualism.[25] Yet in her *Scrapbook, Volume 1*, where she makes the point about the buckle, she writes "Mr. D. D. Home . . . never knew or even saw me in his whole life," but adds that "he has certainly gathered most carefully the dirtiest gossip possible about Nathalie Blavatsky."[26] Nathalie Blavatsky, HPB's sister-in-law, we remember, was the possible mother of HPB's ward, Yuri, by way of Baron Meyendorff.

Now, Home's bad opinion of HPB—which led to a running feud between them—wasn't based solely on Olcott's claims about her unique powers, which Home, understandably, might feel a bit challenged by. He was also piqued because of what he believed was a scandalous affair between HPB and Baron Meyendorff. This was supposed to have happened in Paris in 1858. About this Home is said to have written that he had warned Meyendorff about Blavatsky, whom he saw as a cheap adventuress. But Meyendorff was besotted with her—"massively stout" and all—because he was equally besotted with Spiritualism—hence his friendship with Home—and she had palmed herself off as a powerful medium—which she certainly was not—solely to ensnare him.

Yet Lydia Pashkov, who met and traveled with HPB in Lebanon, later related that she knew Nathalie Blavatsky too, and that she had died in Aden in 1868.[27] And so there is at least some confirmation that there were two Madame Blavatskys—unless we want to believe that Lydia Pashkov was lying for her friend. Jean Overton Fuller examines this somewhat confusing affair in some detail, and concludes that the Madame Blavatsky in question was Nathalie Blavatsky. Home, hearing of the affair with Baron Meyendorff, and irked by reports of HPB's "powers," confused the two, and used the gossip as ammunition against a rival.[28]

At any rate, Olcott was so taken with HPB that he did exactly what she had hoped he would: He wrote about her in one of his reports for the *Graphic*. After that, she became something of a celebrity, and for the rest of her career, was in and out of the papers regularly. But HPB got something more than publicity from Olcott. The two became friends, "chums," as they soon called themselves, and within a week they even had nicknames: he was Maloney and she was Jack (or Mulligan, Latchkey, and sometimes Old Horse). They formed a kind of metaphysical Mutt and Jeff, if readers are of an age to remember the old newspaper comic strip about the two mismatched pals. Or perhaps an esoteric Odd Couple rings more of a bell: Blavatsky the wild, eccentric, unconventional mystic, wrapped in ill-fitting robes, puffing incessantly on her cigarettes, and broadcasting her opinions on all and sundry in often coarse vocabulary, while her magnetic eyes captivated everyone around her; Olcott, the sober, earnest, respectable Yankee lawyer, his long, flowing beard and stolid demeanor announcing his Victorian propriety, while he cringes slightly at his chum's ill manners. Although the relationship was platonic, the "attraction of soul to soul, not that of sex to sex," as Olcott put it, they were pretty much made for each other, at least at that time. In later years, their "chumship"—Olcott again—was less solid. But right now they were on the way to becoming inseparable.

Blavatsky showered the Colonel with confidences, showing him the old wound below the heart that she suffered from in Pskov, which had opened again because of her exertions in Chittenden. She also showed him where the saber had broken her arm in Mentana, and the musket balls still lodged in her shoulder and leg, rather like an old swordsman showing off battle scars. More esoteric intimacies came as well. HPB explained to the increasingly hooked Olcott that the "spirits" he and the other visitors had seen at the Eddys' farm were not those of the friends and relatives who had passed on, but "thought forms" emanating from the living combined with the decaying "shells" of the dead, the etheric skeletons, as it were, left behind when the immortal souls of the departed moved on to higher realms. Unconsciously the Eddys added some of their own astral matter to these spiritual automatons—it is, in fact, what all mediums do—who also absorbed psychic energies from the audience. These etheric simulacra are then innocently accepted by the audience as true visitations by their lost loved ones, but they are really artificially revivified astral corpses, who enjoy the semblance of life at the expense of the living. The practice, Blavatsky told Olcott, was dark and base, and she was here to expose it for what it was, and show the path to true occult knowledge. She was, she told him, "sent from Paris on purpose to America to *prove* the phenomena and their reality"—because they were irrefutably *real*—but to show "the fallacy of the Spiritualistic theories of 'Spirits.'"

That "fallacy" was the notion of human consciousness as a kind of conduit or "channel" for the dead: In the term originating at the time, it was a "medium" for powers outside itself, which it allowed to dominate it. For Blavatsky, who had learned to master her own powers in Tibet, this was an abdication of one's own freedom and responsibility, a kind of psychic slavery, especially as the "spirits" involved were often of a low type, the "larvae" of the astral realm, as she called them, borrowing from Bulwer-Lytton. Linked to this was the notion that the spirits of the departed, once free of the flesh, lingered on in some nearby phantom realm, a kind of etheric

Victorian drawing room, having nothing better to do than politely converse with their living relatives. As she would spell out in detail later, Blavatsky came to teach that every living soul—everything in the universe, in fact—is involved in a vast evolutionary journey, a transformative quest through all forms of being, from the lowest clod to the Godhead itself. Her mission was, in fact, to revive and revitalize the ancient Hermetic, Neo-Platonic tradition, in which the divine spark sunk into creation longs to return to its source, and which came to be known in our time as "occultism." This was why she told her friend in the women's co-operative that she couldn't contact her dead mother. Her mother's real self, the immortal part of her—what Blavatsky would later, borrowing from the philosopher Leibniz, call her "monad"—had indeed "moved on," and was too busy with the challenges of her further evolution to have a quick chat with her daughter—who should herself be busy with more important things.

Fulfilling her mission would turn out to be no easy task, and when it was in full swing, HPB found herself fighting a battle on three fronts. The spiritualists were having a tough enough time as it was, defending themselves against both the Church—who thought them demonic—and scientists—who thought them absurd. But not only would she take on both of the spiritualists' enemies, but the spiritualists too, causing a considerable amount of confusion along the way. If she had hit the barricades in Mentana, battling against the papal army with swords and bullets, the spiritual scrap she was setting herself up for would be no less perilous.

FIVE

ANCIENT WISDOM FOR A MODERN WORLD

As a seasoned journalist, Olcott recognized good copy when he saw it, and in his next article for the *Graphic*, he introduced his new friend to his readers. "The arrival of a Russian lady of distinguished birth and rare educational and natural endowments was an important event in the history of Chittenden," the Colonel announced. In her "eventful life," "Madame Helen P. de Blavatsky" had traveled "in most lands of the Orient." She had searched for "antiquities at the base of the Pyramids," had witnessed "the mysteries of Hindu temples," and—puffing up his new chum's achievements a bit—had pushed "with armed escort far into the interior of Africa." Olcott assured his readers that he had "never met so interesting and . . . eccentric a character."[1] Although most of his readers would probably never make her acquaintance, HPB would soon do everything she could to live up to her reputation.

Her own first appearance in print, at least in the United States—she claimed to have written for foreign publications, but nothing prior to this time has come to light—came in the *Graphic* too. It was a reply to a letter to the newspaper by a Dr. Beard, who had—at least to his own satisfaction—"proved" that the manifestations at Chittenden were fakes. Beard had read Olcott's articles and, as HPB did, decided to visit Chittenden and see for himself. His investigations took all of two days and consisted of poking around in the Eddy brothers' spirit cabinet and demanding that they hold a galvanic battery he had brought along with him. The electric current, he believed, would prevent them from engaging in any trickery. The brothers declined—the battery's current was rather strong—and the meeting broke up into fisticuffs. Dr. Beard returned to New York and produced a letter exposing the whole affair.[2] Blavatsky read it and immediately replied in a manner that would become familiar to her readers.

In a hectoring, table-thumping style, HPB leveled Beard, undermining any qualification he had to investigate the manifestations. If scientists like William Crookes (inventor of the cathode-ray tube), Alfred Wallace (co-discoverer of the theory of evolution), and Camille Flammarion (the great French astronomer) could devote years to the study of Spiritualism, and conclude that the phenomena were *real*, she argued, Beard's "exposé" after a mere two days was pitiful. Blavatsky stayed at Chittenden for another two weeks before she returned to New York, and in her rebuttal to Dr. Beard, she describes in some detail the "Russian" spirits that arrived during her stay. She also challenged him to produce, as he said he could, everything available at Chittenden with "three dollars' worth of second-hand drapery," offering a five-hundred-dollar prize if he succeeded.

Beard did not take up the challenge, nor did anyone else. Yet from the perspective of understanding HPB's "mission," what is most important here is that from the beginning she made a distinction between the reality of the phenomena and that of their supposed source. Crookes, Wallace, and Flammarion had argued that even if "the well-known phenomenon of materialization of spirits did not prove the identity of the persons whom they purported to represent, it was not, at all events, the work of mortal hands; still less was it a fraud."[3] The key phrase here is "did not prove the identity of the persons whom they purported to represent." Blavatsky had already explained to Olcott that the manifestations were not of the dead, or at least not of their "immortal souls," which had moved on to more important business. Yet, although she had made clear to Olcott that her purpose was to reveal the "truth" about Spiritualism—to, in a sense, expose it in her own way—for the time being at least, she had to pretend to be a fellow traveler with it. In her reply to Dr. Beard she calls herself "a Spiritualist of many years" standing. But in her *Scrapbook*, where she pasted her letter as it was printed in the *Graphic*, she crossed out the word "Spiritualist" and wrote "Occultist," and added the comment: "one who laughs at the supposed agency of Spirits! (but all the same pretends to be one herself)."

Blavatsky's work as an esoteric undercover agent—an occultist in spiritualist clothing—would lead to more than a little confusion, and also to some bitter animosity toward her by the people whose beliefs she was ostensibly trying to defend. Sylvia Cranston writes that "in view of her real feelings," that HPB pretended to "champion" the spiritualist cause is "puzzling."[4] True, but it would make sense for her to make a name for herself and gain a reputation as an ardent opponent of the kind of narrow-minded skepticism embodied in a Dr. Beard, and then to lead her followers into the true light of occultism.

Rudolf Steiner, who would become the most famous and influential European Theosophist of the early twentieth century, performed several intellectual backflips, lecturing to Marxists and Nietzscheans in a way that slowly led them to his own brand of German Idealism. Yet like HPB, he too was branded a turncoat when some of his followers felt he had abandoned the "truth" for a different path. (Steiner complicated matters by having an almost pathological need to "identify" himself with an opposite point of view in order to understand it; this "identification" ran so deep that he was often seen, as Blavatsky was, as a champion of the very ideas he was opposing.)[5]

It is, of course, true that such tactics can be seen as sheer opportunism. It isn't too far from the truth to argue that Steiner himself became a Theosophist in order to gain an audience, and that he had every intention of leading his Theosophical flock into the new fold of his own Anthroposophy—which, to the unbiased reader, bears a distinct resemblance to Blavatsky's teaching. Many who became followers of HPB started out as spiritualists for the simple reason that before Blavatsky and the Theosophical Society, there was precious little else for those unhappy with crude materialism and dissatisfied with mainstream religion. To play devil's advocate, we can say that she had to get her foot in the door *somehow*. If temporarily keeping a low profile among the spiritualists was a way to do it, then it was a necessary fiction. Of course, someone like HPB could not keep a low profile for long.

BLAVATSKY HAD ENOUGH media savvy to deliver her attack on Beard to the office of the *Graphic* personally. After Olcott's account, she had become something of a celebrity, and the *Graph-ic*'s editor took advantage of her visit to interview her for a feature. It's not every day that an exotic Russian aristocrat who's traveled around the world walks into your office, especially one dressed like "a badly wrapped and glittering parcel."[6] Yet even allowing for the mistakes that Jean Overton Fuller argues the reporter made, the interview has more than a little bluster. HPB told the reporter that she was sixteen when she married Nikifor Blavatsky, who was seventy-three; she was really just short of eighteen and her groom was in his forties. She also lied about her age, shaving off three years; political correctness aside, at the time this was considered a "lady's prerogative," so perhaps we can't fully fault her for this. But we can see the beginning of "the Blavatsky story" here, and for the next seventeen years the account of her life "in her own words" will be an often frustrating mix of exaggeration, tall tale, and spiritual seriousness, blended in just the right proportions to raise eyebrows, pique curiosities, and engage questing minds.

By the time she delivered her counterblast to the hopelessly outgunned Dr. Beard—it was published on October 30, 1874—HPB had moved house more than once. She eventually settled for a time at 23 Irving Place, just a few doors from the Lotus Club, where Olcott was living while awaiting his divorce (it would be official by the end of the year). Since their meeting in Chittenden they had become practically inseparable. She had begun to tutor Olcott in the occultism it was her mission to bring to the West. She had already explained that the phenomena she could produce were the work of the elementals, and told him that if he was willing to accept the necessary rigors, he could master these forces too. Olcott was eager to meet the challenge, which required, among other things, celibacy, abstinence from drink, and a vegetarian diet. This last proved difficult, and HPB herself admitted that she couldn't as yet give up meat. Her eating habits were, by today's standards, anything but spiritual, and one of her favorite dishes was fried eggs floating in butter, which must have made her cholesterol levels scandalous. In any case, as she would point out later, in the long run "the purely bodily actions and functions are of far less importance than what a man *thinks* and *feels*, what desires he encourages in his mind," a point Rudolf Steiner agreed with when he told a follower struggling to be vegetarian that "it is better to eat ham than to think ham."[7]

Her Masters, though, were chaste in all these things, and she reminded the Colonel that they were not "spirits" but flesh and blood men who had gained mastery over themselves, and through this had acquired remarkable powers. And although her own apprenticeship had taken place in Tibet, the Masters were not all Oriental, but came from all races. She spoke of a Greek, a Copt (native Egyptian Christian), a Venetian, and also an Englishman. There were others too, but all were bodhisattvas, individuals who had attained enlightenment but who remained in the world, rather than enter Nirvana, in order to help their fellow men.

Some fellow men—and women—who needed help at the moment were a spiritualist couple from Philadelphia. Nelson and Jennie Holmes had been publicly accused of fraud when the elder spiritualist Robert Dale Owen—a former congressman and son of the famous Robert Owen, founder of the utopian community New Harmony—admitted to being duped by them. The Holmeses had for a while manifested a spirit known as "Katie King," who purported to be the daughter of the famous spirit "John King," familiar to séance-goers on both sides of the Atlantic. John King had even manifested for Madame Blavatsky, and for a time she included him among her roster of Masters. Katie King was a celebrity too, having turned up in séances held by William Crookes. But a woman named Eliza White had confessed to impersonating Katie, and had sold her story to a newspaper. The Holmeses denied the accusations, but one of the people taken in by the alleged masquerade was Robert Dale Owen, and his admission to being fooled was a great blow to the spiritualist cause. The Holmeses read the *Graphic* articles on Chittenden, and appealed to Olcott to come to Philadelphia and test them.

Olcott did, and after several séances held in January 1875, he concluded that Jennie Holmes was a genuine medium. HPB, however, had more inside knowledge of the affair. She admitted that Jennie Holmes was *sometimes* genuine, but not always. Like many professional mediums, she had little control over her powers, and when an audience demanded results and she was "off her game"—as often happened—she resorted to trickery, a messy expedient that cast much doubt over more than one otherwise genuine medium. Yet more to the point, in a note by Blavatsky that Olcott found after her death, he discovered that it was HPB herself who "saved the situation," by using her own powers—supported by those of Master Morya—in order to manifest "Katie King," and thus prove that she was a "real" spirit. In other words, in order to prove that Katie was "real," Blavatsky had to magically "fake" her. Blavatsky lamented that she "had to identify myself during that shameful exposure of the *mediums* Holmes with the Spiritualists." She was given the mission of proving the reality of the phenomena, and the best way to do that, she concluded, was to supply Spiritualism with ammunition against the skeptics. It was enough for people to see that there was *some* reality beyond the material world; the exact truth about this could be revealed later.[8]

Blavatsky's esoteric rescue had little effect on the Holmeses' reputation, but her involvement in the affair leads to some speculation about what we can call the "occult history" of the modern world. Jean Overton Fuller writes that "there was an epidemic of Spiritualism in America at this time," and another writer remarks that séances, table-turning, and other mystical phenomena were so popular that one could speak of an "invasion of the spirit people."[9] But if there was an "invasion," why did it happen then? Why did the "spirits" pick just then—the second half of the nineteenth century— to invade? After all, people have been dying for ages, and journeys to the underworld and oracles from "spirits" were a part of the Western tradition from the beginning. Why did the dead suddenly start talking to the living in 1848, and carry on for the rest of the century?

John Symonds suggests that, although many people were interested in the other world—séances were often advertised in newspapers alongside traditional church services—there was no real, deep belief in spiritualist philosophy, and that it was "taken up by the public in general only because it was the latest craze."[10] But this tells us nothing. *Why* was it the latest craze? Some esoteric historians have suggested what may have been at work when the spirit people decided to invade.

According to a strange theory developed by the British occultist C. G. Harrison, and later taken up by Rudolf Steiner, by the early nineteenth century, certain occultists were concerned with the rise of materialism, the belief that the only "really real" things in the universe are matter and the forces acting on it. Traditional spiritual beliefs were losing ground, and so the occultists gathered to discuss a plan of action. One group—the "right wing"—were for keeping the knowledge of the higher world secret, afraid that going public with it would only lead to its being profaned. The "left wing" occultists were in favor of putting everything on the table, and wanted to instruct society at large in the reality of the spirit. A compromise was found, in which "experiments" would be carried out with certain people of an unusual "psychical constitution"—mediums—to see if through them, the wider public could be convinced of the reality of the spiritual worlds. This experiment was Spiritualism, and in the end it was deemed a failure, for precisely the same reason that Blavatsky argued it was wrong: the belief that the phenomena associated with it were the work of the dead.

What is remarkable here is the idea that the "epidemic of Spiritualism" wasn't a fluke, or a product of "social forces," or of the "threat of modernity," or of an economic crisis, or of some other "reasonable" cause. Neither was it a result of a war, when many people would understandably want to contact lost loved ones, as was the case in the years following World War I, which saw a sudden rise in interest in Spiritualism.[11] It was, according to this view, the work of conscious individuals, deciding to take action. These individuals were adepts, like HPB's Masters: men and women who developed the kind of powers Blavatsky ascribed to her teachers, and which we've seen are associated with lamas and gurus in Tibet. This naturally leads to the question of *who* these adepts were, assuming they existed at all and that the idea of a direct "occult intervention" isn't absurd. The scholar Joscelyn Godwin has taken the idea seriously enough to research it exhaustively and bring together different threads into what he calls "the hidden hand" theory of Spiritualism. The gist of this is that HPB appears on the scene, not fully formed as Minerva did from Jupiter's brow, but at the head of a rich esoteric current reaching back at least to the seventeenth century, and possibly further still.[12]

Two occult groups that predate the founding of the Theosophical Society seem, according to Godwin, to be the best candidates for those possibly pulling the occult strings behind the "epidemic of Spiritualism." Both are associated with people who would either be involved with the Theosophical Society in its early days, or who would have a profound influence on it and Blavatsky. One of these groups was known as the Orphic Circle, and in a remarkable book published in 1876, *Ghost Land*, mentioned earlier, we can get some idea of what they were about. Some of the material making up *Ghost Land* was originally published in a spiritualist magazine, *The Western Star*, in 1872, whose editor, the spiritualist Emma Hardinge Britten, also edited the book version. Although they would later have a falling out, Emma Hardinge Britten was at one point friends with HPB and, as mentioned, an early member of the Theosophical Society. The actual author of the material is unknown, and both the original "autobiographical sketches" and the expanded "novel" were published under the alias "Chevalier Louis de B." The psychical researcher E. J. Dingwall believed that the true author was Baron Joseph Henry Louis de Palm, a down-and-out European aristocrat who lived with Olcott for a brief time, and who, when he died, left behind a trunk, which some claimed contained significant esoteric writings.[13] Some HPB critics—Emma Hardinge Britten among them—even claimed that her *Isis Unveiled* was plagiarized from the baron's work. The trunk, however, contained little more than some worthless bonds, and a few shirts the impecunious baron had stolen from Olcott; the most significant thing he left behind was a request that his body be cremated. (Olcott fulfilled de Palm's wishes, and his cremation was the first in America.) As Olcott later discovered, the penniless baron was wanted by the police of several European countries. While this does not necessarily preclude him from being a deep esoteric thinker, it does make the idea that he could have written the *Ghost Land* material seem highly unlikely.[14]

Whoever the "Chevalier Louis de B" really was—and some believe he was Emma Hardinge Britten herself—his account of being inducted into the "German branch of a very ancient secret order" remains thrilling. The period covered is the early 1800s, and to the "secret order" Louis gives the name "the Berlin Brotherhood." Wishing to study the spiritual worlds scientifically, the order used a number of methods to initiate a state of "magnetic sleep," stimulating the "animal magnetism" discovered in the late eighteenth century by the Swabian Franz Anton Mesmer (who gave us the term "mesmerized"). This state could be induced "sometimes by drugs, vapours, and aromal essences; sometimes by spells, as through music, intently staring into crystals, the eyes of snakes, running water, or other glittering substances; by intoxication caused by dancing, spinning around [German Sufis?], or distracting clamours." But the most effective method of inducing a "magnetic trance" was through "magnetic passes," slow movements of the hands just over the surface of the body, sending the medium into what was called "lucidity." Louis's account of entering this state resembles later accounts of "out-of-body" experiences, yet this remarkable shift in his consciousness brought other insights.

A crystalline atmosphere surrounded him, and he felt that he could see an "almost illimitable area of space." A "vast realm of perception" opened up, and he felt that he could not only see through the walls of the room, but could also "pass through them with perfect ease." And not only that: "the very furniture itself, if it were only brought into the solvent of the radiant fire mist that surrounded me, would dissolve and become . . . *so soluble* that it could pass . . . through everything material."

This possibility, of matter becoming infinitely permeable, will return when we consider the case of the mysterious Mahatma Letters. Louis's account, however, also sheds light on how the kind of phenomena associated with Spiritualism could have been accomplished by the living. He writes of being brought into "lucidity" through the use of nitrous oxide—first synthesized in 1772 by the chemist Joseph Priestley—and of his "atmospheric spirit" being taken, with two other "lucid subjects," to a castle in Bohemia. There they threw stones, moved objects, shrieked, groaned, and made much noise—exactly the sort of thing associated with poltergeists and other "spirits." And although when they awoke, Louis and his companions didn't remember their "trip," they were shortly afterward shown a newspaper account of the "haunting" in the very castle they visited.

Given the author of *Ghost Land*'s anonymity, it is best, as Godwin suggests, to consider it fiction. Yet Emma Hardinge Britten left an account of her own induction into a secret occult society that closely parallels "Louis B's." Like Louis, she was inducted at a young age because of her somnambulistic abilities. The society's members were ladies and gentlemen of noble rank, and came from all corners of Europe. They were one of a number of such societies whose history reached back to ancient Egypt. They studied Cabala, "philosophical occultism," and also "Practical Magic." This consisted of Mesmerism, crystal-gazing, the use of "magic mirrors," and other forms of evocation—practices designed to bring spiritual entities into physical manifestation and to achieve what we would call altered states of consciousness. Among the people involved was the novelist Edward Bulwer-Lytton, one of the earliest "scientific" psychical investigators, and author, among other works, of the Rosicrucian classic *Zanoni*.[15] Along with practically every occultist in the late nineteenth and early twentieth centuries, Blavatsky was enormously influenced by Bulwer-Lytton; he is even thought by some to be the Master she met in London in 1851. Like Blavatsky, Bulwer-Lytton rejected the idea that spiritualist phenomena were caused by the dead; he believed instead that they were the product of unknown natural forces, which he often referred to as "elementals." These forces, he believed, could be investigated, understood, and eventually even mastered, and this was precisely what Britten's Orphic Circle was about.[16]

While the Orphic Circle was exploring these unknown forces, another group was occupied with a similar pursuit. Exactly when the Hermetic Brotherhood of Luxor, mentioned earlier, began is hard to pin down. Their "official" public appearance was in 1884, a decade after the Colonel met HPB. Yet like many occult societies, they also claimed a lineage going back millennia, and it seems reasonable to assume that an "inner" secret order existed long before the "outer" one broke cover. A more wieldy starting date is perhaps 1870, yet there is reason to believe that the group existed in some guise earlier than this; Emma Hardinge Britten herself is thought to have belonged to some form of it in the 1850s. In the last chapter,

I remarked that when HPB begins to speak about a mysterious Brotherhood of Luxor, she may be referring to people like the radical Sufi Jamal ad-Din al-Afghani and the Jewish-Egyptian playwright James Sanua—whom, K. Paul Johnson argues, she made contact with in Cairo in 1871. I think we also have to accept that it is also possible that the characters Blavatsky had in mind were people like Paulos Metamon and his "son," Max Théon, whom we met in Chapter 4.

Théon is a shifty figure who, except for occasional appearances in the light, tends to remain in the background as a kind of mastermind, or "hidden master." As an associate of Paulos Metamon, Théon would be one of the Brotherhood of Luxor—along with Albert Rawson, al-Afghani, and the other esotericists HPB fraternized with in Cairo. When the Hermetic Brotherhood of Luxor— or H. B. of L., as it was known for most of its existence (even its name was considered an important secret)—started advertising for members, Théon was referred to as its Grand Master and was considered in its writings an "exalted adept," but he had little to do with its actual operation; instead, with his medium wife, he focused on developing what he called his "Cosmic Philosophy," and he would later be the teacher of Mirra Alfassa, who, as "the Mother," would become the leader of Sri Aurobindo's ashram in Pondicherry. Needless to say, the Hermetic Brotherhood of Luxor and the Brotherhood of Luxor sound remarkably similar, and the two groups, who may or may not have had any connection, are easily confused. It is possible that the H. B. of L. in some way grew out of the Brotherhood of Luxor, but it is also possible that the two are related by name alone.

One of the sources of the H. B. of L.'s teaching—which, when it went "public" was available through an "occult correspondence course," possibly the first of its kind—was the work of the eccentric mixed-race spiritualist and occultist, Paschal Beverly Randolph, who probably initiated one of the H. B. of L.'s members, the Scotsman Peter Davidson, in 1874. Davidson himself tells of how he was sought out by Max Théon in 1870, when the "exalted adept" was authorized by his Brother Initiates to take on a neophyte, and train him in his work—much as HPB was sought out by Master Morya. An erratic if charismatic character, Randolph led a life that rivaled HPB's for travel, adventure, and ambiguity. His unstable personality, exacerbated by alcohol and drugs—he used hashish for occult practices, and may possibly be a source for HPB's alleged use of it—led to many crises, and in 1875 at the age of forty-nine he blew his brains out directly after informing a stunned neighbor of his intention. A prolific writer and energetic advocate of his ideas, Randolph is most known today for being an early proponent of the "sex magic" associated with Aleister Crowley and his Ordo Templi Orientis. During his career, Randolph was arrested for promoting free love—as was his contemporary Victoria Woodhull—and his liberality in this area led him to abandon his first wife and their children, one of whom died from neglect. (He later left his second wife, too.) It is possible, as Christopher Bamford suggests, that Randolph founded a form of the H. B. of L. in Boston as early as 1868.[17] It is also clear from most accounts that he was, as Bamford says, "in equal parts authentic and a fake." Something, of course, that was also said of HPB.

What places the H. B. of L. in this curious mix is a remark made by the Traditionalist philosopher René Guénon. "From the beginning of the nineteenth century," Guénon writes, "there . . . existed in Germany . . . secret societies . . . which were concerned with magic and evocations, and also with magnetism" and that "it was precisely the H. B. of L. . . . that was in contact with some of these organizations." This would place the Brotherhood in the esoteric stream much earlier than its "official" appearance. Guénon claims that "indications of this may be found in an anonymous work, entitled *Ghost Land*, published under the auspices of the H. B. of L."[18] Guénon, in fact, was the first to ask why the Hydesville haunting sparked the spiritualist epidemic, when, after all, there were similar cases of "spirit manifestation" earlier than this. And he draws attention to the secret occult societies in Germany—Louis B's "Berlin Brotherhood"?—who were devoted to evocation, and who were operating as early as the late 1770s—which would put them in the context of the beginning of Mesmerism and Swedenborgianism, both of which, in different ways, sought to contact spiritual entities.[19]

AS FASCINATING AS THIS IS, any further digression will take us far from our subject, or entangle us in details it would take the rest of the book to unravel. Suffice it to say that HPB enters this plot in 1871, during her second stay in Cairo. In a way, though, she actually entered it at her birth. According to C. G. Harrison, the "aspect of the heavens" when HPB was born, "frightened" the "right wing" occultists.[20] Exactly why is unclear, but one assumes the stars portended the arrival of some powerful occult figure who would in some way work against their plans. The story is that during her second stay in Cairo, one of the "left wing" occultists told Blavatsky about this. Blavatsky is said to have then rushed to Paris, where she demanded admission to an occult brotherhood. The brotherhood refused, and Blavatsky left for America, where she made a similar demand upon another occult group, thought to be the H. B. of L. Here she was at first accepted, then expelled, and in retaliation, HPB threatened to "close up shop" on the American group. It was at this point that certain occultists came together to put her in "occult imprisonment," a state she remained in during the time she believed she was in Tibet.[21] She was subsequently freed, Harrison claims, by certain Hindu adepts—her Masters—in whose debt she then remained.

We have to note that fairly soon after the "spiritualist experiment" was conducted—at least according to Harrison's account—the "right wing" occultists recognized it had failed and stopped their operation. Yet, according to Rudolf Steiner, taking his cue from Harrison, the "left wing" occultists carried on, albeit now for their own purposes. Those purposes included discrediting the idea of reincarnation.[22] We've already seen that Allan Kardec's "Spiritism" did accept reincarnation, but that with Kardec's death, his teaching lost influence in Europe and America, and that for the most part, "mainstream Spiritualism" did without the notion, as Steiner puts it, of "repeated earth-lives." As with her relationship to Spiritualism, HPB will be accused of flip-flopping on reincarnation as well, underplaying if not actually denying it in *Isis Unveiled*, and making it a central theme of *The Secret Doctrine*. By the time the H. B. of L. begins to act openly—around 1884 to 1885—they will pursue a rigorously anti-reincarnation program, and will be equally opposed to the Theosophical Society, countering its by then Eastern-oriented teaching with their own peculiarly "materialistic" Western occultism. This, according to Annie Besant, later head of the Theosophical Society, "was distinctly allied to the questionable practices of the darker Tantric cults of India."[23]

IF THE READER feels a bit dizzy after all this, I can't blame him, and to be honest I'm not sure that I grasp all the strands of this intriguing scenario myself. Yet while these mysteries "behind the veil" clearly require deep pondering—and the interested reader is advised to consult Godwin's original work—some of HPB's more upfront activities are equally mystifying. Such as why she suddenly decided to marry the Georgian Michael C. Betanelly, whom she met in New York in late December 1874. Betanelly lived in Phila-delphia, and after reading Olcott's *Graphic* articles had written to him, asking if he could meet his countrywoman, to talk about Spir-itualism. HPB agreed and Betanelly traveled to New York. He confessed his deep love and admiration for HPB and followed this up in letters expressing unstinting adoration. Blavatsky snubbed him. When Olcott left Philadelphia, HPB stayed on for a while in the City of Brotherly Love. Betanelly renewed his assault and must have been persistent. Mistakenly believing Nikifor to be dead— her sister Vera had said so, but he was, in fact, still alive—and impressing upon her suitor that sex or other intimacies were out of the question—she did not, she said, wish to live as a married woman—she changed her mind. The fact that Betanelly threat-ened suicide if she refused must have had something to do with it, although it is difficult to think of a woman who had fought on the barricades and trekked across Tibet falling for such neurotic tac-tics. Olcott rightly pointed out that Betanelly was in every way her inferior, and that his Russian import business was about as solvent as her chicken farm (she would, however, win her court case over this and recover her investment). She agreed, but answered that marrying him was a "misfortune" she could not escape. Exactly why is not clear, and one can wonder if it had anything to do with trying to get the "astral mineral" she alchemically and unsuccessfully sought in her first husband? Perhaps the relief of speaking in Russian was the attraction, but if Betanelly was as unsuitable as Olcott says, what could they have talked about? In any case, Betanelly proved incapable of resisting his animal urges, and after fending off his advances, HPB finally left him (as we can see, HPB had no time for P. B. Randolph's ideas about "sex magic"). He later sued for divorce and eventually returned to Georgia.

One incident during her bigamous union stands out. When she exacerbated an already injured knee, her doctor thought it was so far gone that amputation was the only remedy. Blavatsky disagreed and, taking her cue from Francis Bacon, for two nights slept with a puppy—some accounts have a white dog—straddled across her leg.[24] Three days later she was better, and soon after returned to New York.

By this time, Olcott had gathered his research into Spiritualism and produced a book. In March 1875, *People from the Other World* appeared, a work put together from his *Graphic* articles. Needless to say, it featured HPB and, as mentioned, it was Olcott's account of her powers at Chittenden that aroused D. D. Home's ire. Sadly, it aroused little else, and the book was not a success. Although he and HPB had done some damage control on Robert Dale Owen's unfortunate episode with Katie King, interest in Spiritualism was clearly on the decline. Although from the perspective of her mission this should have been a good thing, the immediate result was

increased skepticism about any nonmaterial reality. The Katie
King affair could not have been the sole cause, and the central reason why Spiritualism was losing its steam was that it seemed to lead
nowhere. Tambourines floated, ectoplasm appeared, and voices
were heard, but what they said was not particularly enlightening.
The vast majority of the messages from the dead were numbingly
trivial, and although proof of survival brought solace to many, it
led most intelligent minds to believe that life after death must
be insufferably dull. Like much "channeled" material today, the
"teachings" of the spirits were usually little more than vacuous
meditations along broadly mystical lines. Whether HPB's next
step was motivated by a good nose for the Next Big Thing or by her
mission is debatable, and perhaps the two were identical. Either
way if she was to survive Spiritualism's decline, she had to act fast.
Olcott, impressed with HPB's powers and talk of her Masters, had
already pointed in the general direction and provided the first hint
of the "hidden hand" theory discussed above. In a footnote to his
account of HPB, he raised the suspicion that "this very American
outbreak of spiritualistic phenomena is under the control of an
Order, which while depending for its results upon unseen agents,
has its existence upon Earth among men."

ONE RESULT OF Olcott's book was a letter from the Russian spiritualist Alexander N. Aksakov, who had had his own encounter
with Katie King and found her real enough.[25] Aksakov asked if
Blavatsky would consider translating the book into Russian, and
she seems to have taken on other translation work too, even
tackling Darwin's *Origin of Species*—an ironic choice, given later

developments. More pressing matters occupied her, though. She had received word from M that it was time to speak openly about occultism and to abandon her spiritualist disguise. Exactly how to do this was the question. *The Banner of Light*, which she had written for, would not be interested in the new idea, as it would be critical of Spiritualism, and they already had enough problems in that area. Then she remembered *The Spiritual Scientist*, a small journal published in Boston. Its editor, Elbridge Gerry Brown, had read her attack on Dr. Beard and had invited her and Olcott to call on him if they were ever in Boston. Perhaps her campaign could start there?

Olcott agreed, and wrote a circular letter to Brown, spelling out the new direction he and HPB were taking. When he rearranged the paragraphs so it would read better, his chum pointed something out. The first letter of the first word of each of the six paragraphs spelled a name: TUITIT. It was that of one of the Masters, Tuitit Bey, to be exact (who may or may not have been Max Théon). Olcott had asked HPB if he or she should sign the circular. Blavatsky said it seemed it was signed already, by Tuitit Bey himself. Olcott agreed and sent it off, under the auspices of the "Brotherhood of Luxor." Brown printed it, and a collaboration with him, Olcott, and HPB began.

Not long after this Colonel Olcott received another letter, whose point of origin seemed more exotic than Russia. He had already noticed some funny business with his post. He had received letters in Philadelphia that had not been redirected from his New York office, where he had left instructions about forwarding his mail. Yet who could have known he was there? That is, the senders had addressed them to his office, yet they had reached him directly, without being redirected. How could that have happened? Now another letter appeared. It came in a black, glazed envelope. The address was written in French in gold ink; strangely, it was addressed to his office on Beekman Street, but sent in care of Madame Blavatsky, who rarely visited the office, if at all. It was from Tuitit Bey, the Master whose name Olcott had unconsciously spelled when rearranging his circular. Could that have been sheer coincidence? In a note from HPB accompanying this strange epistle, she explained that the letter had been "ordered at Luxor" and "written out in Ellora"—in India—and entrusted to her to give to him. She warned him about accepting the obligation it entailed, for it was nothing less than an invitation from her Masters to join them. If he agreed, he was, she said, "cooked."

Looking at the strange message, written in gold ink on green paper, and decorated with various Masonic and occult signs, Olcott saw that it was from the Brotherhood of Luxor—the Seventh Section, to be exact—and addressing him as "Brother Neophyte," it read: "He who seeks us finds *us*. Try. Rest thy mind—banish all foul doubt. We keep watch over our faithful soldiers. Sister Helen is a valiant, trustworthy servant. Open thy Spirit to conviction, have faith and she will lead thee to the Golden Gate of truth." After some critical words about "John King"—who would no longer be making appearances—the letter informed Olcott that three Masters, no less, were keeping an eye on him: Serapis Bey, of the Ellora Section; Polydorus Isurenus, of the Solomon Section; and Robert More, of the Zoroaster Section. Entreating Olcott to "Activity and Silence," it was signed "Tuitit Bey, Observatory of Luxor."

Olcott, indeed, was cooked. One part of the message that both Tuitit Bey and his messenger, HPB, especially impressed on him was to "Try." As Joscelyn Godwin has pointed out, "TRY" was the magical motto of Paschal Beverly Randolph, a kind of esoteric "Just do it," familiar today for less noble purposes, and it would appear more than once in the mystical messages that followed. Randolph's work, we know, was part of the H. B. of L.'s curriculum, and with the letter coming from the Brotherhood of Luxor, we can't help but wonder if there is a connection—even as little as HPB hearing of the H. B. of L., and throwing their name into what was fast becoming a very rich mix. Soon Olcott received other letters, mostly from another Master, Serapis Bey, entreating him to have courage and to be hopeful and, more than once, to be patient with his chum, and to do everything he could to help her. For letters coming from a mystic Master, they had a curiously practical tone. One was about the need to complete the divorce from Betanelly. HPB's mad marriage was a calamity, and threatened legal problems, as word was Betanelly was planning to skip the country, leaving his wife responsible for his many debts. The tie had to be severed immediately. (It was and Betanelly returned to Georgia.) Other letters suggested that Olcott borrow money from his ex-in-laws, in order to finance their mission; one even suggested a partnership between them and Betanelly. The Masters quickly changed their minds about this idea, though.

Another concern of Serapis Bey was the collaboration with E. Gerry Brown. Although Brown would publish what Blavatsky later called her "first Occult shot," in which she first publicly declared the existence of the Masters, he turned out to be not quite the staunch supporter that Serapis Bey believed him to be, and was apparently interested in promoting HPB's mission as long as she could pay to have her articles about it printed in his magazine. His collaboration with the chums was short-lived and Brown soon exited the story, but in "A Few Questions to Hiraf," published by Brown in July 1875, Blavatsky makes a kind of dry run for what would soon become her first major occult statement, *Isis Unveiled*.

"Hiraf" was an acrostic made up of the first letters of the names of five amateur scholars who had collaborated on an article published in the *Spiritual Scientist* entitled "Rosicrucianism."[26] HPB read the article and was impressed enough by it to pen a lengthy reply. Although their use of "Rosicrucianism" to cover all aspects of occultism was incorrect, she felt the article was intelligent and insightful enough to warrant clarification. In her response she argues that "Occultism . . . stands in relation to Spiritualism as the Infinite to the Finite," and she affirms the existence of "colleges" of the "Secret Science" in the East. She would reveal, she said, "a little of the little I picked up in my long travels throughout the length and breadth of the East—that cradle of Occultism" in order to help "sincere enquirers" who might want to drink at "the source of knowledge." Those who do wish to learn the "Great Truth" can do so, provided they "try" to meet the right person—again, using Randolph's magical motto. The location of the Brotherhoods, however, will never be revealed, "until . . . Humanity shall awake in a mass from its spiritual lethargy, and open its blind eye to the dazzling light of truth."

One point she emphasized, and which would become a central theme of her later work, is the difference between what she called the Oriental and the Jewish Cabala (Cabala or Kabbalah means "tradition"). The Oriental Cabala, which is "the most secret of all," is "carefully preserved at the headquarters of a Brotherhood in the East," possibly a Sufi sect to which al-Afghani belonged. This mysterious lodge safeguards the "secret powers of the ancient Chaldeans," and, as mentioned, Blavatsky will later make repeated reference to a mysterious "Chaldean Book of Numbers." This Cabala, the original and first, was later altered by Moses, an "ambitious prophet-medium," who passed off his "familiar spirit, the wrathful 'Jehovah'" for the spirit of God himself. The key difference between the Oriental Cabala and the altered Mosaic one is the introduction of a principle of evil. This is absent from the original Cabala, and its introduction by Moses and his descendants has, according to Blavatsky, caused more than a few problems.[27]

As Joscelyn Godwin and K. Paul Johnson have pointed out, a common aim shared by HPB's early occult confederates is a criticism of the Judeo-Christian tradition, not only in occult matters, but in social, personal, and political ones as well. We recall Agardi Metrovitch's passionate anti-Jesuit beliefs, Albert Rawson's researches into the Druzes, Sufis, and other forms of Islamic religion, and HPB's own time in Mentana, fighting with Mazzini's Italians against the papal troops, and we remember the extraordinary hold Judeo-Christian ideas had on the moral and philosophical consciousness of Victorian times. Although she is mostly thought of in occult or spiritual terms, we need to recognize that Blavatsky was also linked to many modern progressive movements, and that she was an early combatant in the struggle against what many felt was an oppressive religious, moral, and social tradition. Whether she was involved in "nothing more nor less than the abolition of Christianity in favour of a freethinking humanism," as Godwin argues, is debatable.[28] Her animus toward the Judeo-Christian ethos, however, is clear, and would soon bring her more than one enemy. Two quotations should give us an idea of her attitude toward it. In an essay entitled "The Esoteric Character of the Gospels," HPB wrote that "the Bible is not the 'word of God' but contains at best the words of fallible and imperfect teachers." And for her, Christianity is "the religion of arrogance *par excellence*, a stepping-stone for ambition, a sinecure for wealth, sham, and power, and a convenient screen for hypocrisy."[29]

ALONG WITH SEEING what would come of working with Brown, the Masters also prodded Blavatsky to try once more to form a society, "a secret Society like the Rosicrucian Lodge," the kind, indeed, to which her great-grandfather Prince Dolgorukov belonged. She had already struck out twice in Cairo, but she and Olcott decided to try again. The result was, as mentioned, something they called the Miracle Club, and its activities were kept to some degree secret. Sadly, nothing too miraculous happened in it, even behind a veil of secrecy. It was for the most part occupied with the familiar spiritualist routine, and those who came to it didn't see anything that they couldn't see elsewhere. But it did provide the setting for what would become an unqualified success.

One of the miracles shared by members of the club was a lecture given on September 7, 1875, by the engineer, architect, and inventor George H. Felt on "The Lost Canon of Proportion of the Egyptians, Greeks, and Romans." The talk, which was held at Blavatsky's rooms at 46 Irving Place—she had moved once again—went over well, and during it a thought came to Olcott (although he later again questioned if it was his thought at all). Wouldn't it be a good idea to start a society that studied this sort of thing, he wondered? Olcott jotted this idea down on a slip of paper and handed

it to a new comrade, William Quan Judge, a twenty-four-year-old
Irish immigrant with an interest in Spiritualism who had only
recently passed the New York bar examination. Judge agreed and
passed the note on to HPB, who nodded approvingly. The lecture
continued and Felt, who it is believed was a member of the H. B. of
L., went on to claim that the men who designed the pyramids were
adepts. Their great structures, which have survived millennia,
were not made of only bricks and mortar—or the ancient Egyptian
equivalent—but were the product of an occult wisdom, carefully
guarded by the high priests. This wisdom consisted of an exact
mystical science, which could be housed in specific geometric
designs. Indeed, these geometric drawings, which involved the use
of the Egyptian zodiac, could, Felt maintained, be used to manifest spiritual "presences," which Felt associated with elementals.
Sadly, although Felt promised that he would give a display of these
mysterious beings, he never did—because he was unwilling or
unable is unclear, but he nevertheless collected a hundred dollars
for his efforts, and subsequently faded from view.[30]

But Felt had manifested something perhaps even more remarkable. During the conversation about the Egyptians and their wisdom following the lecture, Olcott stood up and informed the
audience—there were sixteen or seventeen people in all—of the
idea that had passed between himself, Judge, and HPB. Everyone
thought it was splendid, and an immediate vote was taken, constituting those present into a society dedicated to studying precisely
the sort of thing they were just discussing. Judge moved that
Olcott be made chairman; Olcott reciprocated by nominating
Judge for secretary. Blavatsky herself at this point held no office in
the new society, which was yet to be named. Official elections were

held the next evening, and Blavatsky eventually was made corresponding secretary. But it wasn't until a week later that the society was properly christened. Various names were considered: Hermetic, Rosicrucian, Egyptological, but none seemed right, or to convey the sense those present had that this would be something different. We can be sure that HPB wanted to hit the esoteric nail on the head, having already struck out three times, and with the Master looking over her shoulder. Frustrated, one of those present, Charles Sotheran, a journalist, bibliographer, and antiquarian with an interest in fringe Masonry and radical politics—and who may have known Blavatsky from earlier days—grabbed the dictionary from the shelf and started flipping the pages (today, of course, he'd have gone to Google). Was it chance, fate, or the Master? We'll never know, but Sotheran's eye landed on what seemed a good candidate. "What about 'theosophy'?" he asked. That was it. Everyone agreed. On September 13, 1875, the Theosophical Society was born. Not long after that, at a meeting on November 17, held at the Mott Memorial Hall on Madison Avenue, it was made official, and as the saying goes, the world would never be the same.

SIX

UNVEILING ISIS

lthough unusual, the term "theosophy" was not without precedent. Formed of two Greek terms, *theos* ("god") and *sophia* ("wisdom")—as our word "philosophy," the love of wisdom is—it could be roughly translated as "god-wisdom," or "divine wisdom," or "the wisdom of the gods." This could mean wisdom *about* God or the gods, or the wisdom *possessed* by God or the gods, the one leaning toward theology, the other toward mysticism. In effect, "theosophy" as used by HPB would include both meanings, and a whole lot more—so much, that exactly what theosophy meant would lead to more than one unsatisfactory attempt by Theosophists to define it. William Quan Judge may have highlighted and circumvented the problem by saying that "the strength of theosophy lies in the fact that it is not to be defined." But many people wanting some idea of what the Theosophical Society is about may not be convinced by Judge's belief that in its "evolution," "new truths" and "new aspects of old truths" will expel the need for "dogmas or 'unequivocal definitions,'" which, frankly, sounds like evasion.[1] One wants to ask exactly *what* is evolving, and without agreeing on that, this sounds too much like "anything goes."

Blavatsky herself said that the term came from the Alexandrian philosophers of the second and third century A.D., and she referred to a group known as the Philaletheians, or "lovers of truth," from *philo* ("love") and *aletheia* ("truth"). Neo-Platonic thinkers from the same period, such as Iamblichus and Porphyry, whose understanding of philosophy leaned much more toward mysticism and the occult than any philosopher today would allow, used it, and in more recent times it was associated with the work of the seventeenth century Silesian cobbler-mystic Jacob Boehme. In 1600, Boehme had a powerful mystical experience. While gazing at the sunlight reflected on a pewter dish, he believed he was shown "the signature of all things," the true relation between man and God, the nature of good and evil, and the spiritual structure of the world. In a series of weighty and obscure books, couched in an often difficult alchemical language, Boehme tried to convey his insights. One of these books, his last, was called *177 Theosophic Questions*.

Blavatsky's use of "theosophy," though, would be something more and something less than that of earlier exponents, and the term's vagueness—at least as seen by some—led not a few critics to wonder if it meant anything at all. Peter Washington points out that the understanding of "truth" and "science" that HPB and her Theosophists respected in ancient sages such as Pythagoras and Plotinus was hardly reconcilable with contemporary notions of these pursuits.[2] Part of the new society's aim was to apply "scientific" study to the kind of phenomena familiar to spiritualists, which meant maintaining standards of objectivity, detachment, precision, and neutrality—not qualities usually associated with the "wisdom of the gods." But if you begin by accepting that such phenomena are real—as HPB, Olcott, and the other early members did—then, Washington asks, aren't you already prejudicing your investigations? This muddle, however, is only apparent, as you would have nothing to investigate if you didn't believe it existed, and the other side of the coin is the "hard-nosed" scientist's belief that such phenomena are impossible. If you don't believe they exist, HPB could ask, how can you study them? A greater index of an inherent vagueness in Theosophy—which is not necessarily a weakness—is its inclusiveness. Sometime after the society's founding, it produced a "mission statement," which guides its many branches today:

1. To form the nucleus of a universal brotherhood of humanity, without distinction of race, creed, sex, caste, or color.
2. The study of ancient and modern religions, philosophies, and sciences, and the demonstration of the importance of such study.
3. The investigation of the unexplained laws of nature and the psychical powers latent in man.

Of the three, the last two could, I think, find a place under the more narrow understanding of "theosophy." Yet, in actual practice, at least during HPB's lifetime, it was the first aim to which she devoted the most time and energy. Blavatsky repeatedly reprimanded her followers for wanting to pursue the others—mostly number 3—without securing what, for her, was the most important goal. This seems more attuned to the kind of "freethinking humanism" that Joscelyn Godwin believed she pursued, than any kind of mystical doctrine, although the notion of a "universal brotherhood of humanity" certainly has a Masonic ring.

While it is untrue to say that Theosophy was all things to all men, it did provide a very wide umbrella, under which quite a few things could find a place. This inclusiveness extended to Theosophists themselves. In a late article, "How to Become a Theosophist," published in her journal *Lucifer* (whose title expressed her anti-Christian sentiments and reflected her own, by that time, "fallen" status within society), HPB explained that

> any person of average intellectual capacities, and a leaning toward the metaphysical; of pure unselfish life, who finds more joy in helping his neighbour than in receiving help himself; one who is ever ready to sacrifice his own pleasures for the sake of other people; and who loves Truth, Goodness, and Wisdom for their own sake, not for the benefit they may confer—is a Theosophist.[3]

This, as she often pointed out, meant that there were many Theosophists who weren't members of the society, just as there were many members of the society who were not necessarily Theosophists, a distinction she would repeatedly emphasize in her struggles ahead. If we bracket the word "theosophist," this definition seems to broadly denote what in the West used to be called the philosophical life. In the East, especially in Tibet, it could point to the beginning of a bodhisattva.

In the early days, though, Theosophy meant pretty much HPB herself, and her position as corresponding secretary was a tacit agreement that she would be the new society's theoretician and ideas-person. If the newly christened Theosophists looked to any-one to give them some sense of direction, it was she.

THE GROUP ITSELF, however, was not made up of mere follow-ers. As a report of the first meeting published in a New York newspaper pointed out, those gathered in Blavatsky's rooms on that fateful evening included "several persons of great learning and . . . wide personal influence." Besides HPB, Olcott, and Charles Sotheran, who suggested the society's name, there was William Quan Judge, considered one of the Theosophical founding fathers. Judge had been in contact with occultists and spiritualists in Dublin, Ireland—from where he hailed—and was a correspondent of George Russell, the mystical poet and intimate of W. B. Yeats, who wrote under the pseudonym "A. E." Judge's father had been a Mason, and Judge himself was led to meeting HPB through read-ing Olcott's *People from the Other World*. We've seen Emma Hardinge Britten's association with mysterious occult secret societies; she was accompanied by her husband. The Italian Signor Bruzzesi, known as *Il Conte*, was a sculptor and ex-secretary of Mazzini; he was also, by most accounts, like Agardi Metrovitch, a Carbonaro, who knew HPB from her European travels. C. C. Massey was an English barrister and Freemason. Also present was the Cabalist Dr. Seth Pancost, who had failed to cure HPB's leg in Philadelphia and precipitously advised amputation; William Livingston Alden, editorial writer for the *New York Times*; John Storer Cobb, the editor of a journal called *The New Era*; and a "learned Portuguese Jew," D. E. da Lara. There were also the editors of two religious newspapers; the co-editors of two literary magazines; an Oxford

professor; the president of the New York Society of Spiritualists; and a New York judge and his wife. Although not all would
stay—many indeed soon left or were asked to leave—the initial
gathering showed that HPB's mission was not attracting "flakes"
and "lone nutters," as we might say today, but accomplished men
and women, drawn together by a common interest. And as we've
seen, in its heyday the Theosophical Society would indeed attract
and influence some of the most creative and influential people of
the time.

Although Blavatsky would repeatedly argue that Theosophy
was not a religion—there were too many of them already, she
thought—the next step in her mission seemed obvious: Her new
movement needed its Bible. She had already started to put her
mind to this task, and the result would be a remarkable work, *Isis
Unveiled*, her mammoth compendium of Hermetic, occult, and
esoteric ideas. Yet perhaps even as remarkable as the work itself
was its manner of production. For some months before the founding of the new society, the Colonel had noticed an odd change in
his chum. He felt he was not free to speak of it openly, yet in letters
to her family, Blavatsky herself gave an account of a strange transformation that seemed to be taking place within her. It was
another manifestation of the "double life" she had experienced earlier. Writing to Vera, HPB spoke of feeling a "very strange duality,"
as if there was another consciousness present in her body, which
she called "No. 2." She retained her own sense of self, but along
with this there was *someone else*. She spoke of "the lodger who is in
me," and of the strange experience of *sharing* his knowledge and
memories, which were quite different from her own. This "lodger"
was her familiar Hindu, but now it seemed that he had begun to

infuse his own consciousness into hers, a practice that in Tibetan Buddhism is associated with the phenomenon known as a *tulku*. This is when a yogi or holy man transfers his own consciousness into the mind of another, an experience described by Lama Anagarika Govinda in Chapter 3. Blavatsky spoke of having memories of places she had never visited and knowledge of things that to her "real" self were unknown. Yet, the new consciousness inspiring her was not completely "other," and HPB also told Vera that what she felt was at work was a "higher and luminous Self," thinking and writing for her.[4] This suggests the possibility that the Master HPB had encountered since childhood may have been at least in part a personification of some larger aspect of herself.[5]

Blavatsky's "strange duality" was perceived by others as well. A reporter for the *Hartford Daily Times*, interviewing her a few years later, spoke of her "rare, strange countenance," in which a "combination of moods" seemed to be constantly at play. A "keen, alert, subtle undercurrent of feeling and perception perceivable in . . . her eyes" impressed the journalist with "the idea of a double personality . . . as if she were here and not here; talking, and yet thinking, or acting far away."[6] Many years after Blavatsky's death, the writer Beatrice Hastings—a remarkable character, who, sadly, is for the most part unknown today—argued that parts of *Isis Unveiled* clearly showed that more than one mind was at work in its production. Comparing Blavatsky's style in her letters and more polemical writings to certain passages in *Isis Unveiled*, Hastings observed that while her "private letters frequently halt in expression," and her polemical writings are always expounded with "a thump on the desk," HPB "had nothing of the temperament necessary for the serene expositional expression of which we find so much in *Isis Unveiled*."[7] Hastings would also argue that this marked difference in style was—at least as far as she was concerned—proof that HPB could not have written the notorious Mahatma Letters, whose sonorous sentences seem of a piece with the more stately passages in *Isis*.

Adam Crabtree, an authority on multiple personality, remarks that "human beings possess a mysterious inner malleability or plasticity," and that at "some obscure depth of the psyche, a moulding of discrete mental units can take place."[8] These "discrete units," Crabtree argues, manifest as separate personalities, and one of the most baffling aspects of this remarkable phenomenon, is that the original personality—"No. 1," so to speak—is often completely unaware of his strange partners. In his absorbing history of the discovery and treatment of this often bizarre phenomenon, *Multiple Man*, Crabtree relates how the famed French psychologist Pierre Janet developed a method of communicating with the "other" personalities directly. Janet observed that if the "No. 1" personality was occupied with some activity, he could ask the "other" questions, speaking in a calm, quiet voice, to which it would reply. When the "No. 1" personality was asked what Janet had just spoken to him about, he would not know, and seemed puzzled by the question. It seemed that by catching the "No. 1" personality off guard, when he was distracted by some absorbing activity, "No. 2" could quietly make an appearance. Later acquaintances remarked on HPB's apparent obsession with playing solitaire; in their accounts, it is as ubiquitous as her cigarettes. Archibald Keightley, who knew HPB during her last years in London, remarked that "while solitaire occupied the brain, HPB was engaged in very different work." She could "take part in a conversation going on around her . . . attend to what we used to call 'upstairs,' and also see what was going on in her own room and other places in the house and out of it, at one and the same time."⁹ Yet this "splitting" of her consciousness was with her from early on. When HPB returned to her family in 1858 after her first years of wandering, and entertained them with her raps and strange knockings, she often produced these mysterious sounds while sitting engaged in embroidery. It was as if in order to manifest them, she had to keep her "No. 1" consciousness occupied, much as Janet's patients had to be distracted in order for him to talk to their other selves. The idea seems to be that by engaging in some purposeful but unimportant work—embroidery or playing cards, perhaps even rolling and smoking cigarettes—our everyday consciousness "frees up" some inner space that the "other" self uses in order to appear. This possibility suggests that some activities related to spiritual practice, such as chanting a mantra, repeating a prayer, the rituals involved in ceremonial magic, and even the tea ceremonies associated with Zen Buddhism, are methods of distracting the everyday self, in order for the "other" to manifest.¹⁰

Blavatsky's "other," to be sure, manifested in ways much more monumental than anything Janet's or Adam Crabtree's patients produced. In looking at the enormous effort that went into *Isis Unveiled*, we are tempted to fall back on earlier notions of "inspiration," although the "divine afflatus" associated with this idea can itself be seen as a form of "multiple personality" or even "possession," whether by a "higher Self" or some more external entity.¹¹ Although written under "orders," when HPB began the work, she wasn't exactly sure where it was heading, which was rather the case with the fledgling Theosophical Society itself. Olcott says that at

some point in the summer of 1875—exactly where they were living at
the time is unclear—HPB handed him some pages of a manuscript.
"I wrote this last night," she told him, "'by order,' but what the deuce
it is to be I don't know." She thought it could be for an article, or
maybe a book, or possibly for nothing at all. With this less than
encouraging remark, she pushed the pages into a drawer and forgot
about them for some time. What triggered her return to the work is
unclear, although the publication of a book by Emma Hardinge
Britten, *Art Magic*, might have had something to do with it.

Britten claimed that the book was not written by her, but was
dictated by an adept, none other than the mysterious Chevalier
Louis B, supposed author of *Ghost Land*. Although it spoke of
adepts, white and black magic, and the importance of the Astral
Light—all themes that Blavatsky herself would tackle—neither
Olcott nor HPB was impressed with it. In fact, in many ways they
found it scandalous, not the least because of its assertion that
developing communication with the dead, and accepting them as
spirit guides and "controls," would aid its readers on their way to
becoming adepts, a belief that Blavatsky was determined to under-
mine. Britten was a successful medium and an accomplished
speaker, and although she limited the print run of the book to five
hundred copies, word of it soon spread throughout the milieu that
Blavatsky herself wanted to conquer. HPB's star was rising, but
Britten was at that point the more established figure. Soon, however, it would be clear that no séance would be big enough for both
of them.

That Blavatsky had some major work in mind for some time is
suggested by a letter she wrote in early 1875 to Hiram Corson, a
professor of English literature at Cornell University in upstate

New York. Corson had written to HPB after reading her defense of the Eddy brothers in the *Graphic*; he had turned to Spiritualism after the death of his teenaged daughter, and hoped he could establish contact with her through Blavatsky. In one exchange, HPB remarked that she believed "we . . . are at the threshold of an epoch when a thousand mysteries shall be revealed," and lamented that it was up to "such feeble mortal agencies" as Corson's pen and her own, to determine "how soon the world shall be enlightened." I have not actually counted how many mysteries are revealed in *Isis Unveiled*, but I would say a thousand is a rough estimate.

Corson's and Blavatsky's correspondence led to an invitation by the professor for HPB to come and stay with him and his wife at their home in Ithaca. Here the work on what would become *Isis Unveiled* began in earnest, although the professor had little idea what he was letting himself in for. Blavatsky's letters may have prepared Corson for a "woman of frantic intensity," but having her in his home, and not merely as a correspondent, was another story. HPB's appearance, in a voluminous robe that, according to one account, made her look as if the curtains had fallen on her, was bad enough, but predictably, her tobacco intake was the real shock.[12] HPB had warned him that she would be stealing away every fifteen minutes to have a smoke in his basement; she had come to recognize that even among enlightened folk, in America women smoking in public was still taboo. But her nicotine habit wasn't limited to basements. Corson soon discovered that his flowerpots were full of her stubs, and at one point, while on a carriage tour of the area, she demanded he stop so she could light up somewhere out of view. He estimated she smoked two hundred cigarettes a day, which seems to confirm Hannah Wolff's remark that she could easily get through a pound of tobacco. Corson was also put out by HPB's refusal to try to contact his daughter, and by her adamant dismissal of any such practice, opposed as it was to the teachings of her Masters. She was, he said, "a smart woman, but ignorant of all the graces and amenities of life," and summed up his assessment of her personality by calling her a "great Russian bear."

Yet the crudity of her personal habits was more than made up for by her remarkable ability to work. Holed up in her room, HPB produced some twenty-five "closely written foolscap pages a day." Yet if the sheer volume of words was impressive, even more so was Blavatsky's apparent ability to quote long passages from works neither she nor the professor possessed, and which Corson suspected were not even available in America at the time. Blavatsky explained that she saw the passages "on another plane of objective existence" and simply wrote them down—if need be, translating them from whatever language they were in into English. She employed, it seems, a form of "clairvoyant reading"; either that or she possessed a phenomenal memory, which, as Corson remarked, would be evidence of an even more startling feat than that of getting her references "from the ether."[13]

Corson was not the only one privy to Blavatsky's curious writing habits. By this time, Colonel Olcott and his chum had shared more than one lodging, and in what would become their best-known home, he observed HPB's remarkable "clairvoyant reading" at first hand. Toward the end of 1875, they shared rooms at 433 West 34th Street, where the impecunious Baron de Palm died, his request to be cremated sparking something of an uproar. A cremation society existed in New York, but it had yet to burn any bodies, and in any case, it didn't want to be associated with what it saw as a dubious occult organization. In fact, the baron's funeral and his actual cremation were separated by six months, during which time his body was packed in clay, giving rise to the story that Olcott had built his own clay oven in which to burn it. At the ceremony, which Olcott had devised and which was held at the Masonic Temple in New York on May 29, 1876, the Colonel described God in Theosophical terms as the "uncaused cause."[14] A Methodist preacher took offense at this and shouted, "That's a lie," and started a disturbance. The crowd that gathered laughed at the whole proceeding and the affair garnered some bad press, something that was repeated that December after the baron's body was finally consigned to the flames in the private crematorium of Dr. Francis Le Moyne, which he had built for his own use in Washington, Pennsylvania. News of the "heathen" goings-on was reported around the country and in Europe, and the society was criticized for supporting what was to many a "pagan" custom. Yet Olcott had by now absorbed his chum's sanguine attitude toward publicity. Although lambasted, the debacle did make the Theosophical Society more widely known, and helped to establish cremation as an accepted practice.

In early 1876, the chums found a new roost in Hell's Kitchen, perhaps the most unlikely location for the home of a spiritual movement. At 302 West 47th Street, off Eighth Avenue, HPB and the Colonel came to rest in what would be their last American abode. The apartment's unusual décor led one reporter to dub it "the Lamasery," an apt quip, given the chums' taste for the exotic. Olcott decked the place out with assorted outré bric-a-brac gathered from what used to be called "curiosity shops." Japanese cabinets, a Swiss cuckoo clock, and a stuffed lioness's head greeted visitors as they entered an apartment wreathed in incense and tobacco smoke. An upright piano supported images of the Buddha and other spiritual teachers, and a stuffed gray owl leered eerily from a bookcase. Long, narrow mirrors stood in the corners of the rooms, stuffed monkeys hung from the walls, as did several toy lizards, and potted palm fronds reached to the ceiling. A stuffed bat hung over a doorway, a stuffed crocodile hung over another, and the dining room wall featured a jungle tapestry, complete with a snake, a tiger, and an elephant, surrounded by thick foliage. Another snake curled around the mantelpiece mirror. The most famous *objet d'art*, however, was the celebrated stuffed baboon. This Olcott dressed in a collar, white cravat, and a pair of glasses, and under one of its arms he shoved the manuscript of a lecture on Darwin's *Origin of Species*. They christened the caricature Professor Fiske, after an academic who propounded an extraordinarily narrow materialistic view of the universe. Not all the animals in the chums' menagerie were stuffed, though. Blavatsky liked pets—during one of her stays in the Near East she acquired a collection of monkeys which she was later forced to abandon—and in the Lamasery she kept a pair of canaries, which she often let fly about the rooms. They even made a nest in the chandelier, using scraps from HPB's growing manuscript.

For the next few years, the Lamasery was New York's most famous salon, where Christians, Jews, and "heathens" met with artists, intellectuals, and bohemians, as well as doctors, lawyers, and aristocrats, to discuss "every imaginable subject on earth, in the heavens above the earth, and in the profoundest depths below," with a "curious mix of wit and philosophy."[15] Here HPB also put on occasional displays of her powers, although she was increasingly loath to devote her energies to such trivia, and it was because of her reluctance in this matter that many of the early members of the society left. The demonstrations she did provide seem to leave little doubt that HPB was indeed a mage. Years later, William Quan Judge wrote that in his presence Blavatsky caused objects to move unaided, including a silver spoon that penetrated two walls to reach her hand. She materialized bottles of paint, drew a letter from an unopened envelope and then duplicated it, and created the hallucination of one of her rings, and gave it to a woman who coveted it.[16] From the same period, Olcott described demonstrations of telepathy, materialization (when Olcott balked at lending her his pencil—she invariably kept them—she "materialized" a dozen of them to spite him), the command of elementals, "mesmeric hallucinations," "precipitations"—when an image or writing appeared on blank paper—clairvoyance, and her reading of what she called "the Astral Light" or "Akashic Record," "akasha" being the Sanskrit term for "ether." Many of these displays were accompanied by the tinkling of "astral bells," delicate pings from the spirit world that preceded some phenomenon.

The last power that Olcott describes was most in evidence while HPB labored at what would become her first major work. During the day, Olcott would head to his office, where he maintained the legal practice that provided upkeep for himself and his chum, as well as his ex-wife and sons; when we consider the weird world he was moving in, that he managed to support both Blavatsky and himself as well as his estranged family seems a testament to his industry and sense of obligation. HPB worked on her own during the day, but in the evening, after dinner—which a maid usually prepared, although Olcott occasionally cooked; HPB herself was useless in a kitchen—they sat across from each other at a long desk, the central furnishing of the Lamasery, and worked together into the night. Blavatsky would show him what she had written earlier, and he would comment on it and more than occasionally correct it. Although she had developed a vigorous, idiomatic style, HPB was usually helpless with punctuation, and her syntax would have given Proust a run for his money. She was also less than tidy, and her many pages were often covered with new paragraphs pasted over earlier, rejected passages. Olcott would go over the mess, correcting mistakes, suggesting changes, and occasionally rewriting whole sections. These he would read back to her, and she would either accept them or not. Not infrequently she would throw out what both she and Olcott had written, and start from scratch.

As if materializing pencils were not enough, Olcott was also baffled by the number of quotations Blavatsky stuffed into the work. As they had only a few books in the place, he couldn't understand where they came from. To be sure, she made great use of the books they had, and references to the work of the French occultist Eliphas Lévi; the French writer on India, Louis Jacolliot; the inevitable Bulwer-Lytton; Hargrave Jennings's book on the Rosicrucians; Max Müller's works; those of Samuel Fales Dunlap; Joseph Ennemoser; C. W. King on the Gnostics; and other writers little read or practically unknown today, which came from their meager bookshelves, made their way into Blavatsky's growing *magnum opus*. But as Professor Corson had observed, many quotations came from sources not readily at hand, not even at the public library, which, in any case, Olcott was certain she did not visit. She rarely, if ever, left their rooms, not even for an evening's constitutional.

By some accounts she was housebound for six months straight, and worked seventeen hours a day.

Her manner of writing was anything but methodical and seemed to preclude the conscientious fact-checking of more fastidious authors. She seemed to work to no fixed plan, with ideas rushing through her mind in a ceaseless torrent, her pencil racing across the page in a desperate effort to keep pace. When she did stop, it was not to leave her seat and flip through some tome. Olcott recounts that her pencil would suddenly halt in midsentence, and she would look up into the space in front of her. She would then narrow her eyes, "as though to look at something held invisibly in the air before her," and then resume writing, apparently copying onto the paper what she had just read. When she showed the Colonel the recent addition, it invariably contained a quotation from some work of which neither of them had a copy. If Blavatsky was quoting from memory, then she seems to have been capable of producing "eidetic imagery," one definition of which is "a subjective image of minute photographic detail, which is perceived as a concrete, three-dimensional reality." One famous eidetic person was the inventor Nikola Tesla, who could visualize an entire blueprint in his head and use this to construct some device. Elsewhere I have related eidetic imagery to the phenomena of hypnagogia, the often bizarre, sharply detailed images many of us perceive at the point of sleep.[17] Hypnagogia is linked to the twilight state in between sleeping and waking, and, as mentioned, can be seen as another form of the "duo-consciousness" Blavatsky repeatedly experienced.

One curious characteristic of HPB's apparent astral literacy was a kind of numerical dyslexia. On occasion she would ask Olcott to check some reference she had gathered from the ether at the library, and he often found that the page number she gave him turned out to be wrong. However, if he turned the numbers around, they were correct. So, for example, page 291, which she had given him, would turn out to be really page 192. When asked about this, she explained that "in the astral," it is as if things are seen in a mirror, that is, reversed. Although difficult, she had trained herself to read backward—no mean feat in itself—but for some reason she frequently forgot to turn the numbers around. Later followers who helped organize her other monumentally intractable work, *The Secret Doctrine*, also came across the same problem.

Another curious feature of HPB's writing habits that Olcott observed was a distinct change in her handwriting, depending on the subject matter she was working on. She also seemed on occasion to become another person; this transformation usually took place when she briefly left the room. When she returned, she was "someone else," a strange metamorphosis that was also witnessed on occasion in Gurdjieff.[18] She was not "entranced," nor had she become possessed by "spirit guides," but, she told Olcott, "others" were writing the book through her, and one wonders if the passages of "serene expositional expression" that Beatrice Hastings believed HPB was incapable of matched those supposedly written by Blavatsky's "others." These "others," of course, were the Masters—she spoke of an Indian, Narayan, and of an Hungarian named Rákóczy (a pseudonym of the legendary Comte de Saint-Germain)—but it is worth noting that in his studies of multiple personality, Adam Crabtree more than once came upon cases in which the "No. 1" personality became so different that his patient's actual appearance changed. Crabtree, however, does not recount any cases in which a patient's hair changed as well, but apparently

HPB's did. From its normal state of being fair and crinkly, Olcott and others saw it change to being black and straight. On two occasions, Olcott clipped some of these transformed locks; Blavatsky told him that one came from the head of an Egyptian, the other from a Hindu. She also seemed to sport an invisible mustache and sideburns, which he would watch her stroke, and on one occasion she materialized the head of the Indian to whom they belonged. Olcott himself believed that HPB was not really a woman, but a man, a "Hindu man," and in moments of deep absorption, "his own hair . . . materialized."[19]

By now the reader is no doubt wondering if Olcott was lying, or was a dupe, the victim of a remarkable fraud perpetrated against him by his chum. The fact that these are only some of the incredible events recounted in his *Old Diary Leaves* will not, I am sure, instill greater confidence in the Colonel's account, our recognition that he made a living investigating insurance fraud notwithstanding. Here I will only say that Olcott was not the only one to maintain that, in his presence, Blavatsky did things that, quite frankly, most of us would consider impossible.

ONE SEEMINGLY IMPOSSIBLE FEAT that HPB did manage to accomplish, and to which there were quite a few witnesses, was to gather the chaotic mess of writing she produced each day and fuse it into a coherent whole. In this alchemical task she was not alone. We've already seen that she had help from Colonel Olcott. Another helpmeet was Alexander Wilder, a professor of philosophy who was also a physician and archaeologist, among other accomplishments. J. W. Bouton, whom Olcott had approached about publishing the work, had suggested he let Wilder, who had edited some books for him, read the manuscript. Wilder found it a "truly ponderous document," which "displayed research in a very extended field," and as it related to current thinking, had "a revolution in it." It was, however, too long, and if Bouton wanted to publish it, it needed cutting. Olcott insisted that Wilder meet the author, and one afternoon Wilder made his way to the Lamasery. Wilder found a woman "who had seen much, thought much, travelled much, and experienced much." She was an excellent conversationalist, spoke English fluently, and "uttered her thoughts clearly, concisely, and often forcibly." Evidence for this last trait appeared in HPB's use of the term "flapdoodle" when referring to anything she disagreed with. One suspects Wilder heard the term a lot. Wilder was charmed by the author, and his editing of the enormous work became for him "a labour of love."

Up until shortly before its publication in September 1877, Blavatsky called the work *The Veil of Isis*, referring to the inscription on an ancient statue of the goddess in the Egyptian city of Sais: "I am all that has been, all that is, all that shall ever be, and no mortal has ever lifted my veil." Readers of the book may notice that the whole of the first volume still retains that heading. This is because just before the second volume was prepared for printing, Charles Sotheran told Bouton that a book with the same title had just appeared in England. Bouton agreed that it would be a good idea to change the name, and he and Sotheran apparently hit on the new one simultaneously. HPB herself was never happy with the title *Isis Unveiled*, nor with its subtitle: "A Master Key to the Mysteries of Ancient and Modern Science and Theology," which seems to have been Bouton's idea. Both, she thought, were too immodest.

As today, publishers then reserved the right to decide on a book's title—after all, they have to sell the thing—and as Bouton had already published books on ancient religion, symbolism, and mythology—all of which Blavatsky had written about—he knew there was a ready market for this sort of work, and he wanted potential customers to know exactly what they'd be getting.

Evidently Bouton knew what he was doing. Against all expectation, *Isis Unveiled* was an overnight success, its initial edition of one thousand copies selling out in little more than a week, leaving its predecessor *Art Magic* somewhat in the dust. (As we've seen, Emma Hardinge Britten was so peeved at the book's success that she started the rumor that HPB had plagiarized the work from material found in Baron de Palm's trunk.) More printings followed, many of them, and the work has been in print ever since. Not everyone, though, was happy with it. HPB herself had to be forcibly stopped from adding new material to it, which she did practically up to the minute of publication, making the proofreading something of a hell. The spiritualist papers, expecting another *Art Magic*, were stunned, but many of the mainstream journals were less enthused. One called it a "large dish of hash" (*Springfield Republican*), while *The Sun* thought it a heap of "discarded rubbish." Others agreed, but quite a few didn't. HPB's friends at the *Graphic* called it "a marvellous book," remarking that its index alone, running to some 50 pages, made it unique. (Beatrice Hastings later agreed, saying the "index would be an education to most people."[20] It was apparently Wilder's work.[21]) For the *Boston Evening Transcript*, the book demanded "the earnest attention of thinkers and merits an analytic reading." *The New York World* found it "an extremely readable and exhaustive essay upon the paramount importance of re-establishing the Hermetic Philosophy," and the *New York Herald* called it "one of the remarkable productions of the century." HPB herself, who assumed the book would bring her little more than grief, was so moved by this remark that she pointed it out in a letter to her countryman Alexander Aksakov, emphasizing that it came from one of the most conservative Catholic papers.

One very vocal critic of the book was William Emmette Coleman, who, along with other spiritualists, tried very hard to show that the only veil involved in *Isis Unveiled* was the one being pulled over the public's eyes. Coleman was a scholar and member of several learned societies. He argued that Blavatsky's apparent erudition—astral or otherwise—which amazed everyone, including her family, was a fraud. He diligently scrutinized the work, showing how, while she had indeed quoted from some fourteen hundred works, she neglected to note her *source* for the quotation. This created the impression, Coleman argued, that she had gone to the original works, when in fact she had found the quotations in what scholars call "secondary material," that is, other books that had quoted the originals. In fact, Coleman argued, Blavatsky had really only used about a hundred works of contemporary literature and scholarship, and had not read the many old texts she had claimed to, either in the *akasha* or in a library.

Yet, as Nicholas Goodrick-Clarke points out, Coleman's charge of plagiarism is beside the point, and may be little more than an example of what Beatrice Hastings called a "snippet mind."[22] The point of *Isis Unveiled* is not the erudition that went into it—impressive or not, as the case may be—but what Blavatsky *did* with the material; and we have to remember that, as a spiritualist, Coleman was not a neutral party. Only a dry-as-dust pedant would disregard the original synthesis HPB achieves with her material, basing his argument on the fact that she does not provide correct attribution for her sources. Blavatsky may not have been a particularly logical thinker—her insights are erratic and often jumbled—but she was an enormously vital one, as well as a voracious reader, and she had an enviable ability to make connections between ideas and facts that others may not have recognized. I don't believe she was interested in impressing others with her erudition. If that was the case, then she certainly would have accepted Bouton's offer of a substantial advance, if she would consider unveiling Isis a bit more. The success of the book was so great that any publisher would have jumped at a sequel, yet HPB turned him down, even when he increased his offer to five thousand dollars, a huge sum at the time. She had a mission to accomplish with the book, she said, and she believed she had fulfilled it, and with that done it was time to turn to something else. The torrent of references, quotations, and facts that frequently swamps a reader of *Isis Unveiled*—as Beatrice Hastings remarked, "one is hurled from authority to authority"—is not aimed at impressing us, but at buttressing her argument with so much support that we cannot easily ignore it or dismiss it out of hand. Only someone whose mind was completely numb could come away from this without feeling in some way challenged.

AND WHAT WAS her mission in writing it? What is *Isis Unveiled* about? It is a cliché to say of some works that they "defy description," yet this work of more than fourteen hundred pages and some half a million words is not easily précised. In many ways, its closest relatives are the unclassifiable works of Charles Fort, or Louis Pauwels's and Jacques Bergier's *Morning of the Magicians*, which started the "occult revival" of the 1960s, or even Erich von Däniken's *Chariots of the Gods*, although Blavatsky's is a more serious effort, unlike Däniken's slipshod, frankly commercial work. Yet all three convey with *Isis Unveiled* the hoary truth that "there are more things in heaven and earth than are dreamed of" in our philosophy, and in many ways it is a shame that Blavatsky's first major effort is often overshadowed by her later, more well-known masterpiece. Although *The Secret Doctrine* is seen as the foundation of Theosophy, for my taste *Isis Unveiled* is more accessible, more thought-provoking, and more readable than HPB's later, equally gargantuan opus. It is also filled with more argument—conveyed in Blavatsky's best "desk-thumping" style—that the reader can consider and come to his own conclusions about, unlike that more revelatory, "set in stone" pronouncement.

The central theme of *Isis Unveiled*, as the reviewer for the *New York World* remarked, is the revival of the ancient Hermetic philosophy, and as Nicholas Goodrick-Clarke points out, the value of William Coleman's research is that it shows just how steeped in the Western esoteric and occult tradition Blavatsky was. Nearly all of the works that Coleman argues she cribbed from deal with some aspect of this.[23] Although she would soon turn her sights toward the mystic East, HPB's first major work is firmly rooted in the West. Against a modern, materialist science that considers "magic" and the "occult" mere nonsense, and a Judeo-Christian tradition that sees them as demonic, Blavatsky wants to re-establish the ancient Hermetic, Neo-Platonic tradition, the outlines of which she had discovered in her great-grandfather's library. The third prong of her attack, against Spiritualism, comes from the same source. The kind of phenomena that the spiritualists associate with the dead, she argues, were known to the ancient sages. But they also knew—as did she—that the dead did not produce them, but that they were the work of the "elementals," or were the products of the ancient magicians themselves. The "invasion of the spirit people," then, was not something new; in fact, it wasn't an invasion at all, as the phenomena spiritualists saw as evidence of this had been reported throughout history. They were mistaken that it was the dead who were behind them, and they aggravated their mistake by allowing themselves to be taken over by forces that the magician disciplines himself to master. In fact, Blavatsky even argued that only weak, sick minds could become mediums, as any healthy mind would naturally prevent these lower entities from dominating it—a remark that Emma Hardinge Britten, D. D. Home, and other spiritualists could not have cared for. (It has to be said, though, that as many histories of Spiritualism show, many mediums *were* less than robust—Home is a good example—and a weak grasp on this world was seen as a *sine qua non* of access to the other.)

Although it made her many enemies, this in-house fighting was not the major battle HPB had entered with *Isis Unveiled*. And for today's readers, her equally strong criticisms of Christianity and lavish praise for Hinduism and Buddhism seem nowhere near as scandalous as they did at the time. Precisely because of books like *Isis Unveiled*, our contemporary "multifaith" sensibilities are more open to seeing Christianity in relative terms, as one among many forms of spiritual practice and belief. Although our time has seen a resurgence of intolerant, fundamental forms of religion, we live in an age in which Christian, Jew, Muslim, Hindu, Buddhist—even atheists and agnostics—can generally peaceably coexist. This, as we've seen, was one of the aims of the Theosophical Society, and there is a good argument that the TS was itself a major agent in bringing this about. The World's Parliament of Religions, which took place in 1893 during the World's Columbian Exposition in Chicago, in which Buddhists, Jains, Bahá'ís, Muslims, Hindus, and Theosophists shared a platform with Catholics, Protestants, and Jews, and in which Theosophists like William Quan Judge and Annie Besant were major participants, was precisely the kind of coming together of different faiths that Blavatsky saw as the essence of Theosophy.

A central argument informing *Isis Unveiled* is that *all* of the world's religions spring from a common source, the ancient wisdom religion that Blavatsky identified with the Hermetic philosophy. This idea, of a common, ancient, "primordial" origin for Christianity, Buddhism, Hinduism, and the rest, is found today in the work of the Traditionalist school, whose main theoretician, René Guénon, was, oddly, a strident critic of Blavatsky. The idea has a prestigious pedigree and can be found in the writings of the *Corpus Hermeticum*, a collection of philosophical and spiritual texts attributed to the ancient mythological sage Hermes Trismegistus, but which were most likely written circa 100 to 200 A.D. in Alexandria by contemporaries of the Philalethians and Neo-Platonists. The idea was later revived when the *Corpus Hermeticum*, lost for centuries, was translated into Latin by the Florentine Platonist Marsilio Ficino in 1463. Ficino and his contemporaries believed the Hermetic texts were the source of a *prisca theologia*, a "perennial philosophy," that dated back to the dawn of time, and this idea informed much of the art and culture that we associate with the Renaissance.[24] In reviving this notion once again, Blavatsky was in some good company.

Such an idea seemed peculiarly apt for the time, and if any occult congress wanted to stem the tide of materialism, it would have had better luck with this, I think, than with any murky machinations involving mediums and séances. When *Isis Unveiled* appeared, Western consciousness had entered a kind of metaphysical black hole. Although Christianity was still a powerful presence—hence Blavatsky's criticisms—it was fighting a losing battle against a reductive, exclusively materialist science, the conclusion of which was that the universe, and the life within it, were ultimately meaningless, an assessment it still stands by today. By this time, Darwin's "dangerous idea" had shown that we were really only "trousered apes," and all our pretentions to being something more were mere egotistical delusions. And if this wasn't bad enough, in 1865, the German physicist Rudolf Clausius had introduced the notion of entropy. Clausius had observed that over time, in a closed system, organized energy—for example, heat—tends to move toward a less organized, uniform state. (This is why a cup of coffee cools to room temperature.) As the "second law of thermodynamics," this suggested that eventually the organized energy in the universe would dissipate until it formed a kind of uniform lukewarm "cosmic puddle," unable to support life. This irreversible process was known as the "heat death" of the cosmos. For all the "progress" associated with the Industrial Revolution and the nineteenth century, a sense of futility had entered things, a feeling for which can be found in Matthew Arnold's famous poem "Dover

Beach," where "ignorant armies clash by night" upon "a darkling plain." The Society for Psychical Research, which we will meet shortly, was formed because its members were troubled by this growing sense of cosmic inconsequence, and hoped that the study of Spiritualism and other "psychical" phenomena might help throw light on "the actual truth as to the destiny of man."[25]

Yet while Spiritualism offered some support for the belief in a nonmaterial reality, its nebulous pieties repelled more vigorous minds, eager for some coherent philosophy with which to challenge a science that seemed intent on undermining all human purpose. Faith was little help in this matter. What was needed was knowledge, and with *Isis Unveiled*, Blavatsky seemed to show that she had it on tap.

ALTHOUGH DARWIN'S FIGURE looms over the book, her main targets are his "bulldog," Thomas Henry Huxley, and the scientist John Tyndall, the two high priests of scientific materialism. Although few historians have noted it, in *Isis Unveiled* Blavatsky presents the first major intellectual—not religious—criticism of Darwinian evolution. Credit for this is usually given to Samuel Butler, best known as the author of the utopian fantasy *Erewhon*. In 1878, Butler published *Life and Habit*, the first of a series of brilliantly argued books, criticizing this mechanical account of how species evolved. Butler argued that Darwin had "banished mind from the universe." Blavatsky agreed, but she had made the point first, and this alone should warrant her a secure place in the history of ideas.

Darwinian evolution, she argued, only told part of the story, the part that takes place in our current, physical world. It leaves out what happens before and after this interlude. Basing her vision on the Hermetic belief that the universe and everything in it, including ourselves, is an emanation of spirit—which means that creation necessarily emerges from the Godhead, rather than in the Judeo-Christian account, in which God is separate from a creation that might just as well not exist—Blavatsky argued that the transition from monkey to man is only part of the evolution of men and women into gods, a transformation, she added, that embraces the entire cosmos. Darwin, she said, "begins his evolution of species at the lowest point and traces upwards. His only mistake may be that he applies his system at the wrong end."[26] After passing through a period of necessary separation, spirit returns to itself, enriched by its voyage. Thus, as the late Theodore Roszak remarked, Blavatsky presents "the evolutionary image as the redemptive journey of spirit through the realms of matter" offering "the first philosophy of psychic and spiritual evolution to appear in the modern west."[27]

The evolution of life, then, is not a "chance" occurrence, which "just happened" to take place because of some "accidental" combination of chemicals, and which then carried on, driven by the pressures of survival and the occasional advantageous mutation. As she says, "it is not spirit which dwells in matter, but matter which clings temporarily to spirit."[28] Spirit (or consciousness), then, is primary, and matter a temporary means spirit employs in its work. Evolution is the basic grain of the universe itself, and opposed to the materialist vision which presents a "hideous, ceaseless procession of sparks of cosmic matter created by no one, floating onward from nowhere," and which "rushes nowhither,"[29] Blavatsky offers the Cabalistic aphorism: "A stone becomes a plant; a plant, a beast;

a beast, a man; a man, a spirit; and the spirit, a God." In this scheme, "each perfected species in the physical evolution only affords more scope to the directing intelligence to act within the improved nervous system," a remark that the philosopher Henri Bergson, whose *Creative Evolution* (1907) similarly challenged Darwin, could have made.[30] For Blavatsky, then, mind is not "banished" by evolution, but uses it in order to develop itself. In this way, rather than oppose science to religion or vice versa, Blavatsky synthesizes the two and transcends both, in a way reminiscent of the philosopher Hegel's equally evolutionary account of spirit's journey through matter, *The Phenomenology of Mind*.

Isis Unveiled is such a huge work, both in size and conception, that it can be read on many levels. It is also, as most modern readers discover, not a work that needs to be read cover to cover, and perhaps the best way to approach it is by dipping in and out. (It makes, I believe, excellent bedside reading.) From a historical perspective, we can learn about works that were considered important at the time but which are pretty much forgotten today. One such is *The Unseen Universe* by Peter Guthrie Tait and Balfour Stewart, published in 1875. This once very popular work argues that "the visible universe is not the whole universe but only, it may be, a very small part of it," an idea that physicists today are grappling with under the rubric of "dark matter." Arguing against the universe's eventual "heat death," the authors suggest that the energy of the visible universe might transfer to an invisible one, from which it emerges again in new forms—an idea that Blavatsky, with her Hermetic belief in dimensions of reality beyond the sensory, embraced and which was later revived by the poet Rilke.[31]

On a biographical note, we discover that HPB was impressed

with a work by a Civil War hero, General A. J. Pleasonton, *The Influence of the Blue Ray of the Sunlight*, and because of it she had blue glass windows and blue draperies installed in the Lamasery.[32] Pleasonton believed that blue light was particularly helpful in plant growth and that it was able to eradicate many illnesses.[33] His work is seen as the beginning of chromotherapy—the idea that certain colors affect health—and HPB was not alone in putting it into practice. Around the time of *Isis Unveiled*, there was a "blue glass" craze in America, with many people following Pleasonton's example, using blue glass in their hothouses and for personal ailments.

It should also come as no surprise that many of the themes and ideas that occupy a great deal of contemporary "alternative" literature were first announced by Blavatsky. When she asks her readers, "Do not the relics we treasure in our museums—last mementos of the long lost arts—speak loudly of in favour of ancient civilizations?" we are unavoidably reminded of Graham Hancock's many works on just that theme.[34] When she tells us that "ages before [Columbus] clove the western waters, the Phoenician vessels had circumnavigated the globe and spread civilization in regions now silent and deserted," and asks who "will dare assert that the same hand which planned the pyramids of Egypt . . . did not erect the monumental Nagkow-Wat of Cambodia," we think of Charles Hapgood's ideas about a "prehistoric" maritime civilization that encircled the globe.[35] Even von Däniken, who wrote of "ancient astronauts" and the science of earlier civilizations, is upstaged: "At a period far anterior to the siege of Troy, the learned priests of the sanctuaries were thoroughly acquainted with electricity and even lightning conductors."[36]

An attentive reader familiar with other works of modern esotericism soon sees how much in later systems is rooted HPB. While
a student of Gurdjieff's "work," I repeatedly plowed through his
own gargantuan masterpiece, *Beelzebub's Tales to His Grandson*, and
one idea that baffled me was the notion that "the sun neither lights
nor heats."[37] Gurdjieff, we know, criticized HPB but he was not
beyond borrowing from her, and the same notion can be found
in *Isis Unveiled*.[38] (Its original source is the Pythagorean notion
of the spiritual "central sun," of which our physical sun is only a
reflection.)

Gurdjieff also spoke about the law of "reciprocal maintenance"
at work in the cosmos. HPB speaks of "the reciprocal relations
between the planetary bodies."[39] And when Gurdjieff told Ouspensky that wars were the result of "tensions" between two planets,
Blavatsky told her readers that "certain planetary aspects may
imply disturbances in the ether of our planet, and certain others
rest and harmony."[40] Indeed, for HPB, the planets and other stellar
bodies so influence life on the earth, that at one time they promote
periods of withdrawal—"monasticism and anchoritism"—and at
others frenzied action and "utopian schemes."[41] This seems a pre-
echo of Gurdjieff's gloomy assessment of mankind's inability to
"do," our complete mechanicalness and "sleep." Gurdjieff, of course,
wasn't the only one to borrow from the Madame. Some time ago I
wrote an article for the sadly defunct *Gnosis* magazine about Rudolf
Steiner's odd idea that the earth was "dying," in preparation for its
evolution to a higher planetary level, and how developing our own
inner worlds helps this process along.[42] Although, like Gurdjieff,
Steiner was often critical of HPB, he nevertheless seems to have
picked up this idea from her. Blavatsky asks, "who is able to con-

trovert the theory . . . that the earth itself will, like the living creatures to which it has given birth . . . after passing through its own
stage of death and dissolution, become an etherealized astral
planet?"[43] Gurdjieff, too, talked about the earth "evolving" into a
sun, and the moon "evolving" into an earth, along what he called
the "Ray of Creation." And, as already mentioned, Steiner's
"Anthroposophy"—the "wisdom of man," as opposed to that of the
gods—is in many ways a Western, intellectualized version of
HPB's basic teachings. In saying this I am not arguing that Steiner
and Gurdjieff stole from Blavatsky. As we know, she herself borrowed quite a bit from previous thinkers. But I think it's important to recognize the possible source for ideas that followers of
these two important esoteric teachers may believe originated with
them.

BUT EVEN A READER coming to these ideas for the first time is
sure to learn something from HPB's vigorous, often torrential
accounts of what modern science is unable to fit under its narrow
rubric. Arguments for Mesmerism, hypnosis, precognition, psychometry (the ability to "read" an object's past simply from touching it), the science of the ancients (which in many ways anticipates
our own), the cyclical theory of history (well in advance of Oswald
Spengler's *Decline of the West*), elementals, the evolution of the planets, the unity of all religions, prehistoric civilizations, animal reincarnation (she believed many animals were more deserving of this
than many humans), magic, and much, much more are all presented
in a robust, exuberant manner that often leaves the reader dazzled.
The central message is that the dull, dead, mechanical universe,

which a triumphant modern science was applauding as the height of human consciousness, was, quite simply, false, and that the world was infinitely more mysterious, more fascinating, and more *alive* than what the Huxleys, Tyndalls, and others believed. The ancients knew this and built a deeper, more profound science on that belief, a science that Blavatsky was here to revive.

The style is often breathless and urgent, yet, as Beatrice Hastings noted, there are occasional passages of serene, detached observation, such as this one about what the ancients believed about the inhabitants of the ether: "The universal ether was not, in their eyes, simply a something stretching tenantless throughout the expanse of heaven; it was a boundless ocean peopled like our familiar seas with monsters and minor creatures, and having in its every molecule the germ of life."[44] It was this vision of a universal ether, or, as she also called it, the *akasha* or "Astral Light," that is perhaps the most influential idea to emerge from *Isis Unveiled*. Blavatsky borrowed it from her predecessors, Franz Anton Mesmer, Bulwer-Lytton, Eliphas Lévi, and others, but in her hands it took on a wider scope and meaning. Mesmer had seen his "animal magnetism" as a kind of subtle "fluid," permeating the universe; in the human body, its currents affected health; the mesmerist could learn how to control these, and through this heal his patients. Eliphas Lévi took Mesmer's animal magnetism and transformed it into what he called the "Universal Agent," a medium of such subtle materiality that, through the power of his will and imagination, the magician could impress on it his very thoughts. In his early science fiction novel *The Coming Race*, about a subterranean civilization of supermen, Bulwer-Lytton took Lévi's "Universal Agent" and turned it into *vril*, a mysterious power these superbeings possessed, a kind of laser beam of the mind, a mental force of enormous capabilities. And, of course, material science had its own "luminiferous ether," the medium thought to carry light waves.[45]

Blavatsky linked these notions to earlier ones: the "sidereal light" of Paracelsus; the *anima mundi*, or "soul of the earth" of the ancient philosophers; the sacred fire of Zoroaster; the *akasha* of the Hindu adepts; the spiritual fire of the Rosicrucians; and also to contemporary ideas, such as the *Odic* force of Baron Reichenbach; the "nerve-aura" of Joseph Rodes Buchanan; even electricity, then a still-mysterious phenomenon. To these she added the idea of the Astral Light as a kind of eternal record of everything that has ever happened, what Rudolf Steiner would later call "cosmic memory." For Blavatsky, the Astral Light "keeps an unmutilated record of all that was, that is, or ever will be. The minutest acts of our lives are imprinted on it, and even our thoughts rest photographed on its eternal tablets. . . . It is, in short, the memory of God."[46] So, far from a universe irrevocably heading toward its "heat death," Blavatsky presents one in which even the faintest thought has an eternal life.

"It is on the indestructible tablets of the Astral Light that is stamped the impression of every thought we think,"[47] Blavatsky wrote, and it is the magician's task to *master* this phantasmagoria, this constant stream of images, memories, thoughts, and fantasies. If he fails in this, he can be easily led astray by dreams and alluring visions. Hence the Astral Light or Universal Agent is often symbolized as a serpent or dragon, whose undulating body mirrors the ever-fluctuating surface of the magnetic waves, and the magician is depicted as standing with one foot upon its head. Again, as with

Spiritualism and mediums, Blavatsky insists on the *discipline* involved in becoming an adept; it has nothing to do with "giving way," "letting go," or other passive methods. The magician must *control* the Astral Light, not let it overwhelm him, something that seekers of enlightenment who employ psychedelic and hallucinogenic drugs often disregard.

YET, THE ASTRAL LIGHT is something more than a kind of permanent "cosmic hard drive," containing an infinite number of downloads. It also contains a kind of blueprint for the future, Platonic models of things yet to come. As I have argued elsewhere, in this sense it is similar to David Bohm's "implicate order," and Rupert Sheldrake's "morphogenetic fields."[48] And if we think that only eccentric characters like HPB had access to this, we are wrong. "In the stillness of the night-hours, when our body senses are fast locked in the fetters of sleep . . . the astral form becomes free" and "soars to its parents and holds converse with the stars."[49] ("Astral" means "of the stars.") "No man," she assures us, "however gross and material he may be, can avoid leading a double existence; one in the visible universe, the other in the invisible."[50]

This last remark is the central insight of *all* Hermetic, esoteric, occult, and spiritual philosophy: that human beings are the inhabitants of *two* worlds, the mundane world we unavoidably encounter every day, and *another* world, which transcends this one and in which we are not constrained by the usual limits of time and space.

Again, if we think this is simply woolly "New Age" rubbish, consider, as merely one example, the experience of the historian

Arnold Toynbee, author of the twelve-volume classic, *A Study of History*. In volume 10, in a section called "The Inspirations of Historians," Toynbee speaks of a series of strange experiences that led to his writing the work. All of them involved a kind of "time-slip," in which Toynbee found himself apparently perceiving an event *in the past*, as if he were actually there, reliving it. Perhaps most remarkable was an occasion when, while walking near Victoria Station in London, he found himself "in communion, not just with this or that episode of History, but with all that had been, and was, and was to come." "In that instant he was directly aware of the passage of History flowing through him in a mighty current, and of his own life welling like a wave in the flow of this vast tide." (Toynbee wrote his account in the third person.)

The similarity between Toynbee's words and Blavatsky's is striking, and is more than reminiscent of the inscription on the statue of Isis in Sais. And we should also note the similarity between Toynbee's experience, Blavatsky's Astral Light, and the phenomenon of psychometry, which, as mentioned above, is the strange ability to "read" the past "written" on some object. As one researcher remarks, psychometry "is probably the best authenticated of all 'psychic faculties,'" with "hundreds of impressive examples in the history of psychical research."[51] (William Denton, whose book *The Soul of Things* is the classic work on the subject, receives high marks in *Isis Unveiled*.) Again, we are also reminded of the experience of the neuroscientist Wilder Penfield, who, in 1952, while operating on a patient, accidentally stimulated an area of his brain. As the brain has no pain receptors, the patient was awake, and reported not only a vivid memory but an absolute "re-living" of a past experience in all its detail, and in three dimensions, as if it was happening again (and we are reminded of HPB's "astral reading," which I have linked to "eidetic imagery"). This is practically identical to the famous account that begins Marcel Proust's enormous novel, *A Remembrance of Things Past*, when the hero tastes a bit of cake dipped in tea and is immediately transported back to his childhood, in all its sensory delight.

Colin Wilson has explored this strange ability we have to grasp "the reality of other times and places" and has dubbed it "Faculty X," and elsewhere I have looked at this in the context of the Hermetic philosophy that Blavatsky aimed to revive in *Isis Unveiled*.[52] Whatever we may think of Blavatsky's choice of terms—to some, "Astral Light" is too "occult" and off-putting—she nevertheless pinned down an ability we all have to "transcend time and space," and which seems to be available to us, whether or not we pursue any occult or esoteric studies. If an occultist, a historian, a neuroscientist, and a novelist, who have no connection with each other and are separated by time and space, all seem to be talking about the same thing, reason suggests that it is something objective—that is, *real*. And that Blavatsky argued that it was something the ancients knew of as well, seems to clinch it, for me at least.

Isis Unveiled is full of insights like this, and if all she had done was to produce this unwieldy masterpiece, HPB would warrant credit as one of the most fertile minds of the nineteenth century. But more was in store for her, and shortly after unveiling Isis, HPB and the Colonel were packing their bags for a journey to the East.

SEVEN

A PASSAGE TO INDIA

Isis Unveiled was an unqualified success, but the Theosophical Society hadn't profited by it. The book had caused a stir, but it didn't lead to a flood of new members, and more than a few of the original group moved on. With her *magnum opus* done, the movement itself seemed to have hit a doldrums. Even a brief period as a "secret society" along Masonic lines didn't spark terrific interest, although HPB's Masonic pedigree was recognized by John Yarker, English Grand Master of the Ancient Primitive Rite of Freemasons.[1] "From the close of 1876 to that of 1878," Olcott recorded, "the Theosophical Society as a body was comparatively inactive." Their meetings had practically stopped. They had even stopped collecting fees. What activity there was took place at the Lamasery, and this manifested more as an informal gathering than an official organization, following bylaws and agendas.

Not everything was becalmed. Their correspondence grew, articles appeared, branches in London and elsewhere took shape—C. C. Massey had left for England and started a lodge there—and relations with sympathetic minds developed. One important new recruit was Thomas Edison, who joined the society in April 1878. By this time, "the Wizard of Menlo Park" had made significant contributions to telegraphy. He had also invented the phonograph, developed the first industrial research lab, and was on his way to devising the carbon microphone and electric lightbulb. Edison told Olcott that he had already made experiments along occult lines, and was currently working with pendulums, investigating whether they could be moved by willpower alone. Edison later spoke of making a device to communicate with spirits, although there is some controversy about this, and in a later article HPB quoted him as saying that atoms are "possessed by a certain amount of intelligence," a remark that, some decades later, would seem to be corroborated to some degree by quantum physics.[2] Another famous American who had come into the fold was Abner Doubleday, a Civil War hero, and, as mentioned, the purported inventor of baseball. Doubleday was second in command at Fort Sumter, and a statue was erected at Gettysburg in honor of his bravery there. But even the addition of these stellar notables wasn't enough to prompt wider appeal.

Major events in Blavatsky's personal life had occurred, too. In May 1878, her divorce from Michael Betanelly finally came through, and on July 8, five years and a day since her arrival there, HPB became an American citizen. Yet strangely, taking on U.S. citizenship, and officially renouncing her ties to Russia, were only the prelude to what was perhaps HPB's most fateful decision yet: to leave the United States for good and move to India.

EXACTLY WHY, KNOWING she had already planned to shift her operations to India, HPB decided to become a U.S. citizen, is a

question more than one of her biographers has asked. John
Symonds suggests that she realized carrying a U.S. passport,
rather than a Russian one, would make life easier for her there.
India, we know, at that time was the playground of the Great Game
between Russia and the British. Understandably, the British were
suspicious of Russians coming to India, given Tsar Alexander II's
ideas about a "Russian Asia," and to travel as a U.S. citizen would,
she must have thought, smooth her journey a bit. Debate remains
over whether or not HPB ever worked as a Russian spy, but the
fact that the British *thought* she did is uncontested, and her newly
earned U.S. citizenship did not, it seems, dissuade them from
keeping an eye on her.

But what prompted her to uproot once again and head for the
mystic East is itself a much debated point. Some see it as a purely
practical move. The Theosophical Society was going the way of the
Miracle Club, and rebooting it elsewhere seemed a good idea.
Some, like K. Paul Johnson, believe the move was motivated by
earlier ties she had made on her journeys, connections with spiritual and political societies that would soon resurface. William
Quan Judge relates that HPB had planned all along to go to India
once *Isis Unveiled* had been published, and that further, her plan
was then to go to England, which in fact she did.[3] She apparently
told Olcott something similar as early as the spring of 1876.[4] But in
the standard account of the decision, Olcott is the main player.

Olcott relates how one evening in 1877, he was visited at the
Lamasery by an American, possibly James Peebles, a spiritualist
and occultist who knew of HPB's activities with the *société spirite*
in Cairo in 1871.[5] His visitor had just returned from India, and
on a whim, Olcott asked if he had chanced to meet two Hindu gen-

tlemen the Colonel had met in 1870 on a return voyage from England to America. Olcott had a photograph of the men and showed it to his visitor. As fate would have it, his visitor *did* know one of the men, Moolji Thackersey, a textile magnate whom he had recently met in Bombay. Olcott got Thackersey's address from his visitor and wrote to his old traveling acquaintance, telling him about the TS, his remarkable chum, and her great love of India. He also offered him membership in the society. Thackersey replied, thanking Olcott for his membership, and telling him about a great Hindu holy man, Swami Dayananda Saraswati, who was the leader of a Hindu reform movement, the Arya Samaj ("Samaj" means "society"). Thackersey also told Olcott about Hurrychund Chintamon, who was president of the Bombay branch of the Arya Samaj. Olcott wrote to Chintamon, telling him about the TS, and its belief in an "Eternal and Omnipresent Principle which, under many different names, was the same in all religions."[6] Chintamon replied, explaining that it appeared both groups had identical aims, and as it was pointless to maintain two such societies, it made sense that they combine. Olcott agreed, and after explaining things to the members, they decided to change their name to "The Theosophical Society of the Arya Samaj."

Amalgamating itself with a Hindu reform movement may not seem as logical a step for the TS as Olcott seemed to believe it was, but there was some precedent for it. HPB, we know, had early contact with Eastern beliefs through her experiences with the Kalmuck tribesmen during her time with her maternal grandparents. We also know that she claimed to have traveled in India as well as Tibet, and that her Masters, at least two of them, were Hindus. Her formal conversion to Buddhism was a few years ahead, but as early as 1877, while still in New York, HPB referred to herself as a Buddhist. In a letter in which she explains that she is not a spiritu-alist—at least "not in the modern and American sense of the word"—she calls herself "a benighted Buddhist." By this she means that she is a Svabhavika, "a Buddhist pantheist, if anything at all." This amounts to believing in "one eternal, indestructible, sub-stance," the Svabhavat, an "invisible, all pervading matter," which seems reminiscent of what she means by the Astral Light.[7] In this instance, it seems that HPB's Buddhism is important to her as an alternative to the orthodox Christian view of a supreme, personal, creator God—Jehovah, lording it over the universe. That she did not consider herself a Buddhist in a traditional sense is clear from her remark that, if it was said that she "belonged to the religion that had *inspired* the Buddha"—my italics—and not the one that would have her "turning the *Wheel of the Law*," that would be cor-rect. The religion that inspired the Buddha, it will turn out, is the "secret doctrine" she will later reveal to the world, and of which she makes mention at the beginning of *Isis Unveiled*.

Olcott himself had more than an intimation that his chum was planning a trip back East, and he had asked spiritualist friends to try to dissuade her from the idea. Failing this, he sent out feelers, asking about the possibilities of the "Lodge"—the Masters—sending someone else to shepherd the Theosophical flock in the event that Blavatsky left them.[8] Yet, as early as 1875, in his letter from "the Brotherhood of Luxor," the Indian connection was clear. Although "ordered at Luxor," it had been written out in Ellora, India, the site of mysterious cave temples near Arungabad. The Master Serapis mentioned Ellora more than once to Olcott, and, as Joscelyn Godwin points out, it is in Ellora that the Chevalier Louis B of *Ghost Land* receives an important initiation.[9]

In the public mind, India was a land of magicians, swamis, fakirs, holy men, mystics, and the "Indian rope trick." It was also a land of warmth and sunshine. After completing *Isis Unveiled*, Blavatsky's health, never good, began to suffer. Already large, she began to gain weight—a process certainly helped by her eating habits—and her body started to retain water, with folds of flesh growing around her wrists and ankles, a symptom of a disease in those days known as "dropsy" but today called edema. Her kidneys, too, were not doing well. Combined with other physical problems—not to mention old wounds from her roustabout life— it's no surprise that in her later years, HPB more than once regarded her path as one of suffering. The thought of life under the Indian sun, without having to face another New York winter, more than likely appealed to her.

SHE ALSO HAD another reason for pulling up stakes. In 1878, D. D. Home had published a book, *Lights and Shadows of Spiritualism*, in which he attacked both her and her chum, calling them fakes and charlatans. Never one to take criticism lightly, she erupted with rage—the Colonel was the recipient of it—and in a letter to Aksakov, she explained that as Home had ruined her reputation, where else could she recover it, except India? And there is always the thought that, in some way, HPB or her Masters subtly arranged events to bring her to India. Josephine Ransom, an early Theosophical historian, remarked that on the voyage across the

Atlantic, during which Olcott met them, Moolji Thackersey and
his companion were traveling not on business or for pleasure, but
"on a mission to the west to see what could be done to introduce
Eastern spiritual and philosophical ideas."[10] As Olcott's visitor
knew Moolji, his visit may not have been purely by chance.

But, although the lure of the East was strong, Olcott had ample
reason to hesitate. He had always wanted to go to the East, but
unlike his chum, he had obligations that prevented him. He
thought he should stay in New York until his sons were set up
in their own careers; whatever his relations with his wife, the
thought of no longer seeing them must have crossed his mind. His
own livelihood was another factor: how was he to make a living in
India? These second thoughts must have reached the Masters. One
night at the Lamasery, while he and Blavatsky were still working
on *Isis Unveiled*, Olcott had a strange visitor. Their evening's work
done, the Colonel retired to his room, where he relaxed with a
book and a cigar. Suddenly he found himself in the presence of
"an Oriental clad in white garments," towering above him. Long,
black hair hung down to his mysterious visitor's broad shoulders,
and a yellow silk turban crowned his noble head. He wore a long
black beard in Rajput style, parted at the chin, with the ends curled
gracefully behind his ears. His burning eyes pinned Olcott, and the
Colonel was so impressed by his strange guest's appearance—"so
luminously spiritual, so evidently above average humanity"—that
he bowed before him and bent his knee. The figure placed a gentle
hand on Olcott's head and asked him to sit. He had come, he said,
because he knew Olcott had reached a crisis in his life, and he told
Olcott that his own actions had brought him to this moment. It was
up to the Colonel whether or not in the future they would work

together "for the good of mankind." Great work was to be done, and Olcott could share in it. His link with HPB ran deep, deeper than he could suspect. Olcott was impressed that his visitor could tell him things about himself and his chum that no one else knew.

How long the meeting lasted is unclear—Olcott said it could have been an hour but that it seemed "but a minute." When his guest was about to leave, Olcott, still dazzled, nevertheless had the presence of mind to think that this could be some trick of HPB's. She had, after all, shown remarkable abilities and was not above using her powers to further her Masters' designs. His visitor must have read his mind, for he smiled and, undoing his turban, handed it to the Colonel. As Olcott took it, his guest vanished, but there in his hand was the turban, proof, Olcott wrote, that he had been "face to face with one of the Elder Brothers of Humanity, one of the Masters of our dull pupil–race."[11] Olcott even included a photograph of it in his account of this strange experience in his *Old Diary Leaves*.

This wasn't Olcott's first visit from a Master. Sometime earlier he had a visit from two individuals that, from the description of it in a letter to friends, makes it seem that in some ways the Masters were rather like the Marx Brothers, or at least the mysterious "men in black" that haunt many UFO accounts; they, too, are strange visitors from unknown parts who act in a dreamlike, surreal way. In a letter to the London spiritualist Stainton Moses, Olcott relates how he was visited by a character named Ooton Liatto, a Cypriot, who was accompanied by another individual, a dark-skinned, gray-bearded man he does not name. There's reason to suspect that Liatto and Hilarion Smerdis, the Master Hilarion—who wrote to Olcott as a representative of the Brotherhood of Luxor—are the same. Bidding Olcott remain silent, Liatto materialized a bouquet of flowers, and Olcott watched as it floated to the floor. He then made it rain in Olcott's room, soaking the Colonel, his books, his cigar, and his carpet, yet leaving himself and his companion absolutely dry. The other visitor now showed Olcott a crystal in which he saw fantastic visions. During an earlier visit by Liatto recounted in his *Old Diary Leaves*, Olcott related how the Cypriot made the walls of his room disappear, and how he then gazed on vast landscapes peopled by strange, "elemental" forms.[12]

Olcott told his visitors that they must meet HPB, who lived in the apartment below—this was before they had moved to the Lamasery. Running downstairs, he was stunned to find them already with Blavatsky, chatting like old friends. He then ran upstairs, only to find his apartment empty. He rushed to the window and saw his visitors on the street below, turning the corner. Was his chum playing tricks on him? Yet his wet clothes, the soaking carpet, and the flowers, still there on the floor, argued that his visit had been real. When he asked HPB what had just happened, she said nothing, and only complained that what he had written about her in *People from the Other World* had caused her no end of trouble.[13]

Olcott's fears seemed to have been quieted by his visit from the Master, which appears to have been Blavatsky's old Hindu, Morya. Provisions were made for his sons—William Quan Judge pulled a few strings—and Olcott himself secured a kind of open-ended position as a U.S. trade representative. His reputation even warranted a letter of recommendation from President Rutherford Hayes, which may have done something to assure his ex-wife that he wasn't running out on his alimony payments. Until the last minute, Blavatsky feared that the ex–Mrs. Olcott—whom she referred to as "Kali," the Hindu goddess of death—would prevent him from leaving.

The ostensible impetus for the move was the union with Swami Dayananda's Arya Samaj, and for a time Olcott and Blavatsky believed the swami was in league with the Masters, or at least in communication with them. Letters HPB wrote to Hurrychund Chintamon were full of occult references: *Akasa*, the fourth dimension, and other arcane subjects, such as a request for a photograph of a fakir or *sannyasin* levitating. Chintamon wrote back about the plight of the Hindus under the British Raj, and Blavatsky's sarcastic reply that she would like the Russians to kick the British out of India (only for them and the Muslims to be kicked out by the Hindus themselves) was later used as "evidence" that she supported Russian rule in India. She also asked Chintamon to write letters to C. C. Massey and another London member, Emily Kislingbury, saying that an Indian postmark and Sanskrit signature would do much to impress them. This clearly shows that she wasn't above using a bit of "glamour" to achieve her ends. What Chintamon would say she could easily say herself, but, she explained, she was "but a white-faced idiot not a Hindu," and a letter from the mystic East would carry more weight.[14]

But when Olcott received a copy of the Arya Samaj rules, he and HPB discovered that they amounted to a very narrow interpretation of Hinduism—in fact, a kind of fundamentalism—that was about as far from Theosophical eclecticism as one could get. HPB and Olcott had also communicated with Parsees in Bombay and Buddhists in Ceylon, and the swami had strongly objected to this. The formal union was now scrapped and both chums must have realized that working with the swami wasn't feasible, just as the high hopes about E. Gerry Brown had come to naught. Yet the wheels were turning and whatever might await them, they were India bound.

"Orders" had come that they were to leave New York by December 17. Where the money for tickets and other necessities would come from was unclear. Some of it came from an auction at the Lamasery on December 9, in which the whole menagerie of stuffed animals and assorted other mystical tchotchkes went up for sale. (The fate of Professor Fiske would, I think, make for a good story.) Everything went under the hammer and, as HPB put it, "for a song." Reporters covered the story.

As HPB's arrival in the United States was news, so was her departure. For all her praise of America—becoming a "plain citizen of the U.S. of America," she had told a reporter, was "a title I value far more than any that could be conferred on me by King or Emperor"—on leaving the country, she had some second thoughts. "I am glad to get away from your country," she told one reporter. "You have liberty, but that is all, and of that you have too much."[15] And some practical business had to be settled. Olcott appointed Abner Doubleday president *ad interim* to serve in his absence. Judge, who would later become head of the society in the United States, was made temporary treasurer and corresponding secretary, taking over HPB's post. Judge had intended to make the voyage himself, but concern for his wife, who had no interest in Theosophy, prevented him. Edison was sorry to see them go, and as a parting gift, he gave Olcott a phonograph that weighed nearly one hundred pounds. At a farewell party in the empty Lamasery, many recorded their greetings to their unknown Indian counterparts on this monstrous device, including HPB and Olcott; even

Charles, a Theosophical cat, purred a hello.[16] (Sadly, the recording no longer exists.)

HPB maintained a sense of crisis until the last second. On the day they were ordered to depart, the Colonel had some last-minute business in Philadelphia, and did not return to New York until seven P.M. In his hand were their tickets for the steamship *Canada*, leaving that night bound for London. From there they would journey to Liverpool, and from there—destiny. Things, however, did not go so smoothly, and although they had fulfilled their orders by leaving American soil by the 17th, first bad weather and then a missed tide kept them anchored off Coney Island for a day and a half. Not until the afternoon of December 19 were they on their way, accompanied by two Theosophists, Rosa Bates, a schoolteacher, and Edward Wimbridge, an architect, who would assist them on their journey. Following her Masters' orders, HPB had left her adopted country, never to return.

THERE WERE NOT many passengers on the *Canada*. One of these, an Anglican clergyman, helped HPB pass the time by arguing with her about Christianity. On New Year's Day, 1879, they reached the English Channel and the next day were in London, where they stayed at the home of Dr. and Mrs. Billing, in the suburb of Norwood Park. Theosophists came to see them, as did spiritualists like Stainton Moses. Mrs. Billing herself was a noted medium, with a reputation on both sides of the Atlantic. Inevitably, Blavatsky was asked to produce phenomena, and C. C. Massey, president of the London Lodge, saw her "materialize" an ivory card case.[17] HPB paid a visit to the British Museum and Olcott lectured to the

London Lodge at their headquarters nearby, on Great Russell Street. Later, in Cannon Street, in the City, Olcott had another encounter with the Masters. Walking in a heavy fog with two other Theosophists, Olcott suddenly found himself looking into the eyes of a tall Hindu. Back in Norwood Park, he discovered that the same Hindu had paid a visit to his chum. Although the front door was locked and bolted, that afternoon Mrs. Billing was surprised to find an Indian gentleman in the hallway, asking to see Madame Blavatsky. When Mrs. Billing opened the door to her room, he saluted HPB by placing his palms together, and the two conversed in a strange language.

On January 17, they got a late train out of Euston Station, and that night were in Liverpool. The next day they boarded their steamer, the *Speke Hall*. It wasn't a pleasant voyage. The seas were rough and at one point HPB injured her knee, smashing it into a table leg. Everyone, HPB included, got seasick. Just short of a month later, on February 15, they entered Bombay harbor. Moolji Thackersey was at the dock to greet them, as were some of his friends. In a show of gratitude for finally reaching India's sacred ground—or perhaps simply relief for being off the ship—Olcott kissed the stone quay.

This seems a touch theatrical, but for the Indians it was a powerful symbolic act. The British had been ruling India for more than a century, first under the British East India Company, and then, more recently, under the Crown (the "British Raj"). For most of this time, the Hindus had seen the British as more or less gods, invincible rulers (for the most part benevolent) who had brought them much good: unification, education, higher living standards, peace, and reforms such as the end of slavery, the end of *suttee*—the practice of burning a widow alive on her husband's funeral pyre—the outlawing of human sacrifice, and of the *Thuggee* cult, which performed ritual murder in honor of the goddess Kali. But by 1857 and the Sepoy Mutiny—which Blavatsky just missed during her second Indian adventure—attitudes toward the British had changed. The very education Indians received from their rulers led them to a new, nationalist consciousness. They no longer wanted to be treated as children, and one product of this was Swami Dayananda and the Arya Samaj, who worked to introduce his countrymen to their own culture and religion. And now, here were two influential Westerners, who celebrated the Vedas and Holy India and had abandoned the West for the sacred land. How much Theosophy the many Indians who joined the society actually absorbed is debatable. What is undeniable is the effect that Olcott's and HPB's embrace of their culture had on their self-esteem. For both Theosophy and the Indians, they couldn't have come at a better time.

After the greetings subsided, it was unclear what would happen next. Then Hurrychund Chintamon, who had missed their arrival, turned up. Olcott had asked for a simple house for them, with only a minimum of servants. The house Hurrychund provided was actually one of his own and, as the Colonel had asked, it was very simple, lacking practically all Western amenities. On their second day, at a reception held in their honor, three hundred people crammed into a small hall. Garlands were tossed around their necks—even an Irishman they had met on ship and whom HPB persuaded to join the society was feted. The next day they attended "Shiva's Night," a great feast, and were later brought to see huge statues of the gods, and explored vast caves whose entrances were guarded by giant lingams, large phallic sculptures, that worshipers covered in bright paint (what the asexual HPB thought of them is unclear). Visitors crowded their house, eager to see the Westerners who had joined the Arya Samaj, and holy men engaged them in long philosophical discussions known as *durbars*. One evening they sat through a performance of an interminable sacred drama. By 2:45 A.M., even the chums' love of all things Indian had been exhausted. They got up to leave, but Hurrychund stopped the performance, only to read a lengthy welcoming address.

The next day, out of the blue, their ostensible host presented Olcott with an eye-watering bill for the house, their food, and everything else they had enjoyed on their arrival, even a telegram he had sent them in New York insisting they come. Olcott was staggered, and HPB let loose a barrage of invective. It soon turned out that money the TS had collected for the Arya Samaj and had sent to Hurrychund to be forwarded to Swami Dayananda had never reached its goal. HPB later forced Hurrychund to admit to this and to refund the money, but it was not the best start to their new alliance.

In early March, the chums found a new home at 118 Girgaum Road, in the native section of Bombay, an area few Europeans entered. Here HPB acquired a Gujarati servant boy, the fifteen-year-old Babula, who would stay with her during her time in India. HPB and Olcott had separate bungalows, a symbol, perhaps of the fact that on reaching India, their "chumship," always bumpy, would begin to loosen. As at Hurrychund's house, visitors streamed into the place; they were rarely alone, and Parsees, Hindus, Jains, and others came to see the holy Westerners. Very few British made their acquaintance. HPB's reputation, hardly inviting to the average member of the Raj, may have preceded her, but their reception could not have been helped by the fact that neither she nor Olcott bothered to stop at Government House, more or less standard procedure for any white visitors. Predictably, HPB ignored the "done" thing, and didn't make the expected calls at the "right" houses. This, plus the fact that from the minute they arrived they were under British surveillance, no doubt played havoc with her social standing.

Someone they might have expected to meet was one of the Masters, and soon enough they did. On March 29, HPB had Moolji get them a buggy, a small two-seater carriage. She didn't say where they were going but at each crossing simply gave the driver directions. They entered a suburb, then passed into a wood, and after many turns finally reached the seashore, where they rode to a large estate. At the gate she told the driver to stop. She told Moolji to wait and that under no circumstances was he to try to follow her. HPB then walked down the path to a bungalow. The door opened, and a tall Indian in white welcomed her.

Moolji was surprised that he didn't know of this estate; when he asked about it, gardeners he saw working nearby refused to tell him anything about the owner, not even his name. Finally, HPB and the tall Indian appeared again. One of the gardeners gave the Indian some white roses. He handed them to HPB, who then returned to the buggy and told the driver to take them home. Back at Girgaum Road, HPB gave the roses to Olcott, explaining that they were from Master Morya. She explained that the mysterious bungalow was used by the Masters whenever they needed to come to Bombay from Tibet. It was hidden by what she called a *maya*, an illusion, that prevented unwanted visitors from seeing it. Moolji did try to find it again, with Olcott, but couldn't. Later the Master paid a visit to the chums. Babula told Olcott that someone wanted to see him in HPB's bungalow. There he saw the tall Indian he had seen in New York. Then it was his astral form, but now he was in the flesh. After a few minutes he pointed his finger in the direction of Blavatsky's voice—she was in another room. She came in immediately, and fell at the Master's feet.

More mysterious events happened. In April, on Master's orders, HPB, Olcott, Moolji, and Babula set out for the Karli Caves, ancient Buddhist temples cut into solid rock, a day's journey from Bombay. On the way, Moolji had his own encounter with Morya. At the train station in Khandalla, he suddenly heard his name and in a carriage saw the tall Hindu he had seen at the secret bungalow. He handed Moolji some flowers—they were again for Colonel Olcott—and then his train left the station. Olcott wished he could thank the Master for his gift, and Blavatsky offered to deliver a note. Olcott wrote one, to which he added a question, and handed it to Moolji. HPB then told him to walk along the road ahead of them. Moolji had no idea how the note would be delivered, but HPB simply told him to go on. When he returned a few minutes later he explained that the tall Indian who had just left the station had appeared before him, taken the note from his hand, and then disappeared.

At the Karli Caves, HPB had to be carried up the steep hill; the heat and effort were too much for her. Inside the elaborately decorated temples, the group had a picnic, and Blavatsky told them of secret passageways that led to a hidden inner sanctum, where the Masters still resided. Shortly after, Moolji and Babula went to purchase more provisions, and HPB and Olcott were left alone. HPB then told Olcott to turn his back. He heard a loud thud, like a slam-ming door, and his chum's piercing laugh. HPB had vanished. Sometime later she reappeared and explained that she had passed through one of the secret doors and had been in conference with the Masters within.

The next day, after a night spent sleeping on the temple porch, she announced that the Masters had told her telepathically that they wanted them to go north to Rajputana in the Punjab. Back in Khandalla, HPB was worried that Rosa Bates and Mr. Wimbridge, who were keeping house for them, would think they were heading off on a holiday, using the Masters as an excuse, and wished that the Masters' request had come in a more concrete form—a tele-gram, to be exact. On the train she wrote a note to that effect, ask-ing the Masters to telegraph their friends in Bombay, to make things "official." As she was about to toss the note out the window, Olcott grabbed it, to make sure it wasn't simply a blank piece of paper. She then let it go. When they reached Bombay, they discov-ered that at two that afternoon, Miss Bates had signed for a tele-gram, sent to Olcott by "Gulab Singh," a character in Blavatsky's *From the Caves and Jungles of Hindustan*, who is supposed to be based on Morya. The message was "Rajputana. Start immediately." At a rest house on the way, a Hindu approached Olcott and gave him a letter. It was the answer to the question he had included with his note of thanks to Morya. Olcott had asked if it was possible for him to live full time with the Masters. They answered no: His path was his service to the Theosophical Society. Later, when Olcott had second thoughts about the move, the Master wrote to him again, soothing his worries.

Exactly why they had to go to Rajputana is unclear; it seems the chums were simply waiting for something to happen. At the River Jumma, they met Babu Surdass, a *sannyasin* who had sat in a lotus position on the riverbank for fifty-two years, rain or shine. At Cawnpore and at other places, they met other *sannyasins*, men who impressed Olcott with their powers of physical endurance. Yet when Olcott asked each of them to demonstrate the *siddhis*, or supernatural powers they had achieved, each declined, although one did explain that the secret of materializing physical objects was to discover a "nucleus" around which the adept can gather the "matter of space." (Later, Swami Dayananda would tell Olcott the same thing; again, current ideas about the mysterious "dark matter" apparently missing from the universe as well as the equally mysterious "power of nothing" seem suggestive.[18]) In Agra, they were appropriately stunned by the Taj Mahal, but the main event of the trip was a meeting with Swami Dayananda. At Saharanpore, they were met by the Arya Samaj, who greeted them with a formal reception which everyone attended, even the police agent who had been following them since they arrived. (At the end of the trip, Blavatsky approached him and sarcastically thanked him for his escort. Less humorously, at the U.S. Consul, Olcott brandished his endorsement from President Hayes and made an official complaint against the British, who were intercepting and reading their mail and telegrams; the surveillance eventually stopped.) Olcott, Moolji, and even HPB were impressed with the swami, who conversed with them about Nirvana, God, *moksha* ("liberation"), and also announced that Hurrychund had been expelled from the society. The next day they attended a meeting at which the swami addressed his followers. Olcott addressed them as well, emphasizing the great benefit to be had from a union of East and West. When they left the next day, crowds escorted them to the station and threw flowers after them as their train took them back to Bombay.

At Girgaum Road, Olcott soon "went native," and took to wearing a long cotton cloth and sandals. His chum, however, wasn't happy with all the local customs. When a high-ranking middle-aged gentleman introduced a ten-year-old girl as his "wife," HPB spluttered "Your WIFE? You old beast! You should be ashamed of yourself!" and stormed away. But in general, Olcott and HPB met with tremendous success. In July, they started work on *The Theosophist*, a monthly magazine devoted to the cause. Olcott managed it and Blavatsky was the editor. Its first issue appeared in October and it soon developed a large readership, which brought in many new members. One of these was Damodar K. Mavalankar, a young Brahmin who gave up his privileged life to follow the path. He had read *Isis Unveiled* and when he learned that its author was in Bombay, he went to meet her. When his parents learned of his interest in Theosophy, they demanded he give it up or lose his inheritance. Damodar sacrificed his comfortable life, moved in with the chums, and soon took over managing *The Theosophist*, to which he also contributed. He was the first to start calling the Masters "mahatmas" or "great souls." In his youth he had a vision of a wise sage who helped him pass through a terrible illness; he later identified this figure as Koot Hoomi.

IT WAS AROUND this time that HPB received a letter from her old friend, Emma Cutting, who was now Emma Coulomb. Emma, we remember, knew Blavatsky in Cairo, and was one of the mediums involved in her failed *société spirite*. Emma had seen reports of

HPB's arrival in the *Ceylon Times* and thought it a good idea to reconnect. Emma explained that she had married the son of the owner of the Hotel d'Orient, where HPB had stayed. They had tried to run the hotel, but it failed, and another venture in Ceylon, from where she was writing, was also unsuccessful. If she and her husband, Alexis, could get to Bombay, could her old friend help her find work? Blavatsky remembered the kindness Emma showed her years ago, and Olcott agreed that they should help her. In what would soon prove a major mistake, Blavatsky invited her to join them.

ONE BRIT WHO did go out of his way to make contact with Olcott and HPB was Alfred Percy Sinnett, editor of *The Pioneer*, probably the most influential newspaper in India at the time; among its contributors was Rudyard Kipling. Almost as soon as they had arrived, Sinnett wrote to Olcott, inviting him and HPB to visit him in Allahabad, should they ever come north. Sinnett was a spiritualist with a keen interest in phenomena, and he had been told that *Isis Unveiled* was a major work. In retrospect it isn't difficult to see that, from HPB's perspective, he would make a good alternative lieutenant, should she and the Colonel have a difference of opinion.

In December, HPB and Olcott, accompanied by Damodar and Babula, took up Sinnett's invitation. It was her first real contact with the British ruling class. Olcott records that while Sinnett himself seemed stiff, his wife, Patience, was more at ease, and that a real friendship was struck up between them. Sinnett met them at the Allahabad station with his barouche and pair and two liveried footmen. When they got to his home—they stayed for two weeks—Blavatsky warned Sinnett that she was a "rough old hippopotamus." It didn't take long for him to agree. Not one for small talk, HPB launched into a discussion of phenomena, and when Sinnett admitted that their experiments hadn't produced a rap, she replied "Oh, raps are the easiest thing to get," put her hand on the table and immediately produced a score. Another guest was A. O. Hume, a pro-Hindu secretary for the government and noted ornithologist who later became known as "the father of the Indian National Congress," which eventually led to Indian Home Rule.[19] One of HPB's complaints about the visit was that the smell of alcohol permeated the place. Blavatsky was as teetotal as Carrie Nation, with whom she shared some characteristics, and Olcott warned Sinnett, whom she had watched drink a whole bottle of wine, that she was "under great self-restraint."[20] Although usually loath to do so, HPB agreed to produce more phenomena, and more raps sounded about the house, on a door, a clock, even on her hosts' heads. They felt, they said, like faint electric shocks. They grew suspicious, however, when she was asked to "materialize" a cigarette holder. She made some occult gestures, rubbed the Colonel's pipe between her hands, and then simply pulled one out of her pocket. It may have been a joke, or a subtle hint to Sinnett not to invest so much importance in these tricks, a "teaching strategy," that, like her "abuse" of Colonel Olcott and others, is reminiscent of Gurdjieff. If so, subsequent developments suggest it was lost on him.

The party made a trip to Benares, where they stayed at the palace of the Maharaja of Vizianagram. Swami Dayananda was there, and they also paid a visit to a holy woman, known as the Maji, who lived in a cave near the Ganges. HPB was indisposed and couldn't make the visit, and everyone was impressed when the Maji, who never left her cave, did so to meet the Madame. At a gathering of

Sanskrit scholars, who lauded Olcott for his promotion of Hindu sacred texts, a German professor and protégé of the great Orientalist Max Müller opined that while in the past many yogis possessed *siddhis* and could, for example, make a shower of roses appear, no one could do that now. HPB disagreed, and after a peremptory wave of her hand, a dozen roses fell on the learned heads. After complementing her on her knowledge of Indian philosophy, the scholar thought to catch her in her ruse by asking if she could possibly produce just one more rose, as a souvenir of the evening—she may have prepared for one such trick, he thought, but surely not two. She said, "Certainly, as many as you like," and let loose another bouquet. And to make her point that such *siddhis* were possible today, she also caused the flame of a reading lamp to rise and fall, simply by commanding it. When Olcott expressed his amazement, she said that one of the Masters had simply turned the wick up and down. He disagreed, and believed that she had achieved mastery over the salamanders, or fire elementals.

On their return from Benares on December 26, the Sinnetts became members of the society. Some second thoughts may have assailed them, though. After a lecture Olcott had given on "Theosophy and Its Relation to India," to a packed audience which Hume had arranged, Blavatsky orally pummeled the Colonel because he had left her shawl behind. She had warned them that she was a hippopotamus, and even Olcott admitted that he only put up with her abuse because he knew what lay behind her.

IN MARCH of the new year, the Coulombs arrived unannounced, their passage from Ceylon paid by the French consul. HPB may have forgotten her offer of help, but on seeing her old friend, she instantly asked her and her husband to stay with her—at least according to Emma Coulomb's account. As the Coulombs were penniless, they agreed. Alexis Coulomb was an all-round Mr. Fix-It, with general "hands-on" skills, and Olcott tried to secure him steady work. But he was picky and tended to argue with his employers. Emma could keep house, and so the two eventually became part of the society's household, receiving room and board for their work. As Jean Overton Fuller suggests, this led to problems. If they had been given a wage, then their positions as employees would have been clear. As unpaid members working at the headquarters, their status was altogether more ambiguous. Miss Rosa Bates and Mr. Wimbridge, who had accompanied HPB and Olcott from New York, were beginning to have doubts about the move, and when Olcott put Emma in charge of the house, making Rosa a sub-editor of *The Theosophist*, warning signs should have gone off.

Soon after the Coulombs were installed, HPB and the Colonel sailed for Ceylon (Sri Lanka). The Buddhists there had asked them to come, and already one of their high priests was a member of the society. Mohattiwatti Gunananda, a great Sinhalese religious leader, had praised *Isis Unveiled* and even translated extracts from it. There on May 25, 1880, HPB and Olcott officially became Buddhists, by taking *pansil* (the Five Precepts) at a temple of the Rama-yana Nikaya, although as mentioned, HPB's "Buddhism" was always of a peculiar sort. As in Bombay, the chums were met by cheering crowds, who appeared at every stop on their tour of the island. They were the first Westerners to come and celebrate Buddhism at the expense of the Christian missionaries who, both here and in India, were beginning to feel the effect the chums were having on their flock. Shouts of "*Sadhoo, Sadhoo*" ("Peace be unto you") followed them everywhere. Olcott writes of giving speeches in packed halls, of newspapers filled with accounts of their visit, of dances, rituals, and other performances put on in their honor. Not too long before, they were sitting in Hell's Kitchen, unsure what lay ahead. Now they had a country looking to them as saviors. As in India, the religious revival also fueled a nationalist consciousness, and Theosophy produced a major boost for Sinhalese self-esteem.

As might be expected, the Colonel took it all in with great earnestness, but HPB maintained her sense of humor. On a visit to Kandy at the end of their tour, they were taken to see an ancient relic known as the Buddha's Tooth. When Olcott expressed mild skepticism about the object actually being the Buddha's tooth, or any tooth at all, for that matter—it was quite large—his hosts explained that "they were giants in those days." HPB however had no doubts. "Of course it's his tooth," she said with, one suspects, a smile. "It's one he had when he was born as a tiger."

WHEN THEY RETURNED to Girgaum Road in July, they received some sad news: Moolji had died only a few days before. If this wasn't bad enough, a feud had broken out between Emma Coulomb and Miss Bates. Miss Bates accused Emma of trying to poison her. The charge was absurd but it made clear the tensions in the household. Miss Bates resented being relieved of her duties and wanted to be given more responsibility on *The Theosophist*. She and Mr. Wimbridge had hoped to make a fresh start in India but things weren't working out, and the introduction of the Coulombs did not help. After days of bickering, Wimbridge and Bates demanded the Coulombs be expelled. Olcott and HPB refused, and their two escorts turned on the chums. During an argument, when Miss Bates displayed an invective equal to HPB's, a letter mysteriously fell onto Olcott's lap, apparently from nowhere. It was from Serapis and in essence it advised getting rid of Miss Bates. Whether Miss Bates and Mr. Wimbridge also received counsel from the Masters is unknown, but soon after Olcott received the letter, they decided to return to America.

On the same day that Rosa Bates and Edward Wimbridge announced they were leaving, HPB and Olcott received another invitation from Sinnett, this time asking them to join him in Simla, the summer capital of the Raj. This trip has gone down in history because of what are known as "the Simla phenomena." Much has been written about these strange events, and with the Mahatma Letters, they form the most discussed examples of HPB's powers of "materialization." They took place during a picnic outing with HPB, Olcott, the Sinnetts, a Major Henderson, and a Mrs. Reed (ironically, Major Henderson had been responsible for having HPB and the Colonel shadowed). Just as they were setting out, at the last minute the group was joined by Syed Mahmood, the district judge of Rai Bareilly. When the group decided to stop for tea, the Sinnetts' servants were embarrassed. They had packed the picnic baskets before Mahmood had joined them and, in consequence, were a cup and saucer short. Someone joked that they would have to take turns; someone else suggested that two people share one cup. Someone then asked if Madame Blavatsky could not make a cup and saucer appear? After much encouragement she agreed, and after some time inspecting the ground, she called to Major Henderson and, pointing to a spot, told him to dig. The ground was hard and full of roots from a nearby cedar tree. After some work he had cut through about six inches and there, embedded in roots and the soil was a cup, matching the ones packed by the servants. HPB told the major to dig deeper. He did, and soon discovered the matching saucer, also embedded in the soil and wrapped in roots.

The major was stunned and when he asked Blavatsky to explain how she had managed it, she told him she couldn't speak of it, unless he was a Theosophist. He agreed to join the next day. Mrs. Sinnett asked why he didn't join then and there, and the major asked HPB to produce a diploma on the spot. She asked if he would really join them if she did. The major assured her he would. "Then you shall have it," she said. After looking about for a few moments, she told the major that he would have to find it himself, and that it would be wrapped in blue twine. Everyone joined in the search, until the major came upon the diploma in a bush, wrapped in blue twine and already made out in his name in Olcott's handwriting.

Later, at the house, it was confirmed that the "materialized" cup and saucer did not come from the Sinnetts' pantry. The original set had formed a dozen; three cups had been broken beyond repair and had been discarded, and three remained with broken handles and were set apart on a high shelf. Six cups and saucers were packed by the servants; the ones HPB provided were not from the remaining broken three, yet were a perfect match. Later, Major Henderson had second thoughts about the materialization, and suggested that it was *just* possible for someone to dig a tunnel behind where the cup and saucer had been found and plant them there. When he mentioned this to HPB, and asked for another phenomenon, just to be sure, she burst into predictable rage.

Yet, as Sinnett himself explains in *The Occult World*, a book he wrote about the experience, subsequent examination of the area showed no signs of digging anywhere near the spot where the items were discovered. The whole area was undisturbed. To plant the cup and saucer ahead of time, HPB or an accomplice would have had to have spent a considerable time digging—more than a few hours—then expertly covering their tracks; and for Blavatsky to have planted the items, the tunnel would have had to have been fairly large. But more to the point, she would have had to have somehow known in advance that Mahmood Syed would join them: that is, that an extra cup and saucer would be needed, and that the party would take that exact route. Although the destination *had* been decided on, there was more than one route to it and exactly how to get there was left open until the last minute. And she would also have to have known that the decision to stop for tea would have been made at that exact spot, and which cups and saucers the servants would pack. There was more than one set to choose from, and HPB wouldn't have seen them until they were unpacked for tea. Likewise with Major Henderson's diploma: HPB would have had to have known that he would agree to join the society then and there, and would have had to have been in cahoots with Olcott about it—the diploma and a letter accompanying it were in his handwriting. The picnic excursion was decided on the night before, after HPB told her hosts that one of the Masters was passing through the area and that they might catch a glimpse of him. They had tried the previous day but had no luck, and thought to be in the general area just in case.

There were other phenomena. On the evening of the picnic, the Sinnetts and their guests were invited to dinner at the home of A. O. Hume. His Rothney Castle, decorated with specimens from his ornithological collection, commanded a magnificent view of the Himalayas, and was considered one of the finest dwellings in the area. At the dinner, HPB asked Hume's wife if there was anything she wished for. Mrs. Hume thought for a moment, then said she would like to have a brooch that her mother gave her, but which someone had borrowed and subsequently lost. HPB took her hand and asked her to form a clear picture of the brooch in her mind. Mrs. Hume described the brooch, and even drew a picture of it. HPB then took two cigarette papers and wrapped them around a coin that was attached to her watch chain. She then put this inside her dress. Later, at the end of dinner, HPB said that her cigarette papers were gone, and she announced that the brooch would be found in a star-shaped flower bed in the garden. There was such a flower bed at a distance from the house and, carrying lanterns, the party went to it. There among the nasturtiums they discovered HPB's cigarette papers, wrapped around some object. HPB wasn't there when it was found, and when she got to the flower bed, the discovery was handed to Hume. He unwrapped it; within was a brooch as described by Mrs. Hume.

It later became known that the person who lost the brooch was Mrs. Hume's daughter, and that she had met Madame Blavatsky in Bombay, en route to Europe. Skeptics insist that for some reason, Mrs. Hume's daughter gave the brooch to HPB, who somehow planted it in the Humes' garden. Why Mrs. Hume's daughter would give a family heirloom to a stranger is never explained, but in any case she denied giving the brooch to Blavatsky, and insisted that she really did lose it. But even if she *did* give it to HPB, this would mean *either* that Blavatsky again knew in advance that Mrs. Hume would wish for it, *or* that Mrs. Hume for some reason was in league with Blavatsky, and that the two planned the whole episode together, with Mrs. Hume pretending to want the lost brooch, and someone—Mr. Hume, perhaps—planting it in the flower bed. While conceivable, it raises the question *why* the Humes would go along with it. If the phenomena were engineered to impress people—and that is the general reason given for them— who else would HPB conceivably want to impress, except people like Hume, who could be useful to her in some way. But you cannot use a fraud to impress your fellow conspirators, and it's difficult to see what Hume, an important government official, would have gained from being involved in such business, while it is clear that he had much to lose by being caught out in it.

There were other Simla phenomena, and they all breach the believability threshold, yet they are all also subject to the same logical problems. One concerns another brooch, this time Mrs. Sinnett's. One night Sinnett saw what he believed to be Koot Hoomi in his astral form, and the next day he received a message from the Master, saying that proof of his visit would be given to him. On an outing to Prospect Hill, HPB announced that Koot Hoomi had asked her to ask Sinnett where he would like to receive his proof. The "proof" was something Koot Hoomi had taken the night before, during his astral visit to Sinnett. Sinnett looked around, and finally pointed to a cushion one of his guests was using, and said, "Inside that cushion." HPB agreed and was about to begin, when suddenly Mrs. Sinnett said, "No. Let it be inside mine!" HPB nodded. Mrs. Sinnett used her cushion all the time—it was her favorite—and, following HPB's instructions, she took it from behind her back and put it beneath a cover thrown over her legs. Then HPB asked her to take it out. Sinnett took a knife and slowly cut the threads, stitch by stitch. After he removed the outer cover, he found an inner one, and after Sinnett carefully cut through this, Mrs. Sinnett found a brooch like hers inside, which she had last seen on her dressing table, where she had put it the night before. The initials "K.H." were scratched onto it, and with it was a note, folded into a triangle. It read, "My Dear Brother, This brooch No. 2, is placed in this very strange place, simply to show you how very easily a real phenomenon is produced." It also suggested carrying on communication in a form that didn't require pillows, showing that, if nothing else, the Masters had a sense of humor.

To have a brooch that was pilfered on an astral visit turn up inside your favorite cushion is remarkable enough. But what is truly significant about this phenomenon is that the Masters were beginning to communicate with someone other than HPB and the Colonel. It was the beginning of a whole new era in HPB's life, and it was one that would end in crisis.

EIGHT

A CRISIS IN ADYAR

B y the time Mrs. Sinnett's brooch inexplicably appeared inside her favorite cushion, her husband had already started what has to be one of the strangest correspondences in history. Impressed with HPB's tales about the Masters and their mission, Sinnett asked Blavatsky if he could communicate with them himself. Naturally he would use her as a go-between, an arrangement that he would nevertheless quickly try to get around. (A. O. Hume, equally impressed, would try the same thing.) Blavatsky said she would ask, but there were no guarantees. The Masters were busy men, and, as she told Sinnett, at first none of them were open to the idea. But eventually one agreed, and between 1880 and 1885, Sinnett received over thirteen hundred pages of eloquent, often elaborate communication, collectively known as "the Mahatma Letters," mostly from Koot Hoomi (who wrote in blue ink) but also from Morya (who wrote in red). These made up, for the most part, an extensive instruction in esoteric philosophy.

The essence of this Sinnett compressed into a book, *Esoteric*

Buddhism, which caused quite a stir when it was published in 1883. Among its many readers were a young Rudolf Steiner and W. B. Yeats, both of whom, in different ways, made significant contributions to Theosophy, and to modern thought in general. Yet, although the book had popular appeal and remains a staple of Theosophical literature, it was not appreciated by all. Max Müller, the famed Orientalist, pointed out that however esoteric its teaching, it had nothing to do with Buddhism, and that the idea of an "esoteric Buddhism" itself could not be found in any Buddhist literature and was therefore an invention of the book's author, or of his guru, Madame Blavatsky.[1] Yet Blavatsky herself wasn't happy with the title—or with the book—and took Sinnett to task about it in *The Secret Doctrine*. We've seen that her own form of Buddhism was highly eccentric and had little to do with the Buddhism of scholars like Müller or that of your average Buddhist. As Buddha itself means "awakened" or "enlightened one," Sinnett's use of the term can be translated as "Esoteric Awakening" or "Esoteric Enlightenment." Sinnett himself admitted to the confusion his title triggered, commenting on how people inspired to join the TS after reading his book spoke of themselves as "esoteric Buddhists." He also pointed out that he could easily have called the teaching he transmitted "Esoteric Brahmanism" or "Esoteric Christianity," as a central claim of the work is that it communicated the ancient, original wisdom *behind* these subsequent developments. Brahmanism, Christianity, and other world religions could, through this teaching, be seen to have emerged at various periods "from the same common root of spiritual knowledge." But "since Buddhism had apparently separated itself less widely than other religions from the parent stem," and as in its "exterior form" it was already attracting a great deal of attention in the West, he thought it appropriate to use it as a way of leading his readers into the profound teaching which had been revealed to him.[2]

This may be a way of saying that, as Buddhism was attracting interest in the West, calling his book *Esoteric Buddhism* was a way of attracting attention to it, a successful marketing ploy. In any case, in the long run it led to a great deal of confusion about Theosophy's relation to Buddhism, and in recent years has informed the claim that works like *The Tibetan Book of the Dead* are essentially Western inventions, concocted by Theosophically inclined scholars. As one contemporary Buddhist scholar points out, W. Y. Evans-Wentz, the man responsible for bringing the texts constituting *The Tibetan Book of the Dead* (a title he gave them, borrowing from *The Egyptian Book of the Dead*) to a wide Western readership, was a Theosophist, and the stamp of HPB's ideas lies heavily on his work.[3]

The content of the Mahatma Letters is not, however, the most controversial thing about them. Who actually wrote them is the subject of much debate and, naturally, HPB herself has been seen as their author. Books have been written "proving" this to be the case, most notably *Who Wrote the Mahatma Letters?* by William and Harold Hare, published in 1936. Their conclusion, not surprisingly, is that Blavatsky did, and their argument was vigorously rebutted by Blavatsky's late champion, Beatrice Hastings.[4] Other books, such as *Did Madame Blavatsky Forge the Mahatma Letters?* By C. Jinarajadasa (1934) argue otherwise, and support the case that HPB did not write the letters. (Although the letters in question are generally those Sinnett received, we remember that the earliest date for a Mahatma letter is 1870, when HPB's aunt got word from

Koot Hoomi that her niece was well, and that others, such as Colonel Olcott, received them too; Jinarajadasa also points out that along with KH and M, at least four other Masters wrote letters.) Handwriting analysts, literary critics, and forgery experts have been employed by either side and, frustratingly, have come to opposite conclusions. Although common sense suggests that HPB is responsible, when the circumstances are examined in detail, this doesn't seem as obvious as we might think. And the argument suggesting that whatever her involvement, HPB neither physically wrote the letters nor composed them is more substantial than we might like. But even the question of their authenticity is not the most fascinating or exasperating aspect of the Mahatma Letters. What leads the unbiased inquirer to an often numbing sense of uncertainty about them is their manner of delivery.

Like Mrs. Sinnett's brooch and the miraculous teacup—not to mention the saucer and, aptly enough, quite a few cigarettes—the Mahatma Letters were mysteriously "precipitated."[5] Although some did arrive in the post, most materialized in unusual circumstances via a kind of "astral special delivery," often falling out of thin air.[6] We've seen one appear in Mrs. Sinnett's cushion. Earlier during HPB's visit, another note from one of the Brothers was discovered in a tree. Mrs. Sinnett had asked to receive a letter from the Masters and HPB obliged, passing on Mrs. Sinnett's request by her odd method of jotting it down "invisibly" on a slip of paper, folding this into a triangle, and tossing it into the air, as she did when asking the Masters to send a telegram to Miss Bates and Mr. Wimbridge.

Sinnett's first Mahatma letter appeared on his writing table, in admittedly not particularly mysterious circumstances: It could have been left there by normal means. Yet ironically, its message was the danger involved in trying to use phenomena to convince people of the existence of the Masters, which, one would think, was precisely what the teacup, brooch, and now these mysterious letters were about. Sinnett had asked that the Masters arrange for a copy of his newspaper, *The Pioneer*, to appear in London on the same day as its publication in Allahabad. Normally it would take weeks for copies to arrive in Britain, and one turning up on the same day as publication would, Sinnett thought, be a convincing proof of the Masters' powers. Koot Hoomi disagreed. As HPB herself repeatedly pointed out, he argued that people are never convinced through such things, but would only ask for more and more miracles, and that in any case, the phenomena themselves were irrelevant to their mission. Better, he believed, that Sinnett make known the precipitation of the cup and the other items, and so encourage people to think about them *themselves*—it was preferable to get people taking an active stance toward these things, rather than encouraging their passivity by simply stunning them with miracles. As Sinnett would soon find out, the moral, ethical, and social aspects of their teaching were of infinitely more importance to the Masters, and they were not in the least interested in creating "a college for the special study of occultism," as Sinnett seemed to have in mind. The Brothers worked for the "welfare of humanity" through the foundation of "a universal Brotherhood"—point number 3 in the Theosophical Society's "mission statement"—and from the beginning Sinnett, and even more A. O. Hume, were at odds with this aim.[7] As Koot Hoomi made clear, if Sinnett was to be of use to them, he had to choose between "the highest philosophy" or "simple exhibitions of occult power."[8]

Yet for all Koot Hoomi's argument against the importance of phenomena, one had to admit that the letters in which he communicated this were pretty phenomenal. Although in some, perhaps most cases, some kind of trickery may have been at work, there are some, it strikes me, where that explanation seems inadequate. The phenomena themselves were more complicated than simply having a letter appear out of thin air, as did the roses HPB allegedly produced for her skeptical Sanskrit scholar, incredible enough as that would be. They involved HPB receiving a question from Sinnett (or someone else), and then mentally "transmitting" this to Koot Hoomi. She did this via her "throw-away note method," or by the more immediate means of a kind of telepathy. Then KH would either communicate mentally his answer to one of his *chelas,* or students, who would then "precipitate" this onto a page, or he would "precipitate" it himself. This meant that not only the actual paper the letter was written on, but the writing itself, was somehow paranormally produced. Although KH does remark that he occasionally writes the letters by hand, most of them were "impressed," that is, the writing reached the paper through imagination and will—in other words, magic.

Common sense tells us that, if she didn't write the replies herself, HPB passed on Sinnett's messages through some normal means to whoever did. Yet this very satisfying explanation doesn't seem to fit all the facts. We've already seen how a note HPB threw out of a moving train reached "Gulab Singh," who complied with her request and sent Miss Bates a telegram. *If* the whole thing was not an elaborate hoax (and the idea that it was raises its own problems), how do we account for "Gulab Singh" receiving HPB's request and, immediately after, sending the telegram? The way the story is told, Miss Bates received the telegram almost immediately after HPB sent her request, that is, while she and Olcott were still on the train. This wasn't the only Mahatma letter associated with rail travel. Olcott himself received one on a moving train, and a train was involved in the exchange that convinced Sinnett that HPB couldn't have written Koot Hoomi's letters.[9] On this occasion it was actually a "Mahatma telegram," and it arrived by normal delivery, but it convinced Sinnett that HPB must have been in some kind of telepathic contact with her Master.

On October 27, 1880, HPB and Olcott were in Amritsar, where they visited the Golden Temple of the Sikhs, a place of worship for Sikh pilgrims, which houses the Amrit Saras, "the fount of immortality," and the Adi Granth, the sacred Sikh scripture.[10] The hot weather had ended, and before leaving Simla for Allahabad, Sinnett wrote a letter to Koot Hoomi and posted it in a registered letter to HPB at Amritsar, asking her to forward it to him. When he reached Allahabad, he found a letter from Blavatsky enclosing the registered envelope he had sent her, and a telegram from KH, acknowledging receipt of his letter. HPB received Sinnett's letter at 2 P.M. on the twenty-seventh; the telegram was sent to Sinnett from Jhelum on the same day. In a letter from KH that Sinnett received two days later, KH told him that he had received his letter via HPB while on a train near Rawalpindi (in what is now Pakistan) and had gotten off at the next stop, Jhelum, in order to send him an acknowledgment of receipt. This was at four that afternoon. The distance between Amritsar and Jhelum is roughly 112 miles, and that between Amritsar and Rawalpindi is roughly 175 miles. KH said he received HPB's "transmission" of Sinnett's letter at 2:05 P.M., five minutes after HPB received Sinnett's registered letter (the envelope she returned to Sinnett was stamped with the time of delivery). By train, the fastest transportation available then, it took KH two hours to travel the distance between where he received the "transmission" and where he sent a telegram to Sinnett acknowledging it, roughly sixty-three miles. Were HPB to have sent the telegram acknowledging receipt of Sinnett's letter, she would have had to travel nearly twice that distance in the same amount of time. Sinnett asked the post office for the original message of the telegram. It was in the handwriting he had come to know as Koot Hoomi's. This convinced Sinnett that HPB could not have sent the telegram and could not, then, have written the letters from KH.[11]

This does not, of course, prove that KH or Morya was a Master. But it does show, I think, how difficult it is to account for how HPB "transmitted" Sinnett's letter to KH by any normal means, at least on this occasion. There was no telephone (Alexander Graham Bell had only patented his idea in 1876 and it was still not in general use, and certainly not in northern India), and of course no e-mail. But even if HPB had gotten the message to KH by some normal means, the fact that the original telegram message was written in KH's handwriting and sent from a place that HPB could not have gotten to in time to send it (if she got the letter at two she couldn't have been in Jhelum at four to send the acknowledgment) suggests that she wasn't writing the letters to Sinnett.

To be able to communicate telepathically with KH or her other Masters is, to be sure, a remarkable claim. Yet by now, the reality of telepathy has, I think, been fairly well established. Around the same time as Sinnett was receiving his letters, members of what would become the Society for Psychical Research were collecting data supporting just that conclusion, and since then, numerous studies, as well as a mountain of anecdotal material, confirms, to my mind at least, that telepathy is real.[12] This, again, doesn't prove that HPB did communicate with her Masters telepathically, only that we cannot dismiss the possibility that she did on the grounds that telepathy is impossible.

"Precipitating" letters, teacups, and other items is another thing, but even here there is some evidence in support of such phenomena. In an article for *The Theosophist* HPB spelled out just how precipitation worked. She speaks of a "sort of psychological telegraphy," in which the Master sends his message via "astral currents" to one of his *chelas*. This is picked up by the *chela*'s brain, which communicates the message through his "nerve-currents" to his fingers, which rest on a piece of "magnetically prepared paper." The Master's thoughts are then directed to the paper, which then draws on the "ocean of *akasa*," (the "matter of space" Swami Dayananda and the *sannyasin* that Olcott met had spoken of) and "permanent marks are left."[13] Koot Hoomi himself commented on how he "writes" his letters: "I have to *think* it over, to photograph every word and sentence carefully in my brain before it can be repeated by 'precipitation' . . . we have first to arrange our sentences and impress every letter to appear on paper in our minds before it becomes fit to be read." And he compares the process to the "mystery of the lithophyl . . . and how the impress of leaves comes to take place on stones."[14]

Are there examples of this remarkable ability elsewhere? The medium Stainton Moses, a friend of Olcott's and HPB's, was said to be able to "translocate" objects: photographs, picture frames, books, and other items were said to have appeared in locked rooms during his séances, apparently arriving there through the walls. This "passage of matter through matter"—common during Spiritualism's heyday—came about by some "process of de-materialization," according to Moses' colleague Charles Speer, and we know that such things were speculated on in *Ghost Land*.[15] Other individuals associated with "materializations," "apports," or "translocations" include the late Hindu holy man Sathya Sai Baba and the psychic Uri Geller, and of course much controversy surrounds their claims.

But perhaps the paranormal phenomenon most relevant to the Mahatma Letters are the "thoughtographs" of Ted Serios. In the 1960s, Serios, a Chicago bellhop, claimed he could make pictures appear on Polaroid film through his mind alone, a claim substantiated by the investigations of the parapsychologist Jule Eisenbud in his book *The World of Ted Serios* (1967). Serios's method was to hold a cylinder to the camera and then point this at his forehead. He would then concentrate and force the image in his mind onto the film—a process sounding very much like Koot Hoomi's method of "impressing." Serios also claimed to be able to do this at a distance, and, interestingly enough, he seemed to have more success when under the influence of alcohol.[16]

I should also mention that some of the other phenomena associated with the Masters have a history, too. "Bilocation," which we've already seen in the context of Tibetan Buddhism, is fairly common in the Western world. In 1886, Edmund Gurney, Frank Podmore, and F. W. H. Myers of the Society for Psychical Research published *Phantasms of the Living*, an *Isis Unveiled*–sized tome collecting a monumental amount of anecdotal evidence for the phenomena of someone's "ghost" appearing to others while the person was still alive. In German-speaking countries, this is known as a *doppelganger*, and such esteemed characters as the poet Johann Wolfgang von Goethe were known to have experienced it.[17] In *Psychic Self-Defence*, the occultist Dion Fortune recounts her own experience with creating a *tulpa*, or "thought form," as discussed in Chapter 3. In Fortune's case, it was an "elemental" in the form of a wolf, and as in the case of Alexandra David-Neel, it took some effort on her part to "reabsorb" it. Ouspensky recounts that Gurdjieff was able to project his thoughts *inside* his—Ouspensky's—chest. Gurdjieff was also able to read his mind and, at one point, while traveling alone on a train to Moscow, Ouspensky "saw" Gurdjieff in the carriage with him and carried on a conversation.[18] Again, in mentioning these examples, I am not trying to prove that HPB or her Masters could do such things, merely show that they are not entirely unheard of.

However the Mahatma Letters arrived, soon after their correspondence began, both Sinnett and A. O. Hume ran into some problems. Both Sinnett and Hume asked KH if it wasn't possible to communicate directly, that is, without HPB. Predictably, when "the old lady," as Sinnett called her, caught wind of this, there was hell to pay. Sinnett and Hume had also asked to start a branch of the Theosophical Society independently of Olcott. Both considered him something of a fool and were uncomfortable with his "American ways," as they were with HPB's lack of social tact, and wanted to initiate a more respectable "English" group. KH's reply was a gentle but firm rebuke and a strong defense of the chums; he also asked why, if he was repelled by Olcott's Yankee bumptiousness, Sinnett was ready to take instruction from a "greasy Tibetan." Communication with Hume was soon broken off, and he left Theosophy to focus on what would become the Indian National Congress. Sinnett himself had to be continuously reminded of the importance of furthering a "Universal Brotherhood." He wanted to start an "elite" esoteric school, and KH dropped hints that he had been involved in one that failed some years ago in London, among whose members were Bulwer-Lytton and Eliphas Lévi. From his description, it sounds remarkably like the Orphic Circle spoken of by Emma Hardinge Britten. Other oddly familiar items in KH's letters are the emphasis on the admonition to "try"—which, as we've seen, was associated with Paschal Beverly Randolph and the H. B. of L., and which featured in Olcott's letter from Tuitit Bey—and the American spelling of "skeptic," which suggests that KH spent time in the United States. That the letters fill some thirteen hundred pages also reminds us of HPB's own prolix style.[19]

For students of Theosophical history, Koot Hoomi's discussions about practical concerns and the aims of the Masters are enlightening, but what stunned the readers of *Esoteric Buddhism* was the new vision of man and the cosmos Sinnett was receiving. I can only give the briefest outline here, and interested readers are advised to go to Sinnett's book or the Mahatma Letters themselves, both of which are available online.[20] Contrary to the Christian view, which sees man consisting of body and soul, the Masters told Sinnett that the human being was actually made up of seven "bodies." These consisted of *Rupa*, or the physical body; *Prana*, or the "vital" body, the principle of life; *Linga Sharira*, or the astral body; *Kama Manas*, or the animal soul; *Manas*, or the human soul;

Buddhi, or the spiritual soul; and *Atma*, or the spirit.[21] The first four bodies disintegrate at death—the astral taking a bit longer than the others—and our spiritual development depends on uniting *Manas* with *Buddhi*, or our human soul with that of the spirit, while alive. If we are successful, this will result in a "true individuality" or "monad," which will share in the immortality of *Atma*, the eternal spiritual principle.

This sevenfold system was reflected in the cosmos, with the earth passing through what are called "Rounds," a kind of spiritual evolution of its own. As Jean Overton Fuller remarks, "the Rounds are desperately difficult to understand," and as Jocelyn Godwin comments, their study, as well as that of the "Root Races" and "Sub Races" associated with them, "is a recreation reserved for the few."[22] The basic idea is that our present physical earth is but one in a series or "chain" of seven incarnations that, in KH's homely analogy, form a kind of "necklace." Our earth as the "heaviest" or most material, is a kind of pendant hung between two groups of three. If, following his image, we take our earth as D, then A, B, and C are earlier, less material planetary incarnations, and E, F, and G are future, more spiritualized ones.[23] Each shift from one Round to the next involves huge stretches of time and is occasioned by tremendous transformations and cataclysms, and each Round or "bead" on the cosmic necklace has different "Root" and "Sub" races linked to it, an idea HPB spelled out in considerable detail in *The Secret Doctrine*. The overall picture is of an evolution, but one, as already pointed out in *Isis Unveiled*, that goes far beyond Darwin. It involves the entire universe passing from a pregnant nothingness into its physical existence, then into an increasing spiritual one, until it disappears into a kind of cosmic Nirvana, with a new universe appearing further on, which will go through its own cycle. For a generation already exposed to Darwin and to the vast age of the earth—as presented in the work of the geologist Charles Lyell—that the cosmos itself went through an evolution did not seem too fantastic, and that, united with *Atma*, we could see it through, was a more thrilling version of an afterlife than the Victorian notion of a cloud-filled heaven, populated by chubby, harp-playing angels.

AFTER THEIR VISIT TO SIMLA, the chums traveled through northern India gathering new recruits. Although the English papers in India were critical of them—aside from *The Pioneer*, whose owners were beginning to worry about Sinnett's pro-Theosophy stance— HPB and Olcott received tremendous popular support, and new branches of the society sprang up practically everywhere they went. After a visit to the Sinnetts at Christmas, HPB and the Colonel returned to Bombay at the beginning of 1881. By this time Madame Coulomb, who had ingratiated herself more firmly into the running of the household, had found them a new home. It was a bungalow they nicknamed the Crow's Nest, in the less crowded suburb of Breach Candy. Sinnett was happy at the move. Girgaum Road was much too "native" for him, and as the society was attracting more European recruits, a more respectable location was welcome. The Sinnetts passed through briefly in the spring, en route to England for a holiday, where Sinnett completed his book about "the Simla phenomena" and the Mahatmas. Published that June, *The Occult World* was a popular success, although it received bad reviews; according to the *Saturday Review*, HPB and the Colonel were "unscrupulous adventurers," and Olcott had received his title most likely "in a saloon."

Olcott, however, shrugged off such remarks. Back in Bombay, he had put his mind to more important matters. His thoughts turned to Ceylon and to the influence Christian missionaries were having on the Buddhists there, and he determined that he would help the Buddhist effort. He started a Buddhist Education Fund that would, in essence, bring Buddhism to Buddhists. His chum was not happy with the idea. The Masters, she said, were not in favor of it, and would cut him off, but most likely she was worried about her lieutenant making plans of his own. He would travel without her, and no doubt the signs of independence were a threat. Predictably, she flew into a rage and refused to see him for a week; this may be why she continued to work with Sinnett who, according to a later devotee, was incompetent "to pronounce even the most superficial judgement on one whom he was inherently incapable of understanding," that is, HPB herself.[24]

Whatever doubts the Masters had about Olcott's mission, it was an unqualified success. He gathered support from different Buddhist sects, gave lectures around the island, wrote tracts, raised money, debated with missionaries, and was treated as a savior wherever he went. He was shocked to find how little Buddhism the Sinhalese knew, and to redress the lack, he composed a *Buddhist Catechism*. It was translated into Sinhalese and other languages and became a best-seller. Olcott in fact became a national hero and something of a legend. In the summer of 1882, he returned to Ceylon to continue his campaign, and while there discovered he had some remarkable powers of his own. When a man, Cornelius Appu, with a paralyzed arm and leg made a contribution, Olcott suddenly felt an impulse to "try some healing passes" over him; in his early years Olcott had, we remember, cured some relatives of their ailments through magnetism. Now the power seemed to have returned. Later that evening, Appu returned to thank Olcott, saying his arm and leg were better. Olcott made more passes, and after a few more treatments, Appu could move freely. He came back with a paralyzed friend, and Olcott "cured" him too. Word got around and suddenly Olcott was besieged with the sick and crippled, treating people "from dawn until late at night." By his account, he cured eight thousand people in the course of a year, and only stopped when one of the Masters ordered him to, because his own health was threatened.[25] In recognition of Olcott's efforts on behalf of the nation, in 1967 Sri Lanka issued a commemorative stamp in his honor. Streets in Colombo and Galle are named after him, and a statue of him stands outside Colombo Fort Railway Station. Olcott's work inspired the Buddhist nationalist efforts of Anagarika Dharmapala, the great Sinhalese religious reformer and one of the speakers at the first World's Parliament of Religions held in 1893 in Chicago, at which both W. Q. Judge and Annie Besant also spoke. In many ways Olcott's career resembles that of another Westerner who "went Asian," the Greek-Irish-American writer Lafcadio Hearn, whose celebration of Japanese life and culture led to him being venerated in Japan, much as Olcott is in Sri Lanka.[26]

When Olcott returned to the Crow's Nest from his first Ceylon venture—in December 1881—he was surprised that the Masters had changed their mind about his trip. His chum welcomed him back warmly and gave him a message of congratulations from the Brothers. Olcott was pleased but wondered about the change of attitude. If he had stifled doubts about his chum before, now they started to bubble up. HPB herself had been busy while he was away, traveling, spreading the word, and, in Lahore, meeting her Master. The summer found her again at Simla, and it was during this stay that she exploded over Sinnett and Hume's request to deal with the Mahatmas directly.

The Crow's Nest, though preferable, served as the chums' base for only a short while. During most of it, the two traveled, sometimes together, but also separately. In March 1882, they met in Calcutta, where Olcott lectured and they were the guests of the maharaja. In April, they went to Madras, where they met T. Subba Row, an advocate or *Vakil* in the Indian justice system, who would become one of their most important Hindu supporters. It is said that before meeting HPB, Subba Row was ignorant of Sanskrit literature and anything to do with philosophy or metaphysics, but that after meeting her, he could quote from the Bhagavad Gita, Upanishads, and other mystical texts by heart. The members of the new Madras lodge urged them to move their headquarters from Bombay to their city. The idea appealed to the chums. HPB was beginning to feel the effects of Bright's disease, but the "bags à la kangaroo" that were forming on her body were, she thought, the effect of Bombay's heat and humidity. Her condition, she told her relatives, was so bad that she convinced her doctor that she could "die at any moment as a result of any excitement," and one wonders if the Colonel ever tried his healing powers on her or, indeed, if she would have let him.[27] In November, the Theosophical Society purchased a large estate in the suburb of Adyar. Although HPB herself would spend only a few years there, it would become the permanent home of the society. Before moving to Adyar, HPB took a "rest cure" in Sikkim, on orders from M. She was refused a pass by the British but went "just the same," and spent time in a monastery just across the Tibetan border, and also a few days at her teachers' ashram, where she felt it was "like the old times." In Darjeeling, she met Mohini Chatterjee, a lawyer in the Calcutta Theosophical lodge, who was a descendant of the Hindu reformer Raja Rammohun. It was through Mohini Chatterjee that W. B. Yeats would become involved in Theosophy, when he attended Mohini's lectures in Dublin in 1885. Yeats later wrote a poem about him.[28]

ON DECEMBER 19, 1882, the TS established its new headquarters in Adyar. HPB, Olcott, Babula, Damodar, as well as the Coulombs and various visitors, occupied the new premises, which, with their spacious gardens, mango trees, and view of the estuary and sea, were a welcome change from the noise and bustle of Bombay. HPB's rooms were on the second floor, above a large room on the ground floor which was used for lectures and meetings. A curtain divided her space into a bedroom and living room, but she now thought to have a special space arranged just for the Masters, which became known as "the occult room." Olcott had Alexis Coulomb build an extension for his chum on the bedroom side, and Blavatsky dedicated a recess there as a space solely for the Masters' use. Here she erected what became known as "the shrine." This was a cabinet, about five feet high by four wide, that she hung on the wall. Behind its lacquered folding doors was intricate metalwork, and here HPB put "precipitated" portraits of KH and M, a statue of the Buddha, and other sacred *objets d'art*, all of which was closed off by a curtain. Here followers would deposit letters to the

Masters, which would be "delivered" to them, and here they would receive their "precipitated" replies. Although the most famous Mahatma Letters are the ones Sinnett received, except for one, none of these came through the shrine.

THE YEAR 1883 was relatively peaceful for the chums, but it was only the calm before the storm. Blavatsky wrote and published an enormous amount in *The Theosophist*. This was just as well, as the owners of *The Pioneer* had finally had enough of Sinnett's pro-HPB policy. It was alienating its English readers who saw Theosophy as a native gimmick, and he was asked to leave. The Christian missionaries, who were increasingly resentful of Theosophy's success, were happy about the decision. A plan by KH to start a new paper, *The Phoenix*, funded by Hindu rajas, fell through, and Sinnett returned to England, where he wrote *Esoteric Buddhism* and would soon make a bid to become president of the London Lodge. Anna Kingsford, an upper-class Englishwoman who combined interests in Christian Esotericism with vegetarianism and the anti-vivisection movement (she had even taken a medical degree to fight the practice), had succeeded C. C. Massey as president, but Sinnett had his sights on that position and the two would soon clash. Sinnett's argument against Kingsford was that she doubted the existence of the Mahatmas, a point the Mahatmas themselves thought negligible, as a letter from Koot Hoomi supported her presidency.[29] The Colonel was enjoying his work, which was increasingly independent of his chum. At one point in June, returning from a tour of Bengal, he was unsure whether to accept invitations to Colombo again, or to Allahabad. He put one of the invitations into the shrine and immediately got a reply from Master Hilarion suggesting he go to Colombo. Olcott received several letters that summer, one directing him to write a letter which Sinnett could use to bring the scientist and spiritualist William Crookes over to the Theosophical cause.

One embarrassing moment occurred in September. The spiritualist paper *Light* published a letter by Henry Kiddle, who claimed that whoever the Mahatmas were, they had plagiarized him. In one of the Mahatma Letters Sinnett had published in *The Occult World*, Kiddle was surprised to find phrases that seemed to have been taken from a lecture he had given in 1880 and which had been printed that year in *The Banner of Light*. Everyone rose to KH's defense, but he himself admitted that while making a "clairvoyant survey" of current Spiritualism, he had picked up some of Kiddle's phrases and while "dictating mentally" the letter in question to his *chela*, he had inadvertently fastened on these. He was tired at the time and when Sinnett's book was published had forgotten about it.

A more assuring contact with the Master was made with Olcott in November. On a tour of northern India with a recent convert, W. T. Brown of the University of Glasgow, Olcott received a visit from KH while sleeping in his tent. Touching him lightly, KH placed his right hand over Olcott's, closing his fingers into his palm. When the Colonel opened them, he held a letter wrapped in silk. KH then visited Brown as well. Damodar, who was accompanying them, had his own visit the next night. What made this unusual was that it wasn't an astral visit. Olcott, Brown, and Damodar were convinced they had seen the Master in the flesh.[30]

By December, HPB's health had so deteriorated that she

attended the society's convention on crutches. Her doctors advised a change of climate. Olcott was planning to go to England, both to help settle the turmoil in the London Lodge and also to plead the cause of the Ceylon Buddhist community, which was being repeatedly harassed by Christians; Olcott intended to bring the matter before the British authorities. He invited HPB to accompany him. As the chums would be away for some time, Olcott appointed a Board of Control to run things while they were gone. One of its members was the German-American occultist Franz Hartmann, who had recently arrived from Colorado and whose magnetism HPB once remarked was "sickening."[31] Others included T. Subba Row; another new recruit, St. George Lane-Fox; and Damodar. HPB and Olcott left Adyar in February, and were accompanied by Hartmann and Madame Coulomb as far as Bombay. While staying with Prince Harisinghi Rupsinghi, Madame Coulomb again tried to borrow two thousand rupees from him; she had made an earlier attempt at the December convention. When HPB heard of this, she counseled the prince against the loan, and chided her old friend Emma for the indiscretion. It was a reprimand her friend would not forget.

THEY REACHED MARSEILLES IN MARCH. By now the group included Mohini Chatterjee, who went on to Paris, while Olcott and Blavatsky went to Nice to stay with the Countess of Caithness. The countess was a fervent Theosophist—among other interests— and had founded the French branch of the society, and it is possible that she provided the money that HPB was supposed to deliver to someone in Buffalo on her arrival in New York. The countess invited many notables, including the great astronomer Flammarion, to meet the Madame. The chums then headed to Paris too, where the countess had arranged for them to stay in a suite in the Latin Quarter near Notre Dame. Here she threw a grand fete for them at her home in the Faubourg St.-Germain, which received notices in most of the Paris papers. W. Q. Judge, on his way to India, met them there. By this time HPB was writing Sinnett, commiserating with him about the Masters' support of Kingsford, whom she didn't like (she wore too much jewelry and was a Christian). But she was also unhappy about his attempt to get Laura Holloway, an American medium who had been sent to London by KH to work with Mohini, to work for him. She told him that if he took her away from Mohini, the Masters wouldn't like it. Sinnett no doubt was interested in Holloway as a means of talking with the Masters himself.

On the way to London, Olcott shared an empty carriage with Mohini. Out of the blue—or the ceiling—a letter dropped onto the book he was reading. It was from KH, and it warned him of some trouble afoot back in Adyar. It informed him that they had "harboured a traitor and an enemy" who would help the missionaries against them.[32] What Olcott thought of this is unclear. In any case he had a lot to do already. A meeting was arranged for April 7, to elect new officers of the London Lodge. HPB had been invited to attend, but she refused. At a meeting before the elections, Anna Kingsford had accepted Olcott's offer to head her own branch, the Hermetic Theosophical Society, whose title affirmed Kingsford's preference for a Western rather than Eastern esoteric tradition— one, of course, that HPB herself was well acquainted with. This was later truncated to the Hermetic Society, which eventually

broke with the TS. In Paris, HPB told Judge that M had just given
her an extraordinary "order." She was to go to London anyway.
Why he had ordered this, she couldn't fathom, as the members
there would only think she was doing it for effect. But he had also
taken note of the train timetables, and if Judge would help, she
could just make the 7:45 express.

Whatever the Masters' designs, an effect is exactly what HPB's
appearance at the rooms in Lincoln's Inn, where the elections were
being held, produced. Accounts differ as to details. Kingsford
either decided not to run for re-election, or was defeated by a Mr.
Finch, who became president, with Sinnett a magnanimous vice
president. Among those who watched the proceedings—which
were curiously like a later event, when Gurdjieff made a dramatic
appearance among Ouspensky's London students—were C. W.
Leadbeater and F. W. H. Myers, an important member of the new
Society for Psychical Research, or SPR.[33] According to Leadbeater,
"a stout lady in black" burst into the room and took a seat. After a
few minutes fidgeting, she jumped up and shouted "Mohini," at
which Mohini Chatterjee appeared and prostrated himself at her
feet. Sinnett, who dreaded her ever coming to England, was
stunned, and after a few minutes fumbling announced to the star-
tled crowd that Madame Blavatsky was in the room. HPB asked to
see Anna Kingsford and her colleague, Edward Maitland. The two
apostates presented themselves, and Blavatsky turned her liquid
eyes on them and ordered them to make up with Sinnett. But
Kingsford was no pushover; she claimed to have killed a vivisec-
tionist by thought alone, a feat difficult to square with her Christian beliefs.[34] A showdown was imminent and Olcott, ever the
diplomat, did not want more fractures. He approached his chum

and said that he could not have her mesmerizing Dr. Kingsford. HPB laughed and the tension diffused. But not for long.

One result of the meeting was an invitation by F. W. H. Myers for Olcott to lunch with him and other members of the SPR. Olcott accepted, and investigating Madame Blavatsky and the "precipitated" letters was soon on the society's agenda. HPB wasn't impressed and referred to them as the "Spookical Research Society." But Olcott felt Myers was friendly and posed no threat. He had no idea that the SPR would bang a very big nail into the Masters' coffin, an activity that someone closer to home was engaged in back in Adyar.

MADAME COULOMB WASN'T happy that she wasn't on the Board of Control, nor that her dear friend HPB had spoiled the two thousand rupee loan. On the other hand, the Board of Control wasn't very happy with her. She appears to have fiddled with the house expenses and, perhaps even more egregiously, had made broad hints about revealing "everything" that had been going on at Adyar to anyone who would listen. Emma Coulomb appears to have been a resentful, grasping person, easy to take offense, and she had a habit of poking her nose into other people's business, as well as their mail. As Hartmann, one of her accusers, remarked, "she seemed to consider it her especial purpose in life, to pry into everybody's private affairs, pick up stray letters here and there that were not addressed to her," and if she found a sympathetic ear, she would "insinuate that the whole society was a humbug, the phenomena produced by fraud, and that 'she could tell many things, if only she wanted to do so.'"[35] Although she and Alexis had made themselves indispensable, the board, tired of their insinuations and actual misconduct, thought to dispense with them anyway, and they were asked to leave. The Coulombs refused. The Masters seemed unsure of this decision. KH first thought it best to try to soothe things, but M warned outright that Emma was collaborating with the enemy—Christian missionaries—and he also warned that her talk of "trap doors and tricks" would soon be made good: "trap doors," he wrote, "will be found."[36]

Eager to get rid of them, Hartmann offered the Coulombs a share in a silver mine in Colorado if they would go there. At first they agreed, then demanded three thousand rupees as well, explaining that if they weren't paid, incriminating letters between HPB and her dear friend would reach certain parties eager to read them. These letters, Emma explained, would show how Madame Blavatsky drew her into her scheme to "fake" the Masters, their letters, the precipitations, and their appearances, just as she had been involved in her phony séances in Cairo. Subba Row wrote to Blavatsky of this blackmail attempt. HPB assured him no such letters existed, and the demand was refused. The Coulombs then seemed to have tried to insinuate that Hartmann, Lane-Fox, and others were trying to oust HPB, and that they, her good friends, were being framed.

In May, the board officially charged the Coulombs with several counts, including misuse of funds, accusations of fraud, and blackmail, and they were expelled. They were also asked to return the key to HPB's rooms. They refused. After HPB herself cabled her regrets at developments and bid them both good luck, they relented, but only after displaying to the board the mysterious hole in HPB's room that gave access to the "occult room," and the sliding panels in the wall that opened into the shrine. In her absence, HPB had given the Coulombs the run of her rooms; Alexis was supposedly making some improvements on them. Now the Board of Control discovered exactly what those were. Hartmann remarked that the hole was clearly made very recently and that the sliding panels were stiff and noisy, an assessment with which others, who also examined them, agreed. Neither, they believed, could have been used to fake the precipitated letters, although it was clearly the Coulombs' intent that this "evidence" would prove that they were. About a week later, the Coulombs demanded ten thousand rupees in exchange for keeping quiet about these "discoveries." Again, the board refused, and the Coulombs retreated—for the time being.[37] (The Coulombs, of course, denied any accusations of blackmail or of creating the hole or sliding panels in Blavatsky's room.)

While this crisis was going on, Olcott and HPB were making a favorable impression on the SPR. In May, a committee was appointed to take evidence from TS members regarding the phenomena, and in June, at the SPR's general meeting held in Queen Anne's Mansions in London, Olcott spoke of his astral visit by M, even producing the Master's turban as proof. Strangely, this triggered an onslaught of fury from his chum; she abused him so terribly that at one point he asked if she would like him to commit suicide.[38] Our first reaction is that she was worried that if the SPR investigated the Masters, they would discover they were fake. But HPB's own remarks suggest the opposite: that she was worried that they would be shown to be real, *and their identities revealed*. She was already angry at Sinnett's *The Occult World* and *Esoteric Buddhism* because it had made the reality of the Masters common knowledge, with the result that "Nowadays people call their dogs and cats by the name of Koot Hoomi."[39] Of course, we may decide that HPB was simply afraid of being found out, but her commitment to the Masters—whoever they were—was, I believe, real, and years later she lamented that their name had become "common property" and that the "sacred names of occultism . . . have been dragged in filthy mire."[40] Whatever Olcott's mistake, at Francesca Arundale's home on Elgin Crescent, another meeting between HPB, Mohini, and Professor Henry Sidgwick, president of the SPR, went well. In his journal, Sidgwick wrote that his "favourable impression of Madame Blavatsky was maintained," calling her a "genuine being" with a "real desire for the good of mankind," and also commenting on her "flounces full of cigarette ashes."[41] At two earlier meetings at Arundale's home, members of the SPR, including Myers, had heard astral bells.[42] It seemed that, Olcott's unwitting blunder aside, the Spookical Research Society meant well by HPB.

Then disaster struck. In September, the Madras *Christian College Magazine* published an article entitled "The Collapse of Koot Hoomi," in which its author, Rev. George Patterson, revealed that the Masters and the "phenomena" associated with them were fake. Koot Hoomi himself was a cloth dummy, or, on occasion, someone dressed like him. That someone was Alexis Coulomb. Emma Coulomb had made the dummy herself. Unfortunately, in a fit of pique, after being unceremoniously banished from Adyar, she destroyed it. But the letters she had from Madame Blavatsky told the story. And now the *Christian College Magazine* was telling the world. A *Times* correspondent picked up the account and cabled it to his office in London. When she got the news, HPB was staying in

Elberfeld, Germany, with friends, the Gebhards, working on what would become *The Secret Doctrine*. She immediately wrote the *Times* denying the accusation, saying that aside from a few lines here and there, the letters in question were not written by her. She left Germany for England, and in London told reporters that she was on her way to India to sue the *Christian College Magazine* and clear her name. Olcott was already en route. On November 1, 1884, HPB, accompanied by the Cooper-Oakleys, a Theosophist couple, left for Liverpool, where they boarded the S.S. *Clan Drummond*, heading for Port Said. There they were met by C. W. Leadbeater. The group spent a few days in Cairo, gathering information about the Coulombs. They had, it appears, a history of extortion and general underhandedness, or so at least HPB had discovered. She had cabled Olcott: "Success complete. Outlaws. Legal proofs." HPB was confident she could trump her old friend. But when she finally arrived in Adyar in December, she found another worry. Richard Hodgson, whom she had met while in London, had been sent by the SPR to investigate the phenomena associated with the Masters. He couldn't have come at a worse time.

He had arrived two days earlier and was refused entry to the "occult room" by Damodar; it was, after all, part of HPB's private chambers, so his reluctance is understandable. Then when HPB arrived, Hodgson asked to see the shrine. Damodar explained that it had first been removed to his room, and then inexplicably burned by Hartmann. The hole in the wall from her room to the occult room was also plastered over. If the Coulombs had fixed things so that HPB would appear a fake, the board's actions after discovering this had only thrown fuel on the fire. Subsequent conversations between HPB and Hodgson led Blavatsky to believe that his attitude was hostile. She was correct. In essence, Hodgson bought the Coulombs' story lock, stock, and barrel, and when his report was finally published the following year, he concluded that Madame Blavatsky was, among other things, "one of the most accomplished, ingenious, and interesting impostors in history." She was also most likely a Russian spy.[43]

BUT BEFORE HODGSON'S REPORT was made known, HPB had other problems to deal with. Even though she believed she had sufficient evidence to clear her name and that of the Masters, at the TS convention that year it was decided that taking the matter to court was not a good idea. Several reasons were given for their decision, but the central one, aside from the timidity of the committee in charge, was that the case would give their enemies an opportunity to "injure the cause of Theosophy," and that, if asked questions about the Mahatmas that the Mahatmas had forbidden her to answer, HPB could be charged with contempt of court. No doubt HPB felt plenty of contempt, and not only for the legal system. She fumed, but Olcott and the others held firm. Then the Colonel left for a tour of Burma, leaving his chum on her own. She fell ill and, as in Philadelphia, felt she was near death and made out a will. But once again, a visit from Master Morya revived her. He gave her a choice: She could die now and enjoy a well-deserved rest, or live a few more years and complete *The Secret Doctrine*, which she had begun during her stay in Paris. Yet the stress and scandal were proving too much, and the fact that she wasn't allowed to defend herself in court must have drained her already depleted reserves.

General H. R. Morgan, whom HPB had met in Ootacamund

and who had witnessed the "precipitated" mending of a broken saucer at Adyar, had declared publicly that the "Coulomb letters" were
forgeries.[44] Madame Coulomb's solicitor threatened a libel suit,
but he stood firm, and she relented. But why would she, if the letters were genuine? Perhaps one reason is that, had she sued him,
the letters would have been produced in court, which would have
given the defendants an opportunity to examine them. They never
were, nor were any of the so-called "incriminating" passages ever
made available to public scrutiny.[45] Hodgson himself refused to
show HPB the ones he had in his possession, and she never had an
opportunity to examine the "evidence" against her. The "incriminating" letters themselves have vanished—much like the supposed
"dummy" of Koot Hoomi—and to this day it has never been proved
that Blavatsky wrote them.[46]

Ill, weary, and abandoned, Blavatsky nevertheless remained
fearless and would have taken on an army to clear her Masters'
names, and her own. By this time, in addition to the "incriminating" letters, Emma Coulomb had also produced a pamphlet outlin-
ing in detail HPB's nefarious acts, which included, among other
things, the claim that she had had illegitimate children in Cairo.[47]
And Hodgson seemed to have taken it as his mission not merely to
examine HPB's claims about the Masters and phenomena, but to
turn her Hindu allies against her. (In fact, he never investigated
any phenomena, merely gathered reports about them from others.)
Through his efforts, HPB became a liability to Adyar, and many
felt the society, at least in India, would be better off without her.

No doubt Blavatsky's fiery temper would have worked against
her had she gone to the courts on her own, and she only relented
when Olcott threatened to resign from the society if she did. Her

own departure would be a blow, but without Olcott, everything she had spent a decade working toward would collapse. Her doctor had in any case ordered her to avoid any excitement and to find "perfect quiet and a suitable climate" in order to recover. That meant Europe. So for a second time, Madame Blavatsky said farewell to an adopted home. After resigning from her office as corresponding secretary, on March 31, 1885, accompanied by Hartmann, a Hindu recruit called Babaji, and a visitor to Adyar named Mary Flynn, HPB left India for good. By this time, her health was so poor that she could not use the gangway and had to be hoisted on board in a wheelchair.

NINE

SECRET DOCTRINES
ON THE ROAD

H PB and her party landed at Naples on April 12, 1885 (some sources have April 23), but Italy was only the starting point of a new life of wandering. She stayed briefly at the Hotel del Vesuvio in Torre del Greco, an apt perch for so volcanic a character, with a view of the Bay of Naples and Mount Vesuvius, but found the place cold and uncomfortable and was eager to move on. The essential thing was to find somewhere congenial to work. All she had left now was to finish *The Secret Doctrine*. Working on that kept her alive. She had turned down an offer from her Russian publisher, Mikhail Katkov, to write exclusively for him, a deal that would have "put yearly 40,000 francs at least" in her pocket.[1] She certainly could have used the money, as she was now dependent on a small pension from the TS for her needs. But, as with the offer to do a follow-up to *Isis Unveiled*, Master had said no; she had to concentrate on her real work. Where best to do that was the question. She wanted to avoid any of the European capitals; all she needed, she told Sinnett, was a warm, dry room. She decided to move to Würzburg in northern Bavaria, as it was near to Nuremberg and Heidelberg, where KH had once lived. She wanted to "remain in the shadows," but being solitary was always difficult, and she found herself flooded with guests. Her only helper now was Babaji—the others in her party had left—and he was little use with visitors and correspondence. Another Olcott would have helped, but the chums had taken separate paths. HPB wrote to her friend Mary Gebhard in Elberfeld about her plight, and Mary suggested to a friend, the Swedish Countess Constance Wachtmeister, that she delay her proposed trip to Italy and visit HPB in Würzburg.[2]

The countess had already met HPB in London the year before, at Sinnett's house, where she had also met Mary Gebhard. She had joined the TS in 1880 after reading *Isis Unveiled*. She had been interested in Spiritualism but found Theosophy a revelation. During a later meeting with HPB in Enghien, Belgium, Blavatsky had told Wachtmeister that within two years she would devote her life completely to Theosophy, a prediction Wachtmeister strongly doubted. Now it seemed to have come true.

When the countess wrote HPB proposing a monthlong visit, Blavatsky refused, saying she was too busy working to receive guests. Yet when Wachtmeister was about to leave for Italy, a telegram arrived. It was from HPB. She had changed her mind and the countess was to come immediately. The tactic, if it was one, again reminds us of Gurdjieff, who regularly changed his plans at the last moment. Wachtmeister went, and until Blavatsky's death, she remained her constant companion.

According to the countess, Blavatsky was a hard worker. HPB rose at six, and was at her desk by seven, where she worked until one, when she had a brief lunch, and was back at work until seven

P.M. To relax she played Patience (solitaire) or read magazines and newspapers, mostly Russian, or the occasional French novel, and was in bed by nine. And like Olcott and Hiram Corson, Wachtmeister became privy to HPB's peculiar method of composition. Again Blavatsky seemed to carry an enormous library in her head. Wachtmeister speaks of the "poverty of her travelling library," and of "manuscripts . . . overflowing with references, quotations, allusions" that couldn't be accounted for by the books on hand.[3] On one occasion, HPB asked her to verify a passage that she had taken "astrally" from the Vatican Library. Wachtmeister had a friend with a relative in the Vatican; he verified the passage, even mentioning that the two words HPB had got wrong were nearly indecipherable in the original text.[4]

Wachtmeister was also witness to another aspect of HPB's character that again reminds us of Gurdjieff. Already, at her first meeting, Wachtmeister had experienced difficulties and delays in getting to HPB that she later realized were part of a "probation," something other followers of Blavatsky also encountered.[5] Now, in Würzburg, she saw that she had been "a petted child of fortune," and that her late husband's political position—he was minister of foreign affairs—had given her "a prominent place in society." "It took me a long time to realize the hollowness of what I had hitherto looked upon as being the most desirable objects in life," she wrote, "and it required much training and many a hard battle with myself before I could conquer the satisfaction in self which a life of idleness, ease and high position is sure to engender."[6] As HPB told her, a great deal had to be "knocked out" of her, and no doubt living with Blavatsky did precisely that. "The knowledge of Self," the countess wrote, "was gradually acquired by those who lived in daily contact

with her." Accounts by followers of Gurdjieff, who made things uncomfortable for everyone around him, say practically the same thing.

It was a difficult time for the countess's teacher. While at Würzburg, HPB received Hodgson's report, and when she did, the effect
was crushing. The karma of the TS had fallen on her, she told the
countess in despair, and now she had to pay for the "cursed phenomena," which she only produced to "please private friends and
instruct those around me." She told her friend to leave "before you
are defiled by my shame. . . . You cannot stop here with a ruined
woman."[7] "Letters," Wachtmeister wrote, "came in containing
nothing but recrimination and abuse, resignation of fellows, and
apathy and fear." And those who didn't resign were "paralyzed . . .
all they wanted . . . was to keep quiet and out of sight, so that no
mud should be thrown at them." Babaji and Mohini both turned
against her, but one of the hardest blows came from T. Subba Row.
He broke with his teacher, saying she had brought shame upon
India and had betrayed its deepest secrets to the unworthy. She
was, he said, "guilty of the most terrible of crimes. You have given
out secrets of Occultism—the most sacred and the most hidden.
Rather *that you should be sacrificed* than that which was never
meant for European minds." By this time, Subba Row had moved
to a more fundamentalist position, arguing that the Masters and
their knowledge belonged to Hindus alone.

It was a painful recrimination, but Blavatsky agreed with him.
She said her path was one of suffering, and in one sense she was glad
that Hodgson's "exposé" had made her a "trickster and imposter"
in the eyes of many. It that way, she told a correspondent, "the
whole burden falls upon me, as the Masters are made out to be
myths. So much the better. Their names have been desecrated too

long and too much." If necessary, she told Sinnett, she would "proclaim publicly that *I alone* was a liar, a forger, all that Hodgson wants me to appear" in order to "screen the real KH and M from opprobrium." She was on the "way of blame" and she accepted it.

Yet Subba Row's complaint was not that HPB was a fraud, as the Hodgson-Coulomb accusations argued, and as Babaji, Mohini, and others now believed, but that she divulged "things most sacred and holy that had never been known to the profane before." It was a criticism she herself made of Sinnett, whose books "thrust occultism and its mysteries into the teeth of a prejudiced unprepared public."[8] Yet this was exactly the concern of the "right wing" occult groups we met in Chapter 5, who argued against disseminating occult knowledge freely, and of Koot Hoomi, who refused Sinnett's request to have a copy of *The Pioneer* "precipitated" to London on the day of its publication. It is also, since time immemorial, the charge brought against initiates who divulge holy secrets to the uninitiated. Blavatsky's fiercely democratic temperament compelled her to share what she knew with anyone who showed a serious interest in it. She may have been wrong in this, and she may have been in many ways a poor judge of character. Many she let close to her proved, as Alice Leighton Cleather said of Sinnett, "inherently incapable" of understanding her.[9] We can chalk this up to HPB's essentially trusting nature, which is not the temperament associated with fraudsters and confidence men, who are fundamentally suspicious of others. But it did cause her a lot of trouble.

A DETAILED DISCUSSION of the Hodgson Report warrants more space than I can grant it here. Since its publication in December

1885, it's been subject to numerous criticisms, pointing out its flaws, omissions, prejudice, and bias, and arguing that Hodgson's claim that HPB's "real object" in her Masters and phenomena was "the furtherance of Russian interests" in India, was itself motivated by his own loyalty to the Crown.[10] Through her Russian publisher Katkov, Blavatsky *did* have connections to influential Russians who *were* interested in the idea of a "Russian Asia," as K. Paul Johnson's research has made known. And she did make remarks that *could* be read as supportive of Russia's designs on the subcontinent— but could also be read in other ways. Yet the trigger for Hodgson's conviction that she was, after all, a Russian agent, was her concern over the movement of Russian troops in Afghanistan, which seemed to presage a possible invasion of India. Such a development would, she told Hodgson, "be the death blow of the society." Hodgson read—or misread—this remark as a "blind," to obscure her "real" feelings for such an action. As Sylvia Cranston remarks, Hodgson "could not imagine that her reaction was one of genuine concern for the welfare of the Theosophical Movement."[11] This suggests Hodgson had already made up his mind that HPB was a spy, and was on the lookout for "evidence." But Blavatsky was no more interested in a "Russian Asia," than she was in a "British" or "Hindu" one, and she remarked on more than one occasion that, although the British Raj was bad for India, the Russians "would be a thousand times worse."[12] Like her Masonic antecedents, her vision was international—global, we would say—and concerned a brotherhood of *humanity*, not of Russians, Englishmen, or Hindus.

It's to be expected that friends and followers of HPB would naturally defend her against accusations of fraud, but perhaps the most damning blow against Hodgson's report came not from a Theosophist, but from the SPR itself. In 1986, a century after Hodgson's report appeared, the SPR issued a press release announcing that "Madame Blavatsky, Co-Founder of the Theosophical Society, Was Unjustly Condemned," and declaring that the validity of Hodgson's work was "in serious doubt."[13] Vernon Harrison, a forgery expert and past president of the Royal Photographic Society, examined Hodgson's work and concluded that Hodgson was "prepared to use any evidence, however trivial or questionable, to implicate HPB," and "ignored all evidence that could be used in her favour." "His report," Harrison argued, "is riddled with slanted statements, conjecture advanced as fact or probable fact, uncorroborated testimony of unnamed witnesses, selection of evidence and downright falsity." And he concludes that "The Hodgson Report is not, as has been widely believed for more than a century, a model of what impartial and painstaking research should be: it is the work of a man who has reached his conclusions early on in his investigation and thereafter, selecting and distorting evidence, did not hesitate to adopt flawed arguments to support his thesis." One result of Harrison's efforts is that the SPR itself has disclaimed responsibility for Hodgson's work, in effect saying that the Society did not investigate HPB, only Hodgson, and that he is solely responsible for his conclusions, a somewhat Jesuitical way of sidestepping blame for any possible mistakes. (It is also a means of smoothing over differences between the Theosophical Society and the SPR, both of which share more than a few members.) This maneuver does, however, seem to affirm the remark by Leslie Price, a member of the SPR's Library Committee, that "any writer or speaker who says the SPR exposed Madame Blavatsky is only exposing his own ignorance."[14]

Unfortunately, this disclaimer has not filtered down to many researchers outside the Theosophical fold. In her otherwise brilliant account of the SPR, *Ghost Hunters*, Deborah Blum makes no mention of its retraction of Hodgson's report, and applauds it as his "demolishing a medium's reputation."[15] The idea is not that Vernon Harrison's investigations vindicate HPB completely, a claim some HPB supporters themselves reject, and which we shall return to further on. But it does, I think, show the flaws and prejudices in it. In terms of the British justice system, Harrison's "evidence" would be enough to warrant HPB at least a retrial, and would very likely support a verdict of "unproven" against the charges of fraud, rescinding the earlier one as "unsound." Blum's book, however, does make clear one of the motivations at work in Hodgson's "exposé": the fear members of the SPR had of being seen as "gullible dupes."[16] In *Natural and Supernatural*, Brian Inglis makes the same point: that for much of its history, the SPR adopted a highly defensive attitude and was determined to show that it wouldn't be fooled by any fraudulent activities, resulting in an overly critical and suspicious approach to its material. Given the reductive, dismissive, materialist science of the time—which is still our own—this is perhaps understandable, but it argues that on many, perhaps most occasions, the SPR and its agents began their investigations with the determination that they would not be "fooled." This suggests that they also began them with the suspicion that the mediums under investigation were, more than likely, out to fool them, which is hardly an unbiased attitude. Inglis points out that

Hodgson's investigation of the medium Eusapia Palladino was also highly flawed.[17] Ironically, in the end, Hodgson himself came to believe in the reality of spirit communication.[18]

IN 1886, HPB decided to escape Würzburg's summer heat and move to Ostend, on the Belgian coast. The countess was in Sweden on business, and HPB was accompanied by Emily Kislingbury, an English Theosophist she knew from the early days in New York. Kislingbury had read Hodgson's report and was so outraged that she came to help. In Cologne, Rudolf Gebhard met the party and they decided to spend a few days in Elberfeld, but practically on arrival HPB slipped and sprained her ankle and was bedridden for two months. Her sister, Vera, arrived, and by July they had moved on to Ostend, where Vera left to return to Russia. Here HPB was alone until the countess arrived at the end of August, and she spent her time working on *The Secret Doctrine*. By this time it was extremely painful for her to walk, and she only felt well when she was sitting and writing.[19]

When Countess Wachtmeister arrived, the two decided not to return to Würzburg but to stay in Ostend, where they took a spacious suite, which included a piano, on the rue de l'Ouest. For exercise, the countess wheeled HPB along the sea front in a "bath chair," a kind of early wheelchair. Here they were visited by Theosophists from England, among them Anna Kingsford and Edward Maitland. Kingsford's own health was always poor, and she would die two years later from pneumonia after getting caught in the rain on the way to the Pasteur Institute in Paris.

Another visitor, Friedrich Eckstein, a Viennese Theosophist, was a friend of Rudolf Steiner, at that time a Goethe scholar. It was through Eckstein that Steiner read Sinnett's *Esoteric Buddhism*.[20] Work on *The Secret Doctrine* continued, although HPB's fussiness over materials caused some problems. The ink in Ostend didn't meet her standards and, as she had years before in Russia, she developed her own. She was apparently so successful that she built up a small business. When a poor woman came to their door asking for money, finding her pockets empty, Blavatsky is said to have given her the deed to the business. An item in a Russian paper also gave HPB some amusement. In the fall of 1886, the St. Petersburg newspaper *Listok* ran an article entitled "The Mysterious Hand," in which Madame Blavatsky's "astral hand" was said to have saved a critic of her work from being crushed by a roof that had collapsed after being struck by lightning. Blavatsky herself had no recollection of the event, and her aunt wondered if one of the Masters was involved. Even without her participation, it seemed stories of her miraculous powers were still making news.

A more significant development was a conversation HPB had with her Master around the New Year, in which she was informed that the TS was going through its own "probation," a "final and supreme trial" that would determine its future. Her own destiny was a choice between returning to India to die, or forming a new school of "true Theosophists," which she would run alone, and in which she would gather "as many mystics as I can get." She could do it there, in Ostend, or elsewhere, even in London. Oddly, some of her visitors from England were contemplating just that. Bertram and Archibald Keightley, two Cambridge graduates, told her of their dissatisfaction with the London Lodge. A "deadness" had come over it, which they felt her presence would dissipate. They were also unhappy with Sinnett's approach; he was determined to make Theosophy an upper-class pursuit, an idea he had tried in India, and they, like Blavatsky, believed it should be available to everyone. Not surprisingly, Sinnett himself was opposed to her coming to London. By this time, his *Incidents in the Life of Madame Blavatsky* had appeared, a work that more or less begins the "disinformation industry" around her. Too some extent it helped rehabilitate her reputation—it got some good reviews—although John Symonds thought it "one of the worst biographies ever written," a judgment some readers may share.[21] (Certainly some of Sinnett's contemporaries did: Alice Leighton Cleather believed it aimed "at destroying entirely the bona fides of HPB," and portrayed her as an "ordinary medium, and a fraudulent one at that."[22]) But it also sparked renewed interest in the Coulomb-Hodgson scandal. Blavatsky herself was half-hearted about the project, on which she collaborated with Sinnett, and was again unhappy with its accounts of her contact with the Masters and his obsession with phenomena. Sinnett was by this time determined to be an esoteric source on his own, and having the "old lady" around again would only cause trouble.

Yet trouble was exactly what HPB wanted. She accused Sinnett of leading the London Lodge into a state of "lethargy," and predicted that within another year it would be "covered over with moss and slime."[23] She, however, was a rolling stone, and whether he liked it or not, she was heading across the Channel. Other members of the London Lodge practically begged her to come; she was touched by their need and consented. Her plan was to leave Ostend for London at the end of March, and stay through the summer.

Countess Wachtmeister had decided to sell her property in Sweden, and would join her after that. But then another crisis appeared.

Blavatsky had lamented her fate to the countess repeatedly. She
was "traduced, slandered, not by strangers, but by those . . . most
attached to me, and whom I really love." She was "tired of life
and the struggles of that stone of Sisyphus" and was "wretched
because . . . there is not a corner on this earth where I could be left
to die quietly."[24] Perhaps some angel heard her. Just before she was
to leave for England, HPB was found unconscious in her chair. She
had been feeling "drowsy and heavy" during the day, and a doctor
diagnosed kidney malfunction. Wachtmeister brought in a "sister
of charity," but she brandished her crucifix and told HPB it was not
too late to repent, and was little help. Mary Gebhard fared better,
but HPB was unable to stay conscious, and a Belgian doctor
remarked that he "had never known a case of a person with kidneys
attacked as HPB's were, living as long as she had." The countess
said that her friend had been "compelled to remain in a form which
should have disintegrated two years previously in Adyar," a remark
that again reminds us of Gurdjieff.[25] Ashton Ellis, a London doctor
and Theosophist, was called in. He massaged her organs, which
seemed to help. But everyone thought the end was nigh, and agreed
that she should once again make out her will. She did, and left
"everything" to the countess. When a lawyer contested this, Mary
Gebhard pointed out that "everything" wouldn't have covered her
funeral expenses.

That night, the countess could smell "the peculiar faint odour
of death," and HPB herself told her friend that she was glad to die,
and that "Master would let her be free at last." It seems he had
other plans. When Wachtmeister woke the next morning—having

fallen asleep during her vigil—HPB was sitting up in bed, asking for breakfast, apparently completely recovered. The Master had come to her in the night, she said, and had given her yet another choice: Die here in Ostend or live a few more years and finish *The Secret Doctrine*. According to Wachtmeister, the doctor could only repeat, "But she should be dead." Blavatsky herself asked for coffee and cigarettes.

THE LONDON BLAVATSKY sailed to in May 1887 was the London of gaslight, Queen Victoria, Sherlock Holmes, Dr. Jekyll and Mr. Hyde, and, shortly after she arrived, Jack the Ripper.[26] Her health was not good, and at Dover, after the crossing from Ostend, she had to be carried out of her cabin and onto the train. HPB wasn't the only thing that had to be carried. Blavatsky rarely traveled light—Wachtmeister speaks of the numerous packages that accompanied her in railway carriages—and to this burden was added the growing manuscript of *The Secret Doctrine*, which, at this point, was a three-foot-high stack of densely written pages. Bertram Keightley recalls that HPB worked until the very end, and that no sooner was some item packed away, than she demanded it be unpacked so she could check a reference.

This nonstop writing carried on almost immediately after they arrived at Maycott, the cottage of the Theosophist Mabel Collins in the London suburb of Norwood, where HPB spent her first months in England. Collins, a traveler, novelist, and journalist, is known today as the "scribe" of the Theosophical classic *Light on the Path*, published in 1885. The place was small—HPB compared those living there to "herring in a barrel"—and Blavatsky's few visitors had to sit on her bed. Relations with Mabel Collins, too, were not the best. Unlike HPB, Collins led an active sex life, which included lesbianism, and at one point HPB berated her for carrying on affairs with two Theosophical recruits simultaneously. Yeats tells the story of how Blavatsky, displeased by Collins's promiscuity, berated her, insisting at length that, in order to achieve initiation, one must crush the animal nature and live in chastity, to which she added with perfect timing, "but I cannot permit you more than one"—lover, that is. A more serious fracture occurred when Collins, caught up in a leadership feud within the society, retracted her statement that *Light on the Path* was "dictated" by one of HPB's Masters—Hilarion Smerdis, to be precise—and that she herself was only their channel.[27] She now took full credit for the work, casting doubt on the Masters and HPB. Blavatsky retaliated by calling her a "mystical vampire," and making statements injudicious enough to prompt a libel suit.[28] When HPB's lawyer showed Collins's counsel a certain letter—whose contents remain unknown—the suit was dropped; until the end, HPB had a curious habit of getting into these legal disputes, which only wasted her time and drained her energies. Collins was eventually expelled from the society.[29]

In September 1887, HPB moved on to the Keightleys' home at 17 Landsdowne Road, in London's Holland Park. By this time, the Blavatsky Lodge of the Theosophical Society had started, and many from Sinnett's group left to join it. One of its first acts was to start a magazine, *Lucifer*, which HPB edited, and whose title, as mentioned earlier, suggests her self-image as a kind of "fallen angel." (Predictably, the Anglican Church had it banned from newsstands.) An early issue announced HPB's new "zero tolerance" policy toward phenomena. As in the past, phenomena were only accepted as "miracles, works of the Devil, vulgar tricks, or performances of 'spooks'"; now she would have no part in them. Instead, she was only interested in teaching ideas. "An occultist," she wrote, "can produce phenomena, but he cannot supply the world with brains, nor with the intelligence . . . to understand and appreciate them." It was now time, she said, to "let the ideas of Theosophy stand on their own intrinsic merits."[30] Blavatsky had a nondogmatic approach to editing; she even serialized Franz Hartmann's satiric novel *The Talking Image of URUR*, which poked fun at Theosophists and referred to HPB herself as "mediumistic poll-parrot."

One thing she intended to stand on its own intrinsic merit was *The Secret Doctrine*, the towering pile of which she now handed over to the Keightleys to clean up. They were told to "do what you like with it." Given the size and chaotic state of the manuscript— it was, Bertram Keightley remarked, "without plan, structure, or arrangement"—this was a dangerous suggestion. It was, the Keightleys believed, a great philosophical work, but careful revision would be needed because as it stood now—literally—it was, as Countess Wachtmeister commented, "another *Isis Unveiled*, only far worse."[31] As Wachtmeister politely understated, HPB was "constitutionally . . . unfitted for the task of orderly and patient exposition of her teachings."[32] The Keightleys took it in hand and arranged for a typist—brave soul—to make a clean copy. When they finally managed to get a coherent text to the printers, HPB's changes were relentless. She racked up a three-hundred-pound bill for correcting proofs—a huge sum those days—and had the compositor "tearing his hair out in blank dismay."[33]

At Landsdowne Road, HPB received many visitors, and on

Thursday nights the Blavatsky Lodge held its meetings there, basically an informal Q&A session with the Madame. Alice Leighton Cleather remembered a "double drawing room" in which "a stout, middle-aged woman" (Blavatsky was fifty-six) sat at a card table, playing solitaire. Her rooms were filled with Indian souvenirs and other exotic bric-a-brac, a kind of encore of the Lamasery. She told Cleather that she worked twenty-four hours a day: "in this body all day, in another one, all night."[34] She told Yeats, another visitor, the same thing. "I write, write, write," she said, "as the Wandering Jew walks, walks, walks."[35] Yeats thought she had an "air of humour and audacious power," and some of her remarks suggest it was probably fun being around her. Yeats recalled that her cuckoo clock "hooted" at him, although it seemed clearly broken. After explaining that she had mistaken him for a visitor who thought the earth was flat, she told him not to break her clock. (Wachtmeister speaks of a similar clock with "streams of electric light" radiating from it.[36]) When Yeats remarked on her card playing, she replied "a person of genius has to do something; Sarah Bernhardt sleeps in her coffin."[37] He describes her sitting at a table covered with green baize—the material covering a pool table—on which she would scribble occult symbols in chalk. She was "impatient with abstract piety" and had little time for fools. She told one gullible devotee that the earth was shaped like a dumbbell, and that another globe was stuck to it at the North Pole. Another was informed that "Yes, you have the divine spark within you, and if you are not very careful you will hear it snore."[38] But there was wisdom, too. "Nothing mattered but what happened in the mind," she told the poet. "If we cannot master the mind, our actions are of little importance."[39] Another visitor was her old chum, the Colonel, who believed that "the fact of her being alive at all was in itself a miracle," a sign, perhaps, that the kind of mastery she spoke to Yeats about was in her grasp.

THE FALL OF 1888 saw some momentous developments in Blavatsky's work. One was the founding of what she called the Esoteric Section of the TS. An announcement for this appeared in *Lucifer*. The Esoteric Section, it said, would focus on "the deeper study of esoteric philosophy," and its direction and leadership would be solely in the hands of HPB.[40] Its activities and material were to be kept secret. Blavatsky wrote a series of confidential instructions that were copied—not printed—by members and distributed to others. There was a screening process and only serious applicants were considered. According to one member, "tests" included visits by a Master on the "inner planes."[41] Blavatsky said that the reason she started the Esoteric Section (or ES)— encouraged in the idea by W. Q. Judge—was that there was a great deal that she could not communicate, either in *Lucifer* or *The Secret Doctrine*. Out of those who joined, if she could "place on the right and true path half a dozen or so," she could die happy.[42] Here was her attempt to fulfill the Master's wish that she form a new school of "true Theosophists" with as "many mystics as she could get."

The general aim of the ES was to "prepare and fit the student for the study of practical occultism, or Raj Yoga." This did not mean, however, learning how to produce phenomena or developing magical powers. Except under special circumstances, these were forbidden. What was aimed at was "knowledge of SELF, of the psycho-physiological processes (taking place on the occult plane) in the human body generally," which demanded control and discipline of the "lower passions" and the "PERSONAL SELF." HPB herself, she said, was only the mouthpiece for the real head of the section, which was one of the adepts, although applicants were advised not to worry about which one that was, as it really didn't matter. What was important was that all work was done under the occult law which guaranteed that one receives enlightenment insofar as one deserves it. This depended on the applicant's ability to assimilate the teachings and make them part of his life, his work for humanity, and the Universal Brotherhood, not for personal gain.[43]

Not many made the grade, at least in the beginning. In the first group of "Instructions," Blavatsky reminded members of the "strange law in Occultism," which ensures that, as soon as one pledges oneself to the path, "everything latent" in oneself rises up and confronts one. All vices, vanities, sensuality, and ambitions that we normally keep under wraps appear more powerfully than before, and one is compelled to kill them before taking another step. It was an idea she borrowed from Bulwer-Lytton, who speaks of the "Dweller of the Threshold" in *Zanoni*, and which Rudolf Steiner would also use, and in more recent times appears under the Jungian notion of "the shadow."[44] HPB felt compelled to remind her probationers about this, as, she lamented, "in the last three months . . . several of the most promising candidates have failed ignominiously."[45]

HPB's "Esoteric Instructions" begin with a detailed discussion of the axioms "know thyself" and "as above, so below," in their relation to cosmic and human anatomy.[46] But for many, the other momentous, more exoteric development of this time was really quite esoteric enough. In October 1888 volume 1 of *The Secret*

Doctrine appeared; volume 2 followed that January. As a commercial publisher couldn't be found, with money from the Keightleys and with the countess at its head, the Theosophical Publishing Company was formed. A first run of five hundred copies sold out on subscription—what we today call "pre-order"—and another printing did the same. But if readers of *Isis Unveiled* found HPB's first major work tough going, this second *magnum opus* was even more daunting. It was more mammoth than its predecessor; even so, it was "only quite a small fragment of the Esoteric Doctrine known to the higher members of the Occult Brotherhoods." But its content was baffling. Even HPB herself said that reading it "page by page . . . will only end in confusion," a remark that could apply to other esoteric tomes.[47] Some, however, may think that reading it in any way will do that, and perhaps we cannot blame them.

The Secret Doctrine purports to be a commentary on stanzas from the mysterious *Book of Dzyan*, an unknown text written in an unknown language, Senzar, which, we know, HPB learned, along with English, while studying with Koot Hoomi. It is the "old book" she refers to at the beginning of *Isis Unveiled* and it is the source of the Eastern and Western "wisdom traditions" that have come down to us. What the two volumes of *The Secret Doctrine*, "Cosmogenesis" and "Anthropogenesis," amount to is a cosmic history of man and the universe. The "Rounds," "Root" and "Sub" races of the Mahatma Letters and Sinnett's *Esoteric Buddhism* appear again, but now in complex detail, and it's unfortunate that some of HPB's remarks about the merits of different races, both contemporary and ancient, are what most people know about *The Secret Doctrine*, if they know anything about it at all. In our hypersensitive age, this isn't surprising; we are quick to judge others by our own contemporary views, however anachronistic that may be. Yet the fact that some of Blavatsky's ideas were picked up by outright racist thinkers, and that Theosophists used the swastika, an ancient sun symbol, decades before the Nazis did, clearly doesn't help.

HPB was undoubtedly a "child of her time," and race was an idea central to much nineteenth-century thought, hers included. It's not surprising that some of her remarks about "Sub Races" elicit a cringe. But she can't be held responsible for how some outright racially oriented occultists misused some of her ideas. These ideas themselves, in fact, form only a small part of her total worldview, and appeared in their more extreme form only after her death. I have no doubt that had Blavatsky been alive at the time, she would have fought fiercely to disassociate Theosophy from this abuse, just as she did from any other.

Perhaps the most well-known example of this racist appropriation is the "Ariosophy" associated with Guido von List and Jörg Lanz von Liebenfels, which arose in Austria in the early twentieth century, in the years leading up to World War I. Guido von List was a Viennese poet, journalist, mountaineer, and occultist devoted to reviving German paganism through the mystic power of the ancient runes. In 1902, following a cataract operation, List was near-blind for eleven months. During this time he had a vision of the "Armanen Futharkh." This was an "alphabet" of eighteen runes—ancient German letters—which, he said, opened his "inner eye." In *The Secret of the Runes* (1906) and other books, List promoted "Armanism," a *völkisch*, "Aryan," pan-Germanic philosophy, based on the ancient worship of the "sun-kings," the priestly caste of the Ario-Germanic nation. List drew many admirers, one of whom was Jörg Lanz von Liebenfels, an ex-Cistercian monk, who was also, with Franz Hartmann and many others, a member of the Guido von List Society. Liebenfels, also Viennese, started a magazine, *Ostara*, named after the German pagan goddess of spring. Inspired by the Knights Templar and German paganism, and borrowing elements from Theosophy, Liebenfels promoted a racial, anti-Semitic occultism, which he called "Ariosophy," the "wisdom of the Aryans." This was centered on the belief that "blue blond" Aryans were *Gottmenschen*, "God-men," natural masters of the earth, with the "lower races" and "dark skinned beast men," their natural subjects. In 1904, Liebenfels published a book, *Theozoologie*, arguing this point in detail and suggesting the sterilization and elimination of the sick "sub-men." (Oddly, in his "inspired" text *The Book of the Law*, "dictated" to him in the same year by the extradimensional being "Aiwass," the magician Aleister Crowley was receiving very similar advice.[48])

One regular reader of *Ostara* was an unemployed artist named Adolf Hitler, who subsequently left Vienna for Munich. There, in 1918, a German-Turkish occultist named Rudolf Sebottendorf started the *Thulegesellschaft*, or "Thule Society." "Thule" is a mythical city beyond the North Pole, in a land of mild climate the Greeks called "Hyperborea," "beyond the north wind," a name Blavatsky herself would borrow. The Thule Society was a German-Aryan heritage "study group" with radical right-wing anti-Semitic leanings, and its outlook was influenced by List and Liebenfels. It was very successful and attracted some important figures, such as the evolutionary philosopher Ernst Haeckel, whose ideas influenced both C. G. Jung and Rudolf Steiner. Another member was Rudolf Hess, who would become a high-ranking Nazi. One thing the *Thulegesellschaft*, the Nazis, and the Theosophical Society

undeniably had in common was the swastika. It appears on the
Thule emblem, emblazoned with a dagger, and also in the "Theosophical seal," along with, it should be said, an Egyptian ankh, a
Star of Solomon, the Ouroboros Serpent, and the Sanskrit symbol
for the mystic sound *Om*.

Another member of the Thule Society was Anton Drexler, who
in 1919 started the German Workers Party (DAP). Although Hitler himself did not join the Thule Society, he did join Drexler's
organization, and in due time this became the National Socialist
German Workers Party, or Nazis, for short. Another reader of
Ostara was Dietrich Eckart, Drexler's colleague, who took Hitler
under his wing and, perhaps more than anyone else, was responsible for initiating his rise to power. Later, when the National Social-
ists were in control, both Liebenfels and Sebottendorf tried to
claim credit for the Führer. Hitler took *Ostara* off the newsstands
and banned Liebenfels from publishing, and he had Sebottendorf
arrested. The links between Hitler, the Thule Society, Liebenfels,
List, and much more form the essence of "occult Nazism," by now
a staple genre of modern esotericism.[49]

But whatever we may think of Blavatsky's ideas, she cannot be
held to account for the way in which List and Liebenfels may have
used some of them, nor for whatever "trickle-down effect" their
work may have had on subsequent events in German history, if any.
In many ways, Blavatsky is in the same position that the philosopher Nietzsche occupied, before serious scholars cleared him of his
own appropriation by the Nazis, a false association it took some
time to dissolve. Someone needs to do the same for HPB; the taint
of "racist" clings to her while her more positive influence—on, for
example, someone like Gandhi, which we will look at shortly—is

usually ignored. As I've tried to make clear in this book, paramount on Blavatsky's agenda was the formation of a Universal
Brotherhood, an idea that appealed to Gandhi, and which is not, I
think, on most racist agendas. And it should also be clear that two
white Westerners living among, learning from, and celebrating
Hindus, Sikhs, and Sinhalese, while avoiding their Anglo brothers,
is not particularly racist either.[50]

LIKE ISIS UNVEILED, *The Secret Doctrine* does not admit of easy
summary, and the reader daunted by its length should try Michael
Gomes's excellent abridgement.[51] It establishes, Blavatsky tells us,
three fundamental propositions, any one of which provides much
food for thought. They are:

1. The existence of one absolute Reality, which precedes all
   manifestation and transcends our ability to say anything
   meaningful about it. This is the *sunyatta*, or "void" of
   Mahayana Buddhism, the "Neti-Neti," "not this, not that"
   of the Upanishads, the "negative theology" of Meister Eck-
   hart, and the *Ungrund* of Jacob Boehme. It is, in essence, the
   "rootless root" of everything.
2. The eternity of the universe as a "boundless plane," in which
   an irrevocable "law of periodicity," the "ebb and flow" of cre-
   ation/destruction is ceaselessly at work, bringing worlds into
   manifestation and passing them out of it.
3. The identity of every soul with the Oversoul, a universal aspect of the unknown root of being, which compels
   all souls—or "monads"—to take the evolutionary journey

through all conditions and states of existence, an encore of HPB's earlier reference to the Cabalistic aphorism "a stone becomes a plant; a plant, a beast; a beast, a man; a man, a spirit; and the spirit, a God." This means that each of us—not our "personality" but our "individuality"—passes through all forms of existence, until we achieve complete union with spirit.

Existence itself, HPB tells us, oscillates between the days and nights of Brahma, *manvantaras* being the cosmic days, and *pralayas* the cosmic nights, each of an incalculable length of time. In the beginning there was absolute nothingness, rather like the state of nonexistence cosmologists postulate before the "big bang." Then the vibrations of eternity waken to new life and the primordial essence separates itself into seven Rays that shape the universe. These Rays are really intelligent beings, the *Dhyan Chohans*. Through the energy of *Fohat*, they fashion a new cosmos, eternity being "the playground of numberless Universes incessantly manifesting and disappearing." Our world is the result of a kind of cosmic condensation, stellar matter passing through a kind of whirlwind, collecting into nebulae that will become our solar system.

The earth, as mentioned, goes through seven Rounds, and during these, different beings are created. The first Root Race lived on a continent called the "Imperishable Sacred Land," and were formed of pure spirit, as were the second Root Race, the Hyperboreans, who inhabited a land near the North Pole, which at that time had a mild climate. The third Root Race lived in Lemuria, fragments of which remain today as Australia and

Easter Island. During the fourth Round, higher beings descended to earth, and the beginnings of our physical bodies appeared, as did the separation of the sexes. The fourth Root Race appeared on Atlantis; they had bodies and senses like ours, and were masters of technology and had psychic powers. The Atlanteans, however, had a taste for "black magic" and some unusual sexual appetites: A union between Atlanteans and certain "she animals" resulted in gorillas and chimpanzees. Some Atlanteans were giants and were responsible for ancient sites such as Stonehenge, but they abused their power and knowledge and sank into decadence as Atlantis itself sank into the sea. Fleeing their lost world, some Atlanteans traveled to what we know as Egypt, others to America, and started civilizations there.[52] But they were soon outstripped by the fifth Root Race, the Aryans. The sixth Sub-Race of the fifth Root Race—each Root Race is subdivided into seven Sub-Races—were, according to HPB, being born in her time on the western shore of the United States, with another Sub-Race to appear sometime before the Aryans themselves meet the fate of their predecessors. The aim of these vast cycles of civilizations and races is mankind's ultimate flowering in a Seventh, and final, Root Race.

This, clearly, is the most general of outlines, and there is, of course, much more. I applaud in advance the intrepid reader who goes to the source. My one bit of advice is that, if we read *The Secret Doctrine* as literal "truth"—as some Fundamentalist Christians read the Bible—we may be doing it a disservice. I profited from it most by seeing it as Blavatsky's attempt to create a new myth for the modern age, or as a huge, fantastic science fiction story, something along the lines of Olaf Stapledon's *Star Maker*.

. . .

NOT SURPRISINGLY, most critics of the book point out that both Senzar and *The Book of Dzyan* are unknown to scholars—or anyone else—and most likely have their origin in Blavatsky's own fertile mind. Max Müller thought *The Secret Doctrine* a rehash of badly digested Hinduism and Buddhism. The Cabalist scholar Gershom Scholem thought *The Book of Dzyan* was based on the *Sifra Di-Tseniutha*, a "pompous" Zoharic text.[53] A contemporary Buddhist scholar has called HPB's work "a melee of horrendous hogwash . . . that any Buddhist or Tibetan scholar is justified to avoid . . . ," more or less the standard take.[54] Yet not all scholars agree. The sinologist Giovanni Hoffmann believed that the "Stanzas of Dzyan" origi-nate in the *Book of the Secret Correspondences* (Yu-Fu-King) of the fourth-century Taoist Ly-Tzyn.[55] And Buddhist scholars David and Nancy Reigle argue that Blavatsky's *The Book of Dzyan* is based on the Tantric Books of Kiu-Te.[56] As with so much else about HPB, the debate rages.

One reader of *The Secret Doctrine* who recognized its impor-tance was the journalist, editor, and spiritualist W. T. Stead, friend of Bernard Shaw and H. G. Wells, and later one of the fatalities of the *Titanic*. Stead met Blavatsky at Landsdowne Road and was impressed. When *The Secret Doctrine* appeared, he asked Annie Besant, then a notorious freethinker and atheist, to review it; none of his other writers would touch it. Besant was a political fire-brand; having already been arrested for supporting birth control, she was also a key activist in the "Bloody Sunday" and "Match Girl" demonstrations of 1887 and '88. When she received Blavatsky's book she was doubtful, but as she read, "the disjointed facts were seen as part of a mighty whole, and all my puzzles, riddles, problems, seemed to disappear"; her review, which appeared in *The Pall Mall Gazette* on April 25, 1889, was positive.[57] One writer suggests Besant fell into Theosophy on the rebound of a failed romance with Shaw.[58] Whatever it was, with a fellow socialist who had also turned to Theosophy, Besant visited HPB. Besant noted HPB rolling cigarettes, and that the talk was "worldly," nothing mystical. As she was about to leave, HPB turned to her and said, "Oh my dear Mrs. Besant, if you would only come among us." Her timing was perfect. Besant melted and did come among them, so much that she later became the head of the TS, and in that capacity was instrumental in India winning its independence from the Raj, a tale I tell elsewhere.[59] Besant's conversion from militant progressive to Theosophical aspirant was so complete that she even provided HPB with her last place of residence, at least on this earth.

But perhaps HPB's most celebrated visitor from this time was Mohandas Gandhi, who described Theosophy as "Hinduism at its best."[60] Gandhi first came into contact with Theosophy in London, in 1889, when he was studying law and generally trying to adapt himself to Western, specifically British ways.[61] He believed, as many educated young Indians did at the time, that his people should give up their old ways, and strive to be like the English. He met the Keightleys—whom he refers to as two "theosophist brothers"; they were really uncle and nephew—and they introduced him to the Bhagavad Gita.[62] They were reading the popular Edwin Arnold English translation, and suggested to the young student that they might read it in the original together. Gandhi was ashamed to admit that he had never read it in the original, or any other language. But he was determined to, and the Gita became the most important book in his life; he later said that his doctrine of *Ahimsā*, "nonviolence," was rooted in it. In November 1889, the Keightleys took Gandhi to meet HPB; on the same visit he also met Annie Besant, whose recent conversion to Theosophy was something of a scandal. Gandhi didn't join the society then, but a year and a half later, on March 26, 1891, he became an associate member of the Blavatsky Lodge.[63] Gandhi later said that in 1893, during his time in Johannesburg, South Africa, although he did not join a Theosophical lodge, he had many discussions with Theosophists, attended readings of Theosophical books, and even spoke at some of their meetings.[64] Gandhi's interest in Theosophy was in its goal of a universal brotherhood. He had little interest in its occult side, and in fact was rather critical of it, and his appreciation of the society changed over time. Yet reading Blavatsky inspired Gandhi to study Hinduism and to reject the notion, taught by Christian missionaries, that his nation's religion was mere superstition. It was this belief in the value of his own tradition that sustained him throughout his career. Strangely, some of Gandhi's last words were of Theosophy. On January 30, 1948, the day he was assassinated, Gandhi's journal *Harijan* published some of his reflections on Theosophy and on what he saw as its overemphasis on the occult. He had come to the conclusion, however, that "Theosophy is Hinduism in theory, and Hinduism is Theosophy in practice."[65] It was through Theosophy, too, that Gandhi was introduced to the work of Leo Tolstoy, which influenced him almost as greatly as the Gita.[66]

Before HPB moved to Besant's house at 19 Avenue Road in London's affluent St. John's Wood in August 1890—the lease on the Landsdowne Road house having expired—two more works

emerged from her irrepressible pen. In *The Key to Theosophy*—a
book Gandhi read—Blavatsky tried to answer the many questions
she was asked about the nature of man, karma, rebirth, Spiritualism, occultism, politics, and dozens of other things, in the sack-
loads of letters she received. It's written in the form of questions
and answers and should be, as HPB intended it to be, the first stop
for anyone wanting to grasp the essence of her teaching. Here the
focus and clarity are sharp and the aim is to clear up muddles and
get the reader thinking for himself. After the often baffling pro-
fundities of *The Secret Doctrine*, Blavatsky's *Key* has an air of sound
thinking and healthy common sense. The emphasis is on individual effort. After declaring again that Theosophy is not a religion,
she argues against prayer. It "kills self-reliance and encourages a
still more ferocious selfishness and egotism," because such peti-
tions are directed to an "anthropomorphic God, who is but the
gigantic shadow of man, and not even of man at his best." "This idea
of passing one's whole life in moral idleness, and having one's hardest work and duty done by another—is most revolting to us," she
wrote, and in any case, "being well-occupied people, we can hardly
afford to lose time in addressing verbal prayers to a pure abstrac-
tion," "the inner man" being "the only God of whom we can have
cognizance." Speaking of our "constant failure to find any permanent satisfaction in life which would meet the wants of our higher
nature"—a reflection that warrants repeated consideration—she
tells her readers that Theosophy is "essentially the philosophy of
those who suffer, and have lost all hope of being helped out of the
mire of life by any other means." Theosophy itself is "the store-
house of all the truths uttered by the great seers, initiates, and
prophets" and the "channel through which more or less of truth . . .

is poured out into the world." Duty is key. It is "that which is *due* to humanity at large, to our fellow men," and the Theosophist himself "must be a center of spiritual action . . . from his daily individual life must radiate those spiritual actions [and] forces which can alone regenerate his fellow men." "Selfishness, indifference, and brutality can never be the normal state of the race. . . . Progress can be . . . only attained by the development of nobler qualities," and Theosophy is one means of accomplishing this.[67]

Such development was the theme of her last major work. Like *The Secret Doctrine*, *The Voice of the Silence*—a short, devotional text, unusual for Blavatsky—is a transcription of extracts from a work originally written in Senzar. It was written in France, in Fontainebleau, during a brief holiday from London. *The Book of the Golden Precepts*, from which *The Voice of the Silence* is taken, forms, Blavatsky tells us, "part of the same series as that from which the stanzas of *The Book of Dzyan* were taken."[68] Its maxims can be found, she says, in different forms in Sanskrit works, such as the Upanishads, and the original precepts are engraved on those "thin oblong squares" which are "preserved on the altars of the temples" attached to centers of Mahayana Buddhism, which she learned about during her time in Tibet. Today, Mahayana is the largest and most popular school of Buddhism—Tibetan Buddhism being one offshoot of it—but in Blavatsky's day it was still fairly mysterious, and the *Voice of the Silence* is one of the earliest works celebrating the "Bodhisattva path." The film stars and other celebrities who practice Tibetan Buddhism today and who recognize the Dalai Lama as a spiritual leader owe Blavatsky a debt of thanks. If Colonel Olcott brought Buddhism to Buddhists, his chum passed it on to practically everyone else.

Needless to say, as they do with *The Secret Doctrine*, most academic Buddhist scholars deny that *The Voice of the Silence* originates in anything other than Blavatsky's imagination. Yet some influential names disagree. D. T. Suzuki, who brought Zen, a form of Mahayana Buddhism, to the West, said of *The Voice of the Silence* that "Here is the real Mahayana Buddhism," and remarked that HPB had "in some way been initiated into the deeper side of Mahayana teachings, and then gave out what she deemed wise to the Western world."[69] Edward Conze, the noted Buddhist scholar and translator who brought some of the central texts of Mahayana Buddhism to English readers, told the historian of religion Mircea Eliade that HPB was a reincarnation of Tsong Kha Pa, the fourteenth-century Buddhist reformer and founder of the Gelugpa school, to which the Dalai Lama belongs.[70] In 1960, Christmas Humphreys, founder of the London Buddhist Society, published his influential anthology *The Wisdom of Buddhism*, which included selections from *The Voice of the Silence*. And Lama Kazi Dawa-Samdup, whose translation of the *Bardo Thödol* W. Y. Evans-Wentz published as *The Tibetan Book of the Dead*, remarked that "there is adequate internal evidence" of Blavatsky's "intimate acquaintance with the higher *lāmaistic* teachings, into which she claimed to have been initiated."[71]

That Conze, Humphreys, and Evans-Wentz were all Theosophists suggests to academic scholars that their testimony is biased. To nonacademics, it may suggest that HPB deserves more credit than she's received, a sentiment expressed by the current Dalai Lama when he wrote in a preface to a centenary edition of the work, "I believe that this book has strongly influenced many sincere seekers and aspirants to the wisdom and compassion of the Bodhisattva Path."[72]

Yet even some HPB supporters argue that she wouldn't have needed to have been in Mahayana monasteries to have written it. K. Paul Johnson suggests that Colonel Olcott's friend, the Bengal explorer and British spy Sarat Chandra Das, who traveled in Tibet in the 1880s, brought back hundreds of manuscripts, and this material could have been used by Blavatsky for her "Tibetan" writings.[73] But for most readers, I think, the question of whether HPB gleaned her material firsthand or in other ways is secondary. What strikes them is the quality of the ideas and the sincerity with which she expresses them.

THE MAIN THEME of *The Voice of the Silence* is the contrast between two paths: that of compassion for others, and that of one's own salvation. The followers of Mahayana Buddhism differ from those of Theravada—the form of Buddhism more well known in Blavatsky's time—in their determination to forgo their own liberation—their entering into Nirvana—until all sentient beings are liberated as well. (For Theravada—or, as HPB calls them, Pratyeka—Buddhists, one can only save oneself, no others.) As mentioned, those who are on the threshold of Nirvana and choose to remain in the world (*samsara*) in order to help others reach the same goal are bodhisattvas. *The Voice of the Silence* encourages its readers to do this. It isn't an easy path. Like HPB's own, it is a "way of suffering," of "renunciation" and "woe." As she said in *The Key to Theosophy*, "Our joys and pleasures teach us nothing," "the final goal cannot be reached in any way but through life experiences, and the bulk of these consist of pain and suffering," something Blavatsky herself knew at first hand. [74] Our earth, she tells us, is a "Hall of Sorrow . . . the dismal entrance leading to the twilight that precedes the valley of true light." Yet by walking this path—indeed, by becoming the path itself—one becomes "a soldier in the army of those who work for the liberation or salvation of mankind." One begins the path by seeking stillness and detachment from the senses, by becoming "as deaf to roarings as to whispers, to cries of bellowing elephants as to the silver buzzing of the golden fire-fly." One must, in essence, turn a blind eye to *maya*, the world's illusion, and seek the true vision that comes from within. It is then that we can choose between the "doctrine of the eye," whose followers ignore the sufferings of others as they go about saving themselves, and the "doctrine of the heart," whose followers embrace the suffering of others as their own. As her life suggests, HPB chose the "doctrine of the heart," and whether she learned of it under the tutelage of KH, or from somewhere else, it was a path she had walked for at least a decade and a half, and she knew its contours well.

HER TRAVELS ON IT, though, at least in her earthly form, were coming to an end. On Blavatsky's last day at Landsdowne Road, the countess took her for a drive in Hyde Park, where, according to one version of events, she had first met the Master nearly forty years earlier. When she returned, she lamented that of the many people she saw promenading, there was "not a soul among them." A trip to Brighton to take the sea air was her last out of London—the year before she had hopped across the Channel for the last time, to see M. Eiffel's tower in Paris—and now she seemed to be with-drawing deeper within herself. Her spirits, though, were somewhat brightened by her new home, although not everyone was happy with it. Alice Cleather felt a foreboding at the move, feeling that Annie Besant's "masterful and somewhat intolerant personality" cast a pall over HPB's new address, and did not bode well for the future.[75] If Blavatsky herself felt any hesitation, she didn't commu-nicate it. As she wrote to Vera, the property on Avenue Road was large; she had a spacious room on the ground floor, and she was adding a lecture hall to it. It would fit three hundred people, and its polished wooden ceiling was to be covered with allegorical paint-ings, symbolizing the world's great religions and the zodiac. It was here that the new European Headquarters of the TS was inaugu-rated on July 3, 1890. HPB sat in a huge armchair before the nearly five hundred people who attended—many more than the room could hold, and among them the wife of the Archbishop of Canterbury—and listened to lectures by Sinnett and Besant. Besant was quickly outpacing Sinnett in what would soon become an open contest for dominance in the society. She had been made president of the Blavatsky Lodge, while he remained head of the London Lodge alone. HPB herself was a "regular theosophical pope," hav-ing been elected president of all the European branches. As always, titles meant little to her, unusual among occultists, who generally like dazzling others with esoteric regalia.

It was also here that HPB founded an esoteric group within her Esoteric Section. The Inner Group consisted of twelve mem-bers, six men and six women. Besant, Countess Wachtmeister, Mrs. Cooper-Oakley, Laura Cooper (her sister), Alice Cleather, and Emily Kislingbury formed the feminine half; Archibald

Keightley (his nephew Bertram was in the United States), Walter Old (also known as the astrologer "Sepharial"), Herbert Coryn, E. T. Sturdy, Claude Wright, and G. R. S. Mead formed the masculine. Some members changed over time. E. T. Sturdy became skeptical and left. At some point, the London coroner, Mason, and occultist Wynn Westcott, one of the founders of the Hermetic Order of the Golden Dawn, joined. (One of the Golden Dawn's members would be Yeats, whose interest in ceremonial magic, which HPB loathed, drew him to it.) The Inner Group met in a special seven-sided room with a glass roof, connected to HPB's bedroom. Each wall was covered in a particular metal, and several "magical mirrors," of the kind used by the Orphic Circle, decorated them. Only Blavatsky and the members of the group were allowed to enter it. Here the group sat in front of HPB in a semicircle, always in the same seats, with the men to her right and the women to her left, and she directed them in meditation.[76]

Mead, who became HPB's secretary and was a brilliant spiritual and esoteric scholar in his own right, spoke of her at this time as a "lovable bundle of inexplicable contradictions," a "puzzling mixture of wisdom and folly," a "sphinx clad in motley."[77] Although her energies were flagging and her health in visible decline, HPB could still dish out lessons when necessary. When angry she would "blurt out anything that might come into her head."[78] On one occasion, she berated Mead before Charles Johnston—her niece Vera's husband—over some peccadillo and left Mead crushed. "That was her way, to rate her disciples in the presence of perfect strangers," Mead reflected. "It speaks volumes for her, that they loved her still."[79] As usual, there were plenty of "flapdoodles" around, and HPB let them know what she thought of them. On one occasion, when a visitor droned on about some pet idea, Blavatsky whispered audibly to Besant, "Oh Annie, can you please make him stop!" That was inimitably the Madame.

While taking her Inner Group into esoteric depths, in her last days Blavatsky didn't forget the outer world. In August, on her last trip outside of her new headquarters, HPB traveled to London's slum-ridden East End, scene of the Ripper murders and one of the poorest areas in the country. Crime, poverty, unemployment were rife—a decade later Jack London would write about it in *People of the Abyss*—and Blavatsky was there to open a working-girl's home. Here her bodhisattvic efforts were literally concrete, and the place would be managed by Besant and Laura Cooper. Nearly twenty years earlier, HPB had found herself in tough circumstances in New York's own East Side, and no doubt memories of those days came to her as she sat through the inevitable speeches. But after this, her only excursions were brief forays across Prince Albert Road and into the Regent's Park, wheeled in her bath chair by the countess. On one promenade, HPB nearly fell out of her chair when she bent down to help a child whom they almost ran over.

She kept working until the end. There was her *Theosophical Glossary*, a handy guide when plumbing the depths of *Isis Unveiled* or *The Secret Doctrine*, and she also edited some of her occult stories, which an enterprising publisher should reissue; HPB is a find for fans of ripping occult yarns. But as Mead and others felt, it seemed she was arranging things and preparing her flock for her departure. Her followers saw less and less of her. Gone were the open evenings, with visitors coming and going, when mystical pearls were dropped amid the confusion. She may have wished for quiet, now that she was getting ready to move on, but even her last days were filled with controversy.

One last legal squabble flared up. Elliot Coues, who had founded a branch of the TS in Washington, D.C., had kicked up a storm when, in league with Mabel Collins, he started the story that HPB had somehow forced Collins to say that her *Light on the Path* had been dictated by the Masters. He then tried to get control of the TS in the United States, and asked HPB's help in taking its leadership from W. Q. Judge. Blavatsky would have no part in this, and Coues was eventually expelled. Coues retaliated by publishing articles denouncing Theosophy as "humbug" and HPB as a "fraud," and on July 20, 1890, *The Sun* published a long "interview" with Coues, in which he brought together every calumny ever made against Blavatsky, including the charge that she had had an illegitimate child, this time with Prince Emile de Wittgenstein, a longtime friend of her family. HPB replied in a letter in *The Path*, denying the charges and denouncing Coues; in September, libel suits were brought against Coues and *The Sun*. In the end, it turned out that Coues's "interview" was written entirely by himself, and on September 26, 1892, *The Sun* printed a retraction, stating that there was no evidence supporting Coues's statements. Coues gathered much of his "evidence" against HPB from her nemesis William Emmette Coleman (Chapter 6), who supplied Coues with the disinformation about her affair with Prince Wittgenstein, drawing on the dubious letter from D. D. Home to Dr. Bloede (Chapter 4). Coleman also gave Coues the originals of the infamous HPB-Coulomb letters, which he had bought from George Patterson, the Scottish missionary who had published them. The letters were never seen again, and are said to have been either lost or destroyed while in Coues's possession. Although they are still referred to as having proved that Blavatsky was a fraud, their loss makes any definitive judgement about their authenticity impossible.[80] Some HPB supporters suggest that Coues, realizing the letters were faked, destroyed them in order to conceal the forgery.

Sadly, HPB never saw *The Sun*'s retraction, and so didn't have the chance to appreciate her victory. By the time it was printed, she had been dead for more than a year. The winter of 1891 was harsh, and in April, an influenza epidemic hit London. Everyone at Avenue Road was struck, HPB especially. Besant was in America, bringing HPB's last message to the TS convention there. Blavatsky's temperature ran high and she had trouble swallowing. Laura Cooper tended her. Mostly she kept to her bed, but on May 6 and 7, she got up and walked a bit around her room. She rolled her last cigarette on May 7, for her doctor, who told her she showed courage when he found her sitting in bed playing solitaire. The night before she died she was restless, but that morning, May 8, 1891, she seemed to quiet a bit. But by 11:30, she had taken a turn for the worse. As she sat in her big armchair, Walter Old and Claude Wright knelt before her, holding her delicate hands, something she would have erupted at had she been well—Mead tells the story of how she "cried out in genuine alarm" when a zealous devotee once tried to kneel before her.[81] Isabel Cooper-Oakley had relieved her sister and was supporting HPB's head with her arm. By two that afternoon, the end was close. Her last words were, "Isabel, Isabel, keep the link unbroken; do not let my last incarnation be a failure," a tough admonition to take on. That enormous vitality and will, which kept her going when others would surely have been crushed, was finally coming to a halt. Her breath slowed, and she died so quietly that no one knew quite when it happened.

Or almost no one.

The Colonel was in Australia at the time, and he had last seen his chum on December 26, 1889. He had just been in Japan then, where he had been asked to head all the Buddhist sects in the country; only he, they believed, could bring the different schools together. It was an honor he had to decline, as Master Morya wouldn't let him resign from the presidency of the TS. Now, on the other side of the planet, he felt his old chum was sending him a message, telling him her path, at least in this world, was coming to an end. The next day, on May 9, Olcott wrote in his diary that he felt a foreboding of Blavatsky's death, a remark he repeated in his entry on the following day too. On May 11, he got the telegram letting him know. They both were a long way from Chittenden. The Master had finally set her free.

May 8, the day of Madame Blavatsky's death, is celebrated by Theosophists all over the world as White Lotus Day. Although practically nothing about her life is certain, one thing is for sure: The world is a far less interesting place without her.

TEN

THE MASTERS REVEALED?

HPB's body was cremated at Woking Crematorium on May 11, 1891. As fire had marked her entry into the world—we remember her young Aunt Nadya setting the priest alight at her niece's baptism—it seems fitting that it should mark her passage from it. Cremation was still a controversial practice at that time. The first cremation in England had taken place at Woking only a few years earlier, in 1885—a decade after Baron de Palm's in Pennsylvania—and the practice was only declared legal the year before. So once again, the "old lady" was causing trouble.

Yet the real trouble HPB's death had started had little to do with the disposal of her *rupa*, or physical body. As happens with practically all occult groups and societies once their leader dies, Blavatsky's passing triggered a contest among the Theosophical higher-ups to assume her place in the hierarchy. What this meant more than anything else was assuring one's own contact with the Masters. Although those close to her knew that HPB's authority was anchored in her own personality, for rank-and-file Theosophists, having a direct line to Morya, Koot Hoomi, and the rest was what guaranteed one's esoteric credibility. Now that HPB was no longer around to pass on messages, who was going to fill the gap? The Colonel was still president of the TS and would remain so until his death in 1907, when Annie Besant would succeed him. But his position had always been more administrative than spiritually authoritative, his own deep commitment to Buddhism and evident healing powers notwithstanding. Although attempts to dislodge him from power were made, he remained relatively secure. Others, however, jockeyed furiously to get even the slightest advantage in the race to reach the Masters. The result was an exercise in what Alice Leighton Cleather called "the extraordinary pettiness and narrow-mindedness" of many of HPB's early followers.[1] For a society built on the idea of a universal brotherhood, it's most important members certainly had a very difficult time getting along.

Sinnett, we know, had already tried to make direct contact with the "old lady's" adepts, but had been rebuffed. With HPB's arrival in London and the start of the Blavatsky Lodge, he had already felt that he was losing ground in his own backyard. And now it was clear that Annie Besant was in line for the throne. She had already been appointed co-editor of *Lucifer* and president of the Blavatsky Lodge; with Blavatsky's death, she became head of the Esoteric Section, too. Alice Cleather's sense of an "impending disaster" accompanying Blavatsky's move to Avenue Road may have been a product of hindsight—her reminiscences of the time weren't published until more than thirty years after the event—but one wouldn't have needed precognition to see that Besant would quickly rise to a position of power. Whatever her Theosophical credentials, Besant was a woman of action and an inspiring speaker.

And she was only in her early forties, so still relatively young. The-osophy has always seemed much more of a woman's game than a man's. Aside from Rudolf Steiner, who eventually broke away to start his own movement, the dominant personalities in Theosophy have been for the most part women. There's HPB herself, Besant, Anna Kingsford, and later, Katherine Tingley and Alice Bailey. Certainly there was Sinnett, Judge, C. W. Leadbeater, and of course Olcott. But none of them had the personal power that HPB or Besant and the others had.

Yet although Besant clearly was a dominant character, that in itself wasn't enough to fill HPB's shoes. Alice Cleather could lament that "when HPB left us, there was no longer any possibility of direct communication with the Great Lodge of Masters," but not everyone agreed.[2] One in fact who had other ideas was William Quan Judge, who had remained vice president of the society.

When his fellow founders had relocated to India, Judge stayed in America, building up a powerful Theosophical section there, and publishing an important journal, *The Path*. Judge had got closer to HPB in her last years, and now, with her gone, he decided it was time to challenge Olcott for the society's leadership. While acknowledging the Colonel's valuable powers of organization, Judge put it out that he, on the other hand, was the "spiritual" heir of HPB, and that the decisions for the society's future directions should lie with him. Initially he had support from Besant in this. During her trip to the United States—she was there when Bla-vatsky died—she and Judge had become good friends. Now, as head of the Esoteric Section—a development that Olcott had agreed to but had never really liked—she was open to Judge's criticisms of the Colonel, who, he said, was losing the spiritual plot with all his focus on administration. Judge should be the one to put the society back on its proper course, and to prove his point, Judge produced letters from the Masters more or less saying so. Besant even found one communication among her personal papers, informing her that "Judge's plan is right." Besant was so impressed by this that, in August 1891, at her farewell speech to the National Secular Society, given at the Hall of Science—she could hardly belong to a secular society and remain a Theosophist—she declared that HPB herself was sending her messages from the spirit world.[3]

Olcott had come to London to secure Besant's support against Judge, and was there when she made this announcement. Besant may have been impressed by Judge's "letters," but not the Colonel. Every other time Judge had had communication with the Masters, it had gone through Olcott. How was it that Judge was communicating directly with them now? What made things even more suspicious was that the letters were stamped with Master Morya's "seal." But this seal had been devised by Olcott himself, and had been given to HPB in 1883, but subsequently "misplaced." Olcott threatened to expose Judge's apparent fraud. Judge responded by threatening to tell the truth about the Master's seal, which most members assumed was genuine, or at least made in Tibet.[4]

The two had reached a standoff, and this quickly descended into farce when Judge, through the Masters, tried to convince Besant that if she went to India, Olcott would poison her. Perhaps convinced by Judge's warnings, in 1892, Judge and Besant plotted to force Olcott to resign, gaining support from KH, who wrote to Judge approving of their plan. Master Morya, however, disagreed, and told Olcott to stay put.[5] (We remember that the Masters disagreed at first about the Coulombs, so perhaps this difference of opinions shouldn't be surprising.) Olcott did resign briefly, but quickly reinstated himself. The European Section seemed in favor of Judge, but they also wanted Olcott to stay in power. The balance shifted in Olcott's favor when Besant visited him in Adyar in 1893, ignoring Judge's warnings of certain death. Olcott won her over, and she initiated proceedings against Judge, charging him with fraud. This accusation was eventually dropped because the committee convened to try Judge admitted that, as belief in the reality of the Masters was not incumbent on members of the society, there were no grounds for the charge of fraud. Which is to say, one can only be accused of forgery if the existence of the genuine article is accepted, and the reality or not of the Masters is something each Theosophist must decide for himself; it is not part of the rules of the society. So Judge avoided charges of fraud through a loophole that put the existence of the Masters—the raison d'être of the TS—in question. This absurd situation wasn't lost on the press, and in a series of articles entitled "Isis Very Much Unveiled," the *Westminster Gazette* was not slow to point out that the very letters Besant accused Judge of forging were those that she solemnly told her audience at the Hall of Science had been sent to her by HPB from beyond the veil.

Along with the questionable letters from Master M, Judge later claimed he had made contact with HPB via the psychic powers of the American Katherine Tingley. Judge met Tingley in a New York soup kitchen in 1894. Like Besant, Tingley had thrown herself into a number of philanthropic efforts and was running the kitchen in support of striking workers. She was converted to Theosophy almost immediately.

Judge seceded from the main TS body in 1895, bringing his several thousand followers into the new Theosophical Society in America. He died in 1896, and Tingley succeeded him as head of the American section. Like Judge, Tingley had big ideas, and on a visit to India, she arranged to visit one of the Masters herself, a meeting she described in her book *The Gods Await*. She met HPB's "Teacher," as she calls him, in Darjeeling. He was dressed in a plain Tibetan style and was whittling a small wooden peg to be used by his *chela* in the yoke for his oxen. The Teacher told Tingley that "the atoms of the human body become weighed down . . . by the burdens of the mind," but that his *chela* had achieved mental balance, simply by conscientiously plowing his field.[6]

Much as had happened between HPB and Anna Kingsford, but on a larger scale, for a decade, Tingley and Besant locked etheric horns in a relentless battle for Theosophical dominance. Tingley had renamed the American Section "the Universal Brotherhood and Theosophical Society," and set out on a worldwide tour to draw support for the new movement. Her crusade was not particularly successful, and Besant retaliated by embarking on a tour of her own, winning over several thousand new recruits in the United States alone. Through the weird twists of karma, at one point Tingley actually purchased Besant's old home on Avenue Road—Besant had by now relocated to India. But Tingley's real success was in establishing what must be one of the earliest "alternative communities" in America, her Theosophical "white city," Lomaland, at Point Loma, San Diego, whose foundation stone was laid in 1897.

Here the "Purple Mother," as Tingley liked to be called, presided over a spiritual enclave that included education, the arts, architecture, agriculture, and other necessities for a self-sustaining, what we would call "off-the-grid" establishment, as well as her own version of Theosophical spirituality. Tingley's eclectic taste in architecture—which included Muslim domes, Hindu temples, Egyptian gates, and Greek theaters—seems to have presaged the kind of architectural extravagance that would be associated with Southern California in later years, and her early communal farms made an equally lasting contribution by introducing the avocado to the Californian diet.[7] One of Tingley's closest allies was the Swiss-American Gottfried de Purucker, who went on to write several Theosophical works. Another was the pulp mystical adventure writer Talbot Mundy, whose works, such as *Om: The Secret of Ahbor Valley*, are full of Indiana Jones dash and Theosophical mysticism. (His novel *The Nine Unknown* is based on an ancient Indian legend of a secret society dedicated to preserving esoteric knowledge that HPB herself would draw on.) Although initially successful, Lomaland slowly ground to a halt, mostly because of the lavish eccentricities of the "Purple Mother," and it eventually came to an end following her death in 1929.[8]

Although Besant was the clear front-runner for the Theosophical throne, a direct link to the Masters was needed to make this a fait accompli. Following in Theosophical tradition, in order to secure this, Besant needed a man. In fact, one could say that behind every successful Theosophical woman was a competent, but less dominant man. HPB had Olcott. Anna Kingsford had Edward Maitland. Katherine Tingley had W. Q. Judge. In Besant's case, it was Charles W. Leadbeater.

Leadbeater is one of the most colorful and dubious characters in Theosophical history and is perhaps best known as the man who discovered Jiddu Krishnamurti, himself a Theosophist saint until his rejection of the society in 1929. Picked by Leadbeater as the incarnation of Maitreya, the avatar of the New Age, following his rejection of Theosophy, Krishnamurti went on to become an influential spiritual teacher, inspiring figures as different as the composer Igor Stravinsky and the physicist David Bohm. Leadbeater's "discovery," however, which involved his ability to "read" auras as well as his predilection for young boys, led to charges of pederasty, as well as acclaim as the mentor of a new "world teacher." At least twice before, Leadbeater's enthusiastic tutoring of Theosophical adolescents got him into hot water, and it was only Theosophy's high standing in India that saved him from a lawsuit, brought against him by Krishnamurti's father, involving pedophilia and deification, unique in the annals of the Raj.

Leadbeater, who was ordained in the Church of England in 1878, read Sinnett's books and joined the TS in 1883. His enthusiasm led to his own attempts to reach the Masters through a medium named William Eglinton, and when these failed he approached HPB about it herself. She passed on his request and got a reply that Leadbeater should accompany HPB on her return to Adyar. Leadbeater was among the audience shocked by HPB's appearance at the London Lodge meeting when she and Anna Kingsford faced off. During his voyage, Leadbeater claims that he had a vision of Djwal Khool on board ship. It was the first of many such sightings, at least according to Leadbeater. Leadbeater remained at Adyar, undergoing a crash course in Theosophy, Blavatsky style. Like Countess Wachtmeister, he endured his probation, and soon was learning the basics of clairvoyance from KH himself. After that, as Peter Washington puts it, "the Masters couldn't keep away from Leadbeater," visiting him almost every day. HPB wasn't pleased with her new *chela*'s progress. The Masters themselves had repeatedly insisted that she was the sole source of contact with them. Now this renegade clergyman was chatting with them regularly. As we will see, more than anyone else, Leadbeater is responsible for leaving the astral door wide open and for encouraging the kind of purely "spiritual" contact with alleged adepts that resulted in the plethora of "ascended Masters" stuffing many New Age books today.

Like Olcott, Leadbeater embraced Buddhism, and in Ceylon, he became the first Christian minister to become a Buddhist. It was in Ceylon that he met a young boy, Curuppumullage Jinarajadasa, and became so attracted to him that he more or less tried to kidnap him. He was only stopped by the boy's father and his revolver, but when he explained that his intentions were purely pedagogical, Jinarajadasa's parents allowed him to take the boy to England, where Leadbeater promised he would be educated. For all his adoration of the East, Leadbeater was miserable in Ceylon, and he had written to Sinnett asking him to find some congenial work for him in London. Sinnett suggested he come and tutor his son, but another reason for the invitation was that he wanted to use Leadbeater's psychic powers to contact the Masters. They had by this time stopped their correspondence and Sinnett was eager to start it up again. Sinnett had apparently already tried other psychics and mediums but with little luck. For a time, Leadbeater taught Sinnett's son, as well as Jinarajadasa and George Arundale (the nephew of Francesca Arundale, whose guest HPB had been), but then something happened, and he was asked to go. That "something" remains unclear, but it seems likely that Leadbeater's instruction included some doubtful extracurricular activities. Both George Arundale and Jinarajadasa would later become presidents of the Theosophical Society Adyar, the name adopted by Olcott and then Besant to differentiate their organization from Judge's American society.

Leadbeater met Besant in 1890, and soon the two became close colleagues; both were much too formal to be "chums." In some ways their relationship was the reverse of HPB's and Olcott's. In this version, it was Leadbeater who found sex beastly—ironic, given his track record with boys. At least he had a paranoid aversion to women, and the only one he could stand any close contact with was Besant. By 1895, Leadbeater and Jinarajadasa were living in Avenue Road, and with HPB out of the way, the clergyman could let his psychic vision rip. He did, and through tutoring Besant herself— whose psychic abilities were less powerful than her oratory ones— she could join him on clairvoyant visits to the Masters.

What followed was a series of books which more or less set the tone for post-HPB Theosophy. Through the Masters, Leadbeater and Besant journeyed to the earth's remote past, visiting Atlantis and Lemuria. They traced the true life of Christ, discovering that he had actually been an Egyptian adept. Modern science was also open to them, and in their book *Occult Chemistry*, the two explored the new world of the atom, clairvoyantly entering into its complex structure. One book, *Thought Forms*, can be seen as the inspiration for abstract art. One of its most important readers was the Russian artist Wassily Kandinsky, who was also a deep reader of Rudolf Steiner. Leadbeater and Besant's descriptions of thoughts and their auras as "radiating vibrations" and "floating forms" inspired Kandinsky, who is commonly accepted as the first abstract artist, and led to his own influential work *Concerning the Spiritual in Art*.[9]

Besant and Leadbeater also journeyed into their and others'

past lives, tracing the karmic connections of their fellow Theosophists through countless eons. And they also took more than a few peeks into the future. In one of them, Leadbeater saw that a new "world teacher," the Lord Maitreya—a coming bodhisattva—would soon appear in human form, and he realized he should be on the lookout for him. Hence his delight when, on a riverbank near the Theosophical compound in Adyar, he saw Krishnamurti's aura. Leadbeater had already pegged another boy, Hubert van Hook, son of a staunch American Theosophist, as the avatar of the New Age, and had duly taken him under his wing, but apparently he was mistaken. What Hubert thought about this is unclear, and one wonders how far he had gotten in his instruction. This time, however, Leadbeater was certain, and Besant soon agreed. This was in 1909. In 1906, Leadbeater had been expelled from the TS because of a scandal involving some young Theosophical boys he had instructed in masturbation. But all that had been forgotten now, at least by Besant.[10]

Sinnett and G. R. S. Mead, however, hadn't forgotten it, and with some seven hundred other members of the British Section, they resigned from the society over Leadbeater. Sinnett continued to write; his posthumously published *Early Days of Theosophy in Europe* was one of the first books of Theosophical history. He died in 1921. Mead went on to become a respected scholar of Western esotericism, his work inspiring figures as important as the psychologist C. G. Jung and the poet Ezra Pound. Following his departure from the TS, he formed the Quest Society, which promoted an eclectic approach to the study of religion, philosophy, and science, much as the early TS had. Although Leadbeater's return was the trigger for Mead's resignation, Mead had long been unhappy with what he felt was Besant's dictatorial style. He died in 1933.

Besant and Leadbeater would call the Theosophical tune for the next two decades. Besant would also die in 1933, Leadbeater in 1934, but Theosophy itself would bottom out in 1929, when Krishnamurti famously dismissed his avatarship. Krishnamurti himself survived, however, and, as mentioned, went on to become a spiritual teacher in his own right. But there were many who felt that whatever it was Besant and Leadbeater were doing, it wasn't Theosophy. With their headlong plunge into the *akashic* and easy access to the Masters—accompanied by what seemed an inexhaustible appetite for ritual and showy initiation—Besant and Leadbeater's approach was very different from HPB's, and those who remembered the "old lady" weren't happy with it. A "Back to Blavatsky" campaign started up, arguing against what it saw as an unhealthy revisionism. Granted, HPB's own link with the Masters wasn't exactly transparent. But at least she had always insisted that they were real people, made of flesh and blood, existing here and now in space and time, somewhere on the planet. With Besant and Leadbeater, the Masters had become something much more like gods, or certainly almost entirely "spiritual," and their astral open-door policy suggested that practically anyone could say they had chatted with the Masters on Venus or Atlantis the night before, and there was little one could say against them. The result, as mentioned, was a string of increasingly godlike "ascended Masters" having little or nothing to do with HPB's original brotherhood.

THE IDEA OF "hidden masters" did not, of course, begin with Blavatsky. Although many "occult histories" root it in dim ages past, for the modern period at least, the notion begins in Germany in

1614. As we saw in Chapter 1, that year, strange documents known
as the Rosicrucian manifestos appeared, announcing the existence
of a mysterious Brotherhood of the Rosy Cross. As we saw, when
the many who tried to find and join the Rosicrucians could not
locate them, they were sarcastically nicknamed "the Invisibles,"
and some Rosicrucian defenders claimed they had decamped to
Tibet. This idea of "invisible" adepts was later reprised in the Freemasonry of Baron von Hund, with its Rite of Strict Observance to
"unknown superiors." Blavatsky had found tales of these mysterious figures in her great-grandfather Prince Pavel Dolgorukov's
library, and to them she later added other accounts of enigmatic,
powerful adepts. In Bulwer-Lytton's *Zanoni*, she met the figure of
Mejnour, a Rosicrucian mage who had lived for countless ages, and
in *Occult Science in India*, by the Frenchman Louis Jacolliot, she
came across mention of the "nine unknown men," who, Jacolliot
claimed, really existed in India and secretly influenced world
events. As mentioned above, these "nine unknown men" would
reappear in pulp adventure fiction, but also in the best-selling *The
Morning of the Magicians* by Louis Pauwels and Jacques Bergier—the
book that kick-started the occult revival of the 1960s—and also as
the source of some paranormal communications received by the
psychic Uri Geller.[11]

Post-Blavatsky, the idea of "hidden masters" took a dark turn in
the work of the French occultist Saint-Yves d'Alveydre, who spoke
of a mysterious, all-powerful "Sovereign Pontiff" who secretly rules
the world from his subterranean kingdom of Agartha, mentioned
in Chapter 3. As we saw, this notion of a subterranean kingdom
of supermen, preparing to invade the surface, had already been
explored in Bulwer-Lytton's early science fiction novel *The Coming*

Race. It was from Agartha and its Sovereign Pontiff that d'Alveydre developed his ideas about "synarchy," a form of occult totalitarianism that d'Alveydre had some success in promoting in the early years of the last century. The Traditionalist thinker René Guénon also spoke of Agartha and a "King of the World" who resides there. His ideas about both were inspired by the account of Agartha given in the Polish traveler Ferdinand Ossendowski's book *Beasts, Men, and Gods*, in which he speaks of legends of an underground kingdom in Mongolia, told to him by a Mongol guide. Tibetan Buddhism itself speaks of a hidden city, Shambhala, which the Russian artist, traveler, and Theosophist Nicholas Roerich tried to locate during two expeditions to the Himalayas in the 1920s and '30s. Roerich claimed that at least one of these journeys was overseen by Master Morya, and the Theosophist Alice Bailey also spoke of an "invisible brotherhood" living in Shambhala.[12] Agartha and Shambhala also make appearances in Pauwels's and Bergier's *Morning of the Magicians*.

Other forms of "hidden masters" populate much of Western esotericism. The Hermetic Order of the Golden Dawn spoke of "Secret Chiefs," and there is some speculation that the origin of this term goes back to Baron Hund's "unknown superiors" and the mysterious career of the enigmatic Rabbi Samuel Falk, a Cabalist from eastern Europe who was at the center of an occult community in London in the 1740s.[13] Aleister Crowley, an early member of the Golden Dawn who broke with it to start his own occult society, took a Besant-Leadbeater turn and declared that he had contacted a Secret Chief psychically in a hotel room in Cairo. He spoke of an extraterrestrial intelligence he called Aiwass, who, Crowley claimed, dictated to him his notorious *Book of the Law*. How

different Crowley's "Aiwass" was from run-of-the-mill spirit communication is unclear, but many of Crowley's followers, such as the
late Kenneth Grant, also tried to establish contact with this disem-
bodied "Master." Gurdjieff talked about the mysterious "Sarmoung
Brotherhood," and the "inner circle of humanity." Some, like his
follower J. G. Bennett, traveled in Central Asia in search of these
"Masters of Wisdom," believing they had some link to present-day
Sufi brotherhoods. Ouspensky, Gurdjieff's most brilliant student,
began his "search for the miraculous" by trying to make contact
with what he called "schools." At first he considered "the possibility of a non-physical contact . . . a contact, 'on another plane.'"[14]
Later, this idea of "schools" became "more real and tangible," and
with his meeting with Gurdjieff in a Moscow café, he believed he
had finally found one, or at least someone who had. After break-
ing with Gurdjieff, Ouspensky spent the rest of his life trying to
reach the esoteric source of his ex-master's teachings. Sadly, he
never did.[15]

One thing that differentiates HPB's approach to her Masters
from some of these accounts is that, regardless of whether they
"really" existed or not, one soon grasps that, whoever Blavatsky is
talking about, they are actual people. Although Blavatsky claimed
to communicate with her Masters mentally, we never have the
sense that the Masters themselves are "spirits" or "entities" or
"higher beings." They are men. Remarkable men, possessed of
remarkable powers, with high aims and a noble mission, but men
nonetheless. And if we accept the possibility that they really did
exist—putting aside the question of whether they really were
Masters—one can't help but ask: Who were they?

Oddly, it seems that until relatively recently, no one, whether

Theosophist or skeptic, tried to answer this question. Over the years, Theosophists more or less seem to have accepted Blavatsky's account, and with the rise of Besant and Leadbeater's neo-Theosophy, regarded the Masters as entirely spiritual beings, existing on the "higher planes." Skeptics took the Hodgson route and regarded them as sheer fabrications. One attempt to pin the Masters down—or at least one of them—was made by Jean Overton Fuller. In *Blavatsky and Her Teachers*, Fuller provides a list of dignitaries who accompanied the Premier of Nepal during his visit to Queen Victoria in 1850, and suggests that "Master Morya" was among these. Although HPB says her first physical encounter with Morya occurred in London in 1851 during the Great Exhibition, and not 1850, Overton speculates that either Morya returned to London the following year, or had simply stayed on to see the exhibition. It was one of the most important attractions of the time and drew people from around the world, so it would not be unusual for a high-ranking Nepalese either to extend his stay in London in order to see it, or to return.[16]

Yet the most extensive and convincing investigation into the "real" identities of the Masters was undertaken by the Theosophical historian K. Paul Johnson. His work remains controversial, but it is highly stimulating and, perhaps more than anything else, is responsible for a kind of "Blavatsky revival" taking place on the Internet, with scholars, Theosophists, and simply interested readers, engaging in a lively and passionate debate. (Others involved in the "Blavatsky revival" are Michael Gomes and Daniel Caldwell.) Whether or not Johnson is right, he has done HPB and Theosophy a great service by reinvigorating discussion about her and re-evaluating her importance to modern thought and culture. If the

"Back to Blavatsky" movement of the early twentieth century failed to attract much attention, Johnson's work may achieve what those stalwart devotees of HPB set out to do.

Johnson argues, in essence, that Blavatsky's Masters were a combination of three things: her youthful romantic fantasies of Rosicrucian adepts and Masonic "unknown superiors," stimulated by her discovery of her great-grandfather's occult library; her own fertile self-mythologizing; and her actual encounters during her travels with a variety of men and women who, like herself, were engaged in the pursuit and study of esoteric knowledge. Johnson does not comment on HPB's powers, nor on how the Mahatma Letters could have been precipitated, and unless we decide that she had no powers and the precipitations were faked, I think we must keep an open mind about these. But, as HPB herself repeatedly pointed out, this is the least important aspect of her work, and, as we know, she herself regretted the attention her phenomena drew. I have no idea how she could have made a teacup material-ize in solid earth—if she did—not to mention a brooch in a pillow, or how she could perform some of her other phenomena, and more than likely I never will. But I have, by now, stopped losing sleep over it. When you write books about the kind of people I do— Swedenborg, Rudolf Steiner, C. G. Jung—you start to accept strange phenomena as part of the territory.

Johnson points out that HPB's ideas about her Masters changed throughout her career. Who might qualify as a Master seemed rather fluid, ranging from the spirit guide "John King," to the Egyptians Tuitit and Serapis Bey, to their last incarnation in her Indian Mahatmas. We must remember that it was Damodar Mavalankar, and not Blavatsky, who started calling the Masters

Mahatmas. Blavatsky herself pointed out more than once that, although she herself received her training in Tibet, it was not the home of the Brotherhood, and that they had bases across the globe. Blavatsky's habit of providing prequels to her life at various times, that linked up her past activities with those of her present, gave the impression that Master M was *one* individual who was involved in her life at different times over many years. Yet the possible candidates for Master M include different people, involved with her at different times. "M" could have been the Italian radical Giuseppe Mazzini in London, Paulos Metamon in Cairo, and even the novelist Bulwer-Lytton: Each have been suggested as his "true" identity. We have even seen that she could be wrong about a Master. Before arriving in India, Blavatsky believed that Swami Dayananda Saraswati was a Master, or at least was working with them. But once she and the Colonel met him, she realized he wasn't. And we've seen, too, that the Masters themselves could be wrong. Elbridge Gerry Brown, the editor of *Spiritual Scientist*, the journal that published HPB's "first occult shot," turned out to be a dead end.

"Master" seems a title of honor and respect that HPB bestowed on different people throughout her life. I don't doubt that she had an "inner" Master, something along the lines of a guardian angel, or Socrates' "daimon," who guided her at difficult times and who first came to her in her childhood. Later, this "inner" Master, which I think we can associate with her accounts of a "double life" and a kind of "controlled multiple personality," came to be linked to the "real-life" Masters she read about in her great-grandfather's library. Then, as she began her travels, she met people who so impressed her, that she regarded them as Masters. We have met some of them in this book: A. L. Rawson, Max Théon, Agardi Metrovitch, Paulos Metamon. Whether they considered themselves Masters or not—or whether anyone else did—isn't the point. HPB did, and her contact with them fueled both her romantic, adventurous spirit, and her omnivorous appetite for knowledge.

As Johnson says, HPB's Masters were "real persons systematically fictionalized in Blavatsky's accounts." This is not to say she "lied" about them, but that they became "Masters" in her eyes, and in this way, part of her ongoing self-mythologizing. Again, self-mythologizing does not simply mean lying; only an irredeemably literal-minded person would think so. But from an early age, Blavatsky was on a search, a quest, which she believed was guided by an inner destiny, and at different points, different people came to her as guides, instructors, and role models. The philosopher Nietzsche remarked that "the great man is the play-actor of his own ideal." This means that in order to become who you want to be—which is who you "really" are—you have to pretend to be that person already. By believing in her quest, her mission, Blavatsky made it true.

Part of this belief meant telling stories, "true lies," an idea we will return to shortly. In this sense it is pointless trying to discover which of the several accounts of Blavatsky's first meeting with Master M is the "real" one—and it may be the case that Blavatsky *purposefully* changed her story in order to get this point across, and not, as literal-minded skeptics might say, in order to "cover her tracks." What is "real" is that she met Master M, he gave her a mission, and she accepted it. The rest is "histery," an awful coinage that conveys the fact that HPB's life was made up of more or less equal parts of history and mystery, some of which I've tried to outline in this book. Whether she met M in London or Ramsgate, in Hyde Park or on Waterloo Bridge is, in a very real sense, unimportant, although biographers and historians may wrack their brains over it and rummage through more than a century and a half of wreckage searching for clues. Writing this book, I've sometimes wondered if I am in the position of that visitor to Holland Park who was told by HPB in all earnestness that the earth is shaped like a dumbbell. I ask myself: Are all the "blinds," tall tales, wild adventures, and improbable claims pointing to *something else*, and have I been too thick to see this?

Johnson's most controversial claim is that he is fairly certain of the identity of the two main Masters, at least for the period in HPB's life when they were most in public notice. These are, of course, Morya and Koot Hoomi. His suspects are Maharaja Ranbir Singh of Kashmir, in the role of M; and Thakar Singh Sandhawalia, founding president of the Amritsar Singh Sabha, a Sikh reform movement, in that of KH. Johnson points out that in its early years, the TS focused on the revival of Western occultism as a viable alternative to both materialist science and dogmatic Christianity. Although HPB claimed that she always had her eyes on India, it wasn't until her arrival on the subcontinent's shores that the TS's focus shifted to the revival of Indian culture and the reform of Indian society; hence its early but mistaken union with the Arya Samaj. These concerns, Johnson argues, were motivated by HPB's alliance with Ranbir Singh, who supported her work openly, but, he argues, was also in a secret confederacy with her. Johnson's argument is detailed, but according to him, both Ranbir Singh and Thakar Singh Sandhawalia were committed to advocating religious brotherhood. In the maharaja's case, his subjects included Muslims, Buddhists, Christians, and Sikhs, so the kind of religious tolerance promoted by the TS was a political necessity for him. HPB, we know, was associated with different progressive, if not radical, political movements, and the idea that she got involved with them in India too shouldn't be too surprising. HPB lent her support to the Singh Sabha and to what Johnson calls "a network of Sikh and Hindu maharajahs in a secret coalition opposing Christian missionaries."[17]

Although HPB wasn't a Russian spy, the British were right to be wary of her, as her "silent partners" in India did include powerful leaders who could make trouble for the Raj. This comes through in the Mahatma Letters; at one point, KH informs Sinnett that, at a signal from him, forces could be unleashed against the British and the "white race which subjugates and daily humiliates mine." It also makes clear why Sinnett was important to them. As an influential part of that "white race," who had thrown his support behind their "agent"—HPB—he was an excellent means, at first, of getting their message across. Johnson points out that with Sinnett's departure from *The Pioneer* and the failure of "the *Phoenix* venture," the attempt to start a Maharaja-funded newspaper (mentioned in Chapter 8), KH lost interest in the plan. KH/Thakar Singh Sandhawalia was also deeply involved in a conspiracy to return his cousin, the disposed Dalip Singh, the last Maharaja of the Sikh empire, from England to northern India as ruler of an independent Punjab; and it is in his company that most accounts suggest that Blavatsky has another meeting with Morya "in the house of a stranger" (Chapter 2). The plan was thwarted by the British, but by this time, Johnson argues, the KH identity was of no further use to Thakar Singh Sandhawalia, and he drops out of

view. Yet by then, A. O. Hume was on his way to founding the
Indian National Congress, a movement he claimed was inspired by
"advanced initiates."[18] Gandhi wrote of the early days of the Congress that all "the top congressmen were theosophists," so it is not
an exaggeration to say that Theosophy was a threat to the British
in India after all.[19]

Johnson is also controversial among Theosophists for his belief
that Blavatsky, and to some extent Olcott, were involved in *some*
deception with the Mahatma Letters. Not in the way that Richard
Hodgson believed—although here, too, Johnson's opinions have
drawn much criticism. Johnson accepts that Hodgson's investigation was flawed and that he was wrong to accept the Coulombs'
account at face value. But he doesn't believe, as some Theosophists
do, perhaps rightly, that Vernon Harrison's examination of Hodgson's report exonerates HPB completely. In fact, Johnson argues
that the whole "Tibetan adventure" was one of Blavatsky's "blinds,"
and that during the time that she claimed she was in Tibet, she
was really in northern India. The "Tibet blind" was devised to
draw attention away from her "real" Indian Masters in order to
protect their identities, and it was a device she used even with her
followers. But when first the Coulombs and then Hodgson drew
unfriendly attention to them, Blavatsky realized her Masters were
in danger.

Even earlier, Blavatsky had second thoughts about using the
Masters as a means of drawing recruits into her mission. In a letter
to Franz Hartmann, she wrote that when Olcott met a Master in
Bombay, he "went crazy," and that this started an uncontrollable
process of turning her Masters from real, if incognito, people into
"Gods on earth." With each new meeting with a Master by new

members, their status grew, and Blavatsky must have realized that soon the whole game would explode. But it was the Masters and the belief in them that were drawing people to Theosophy and, perhaps even more important, were giving many Hindus a renewed sense of self-esteem and cultural awakening. Hodgson's conclusion that the Masters were a fabrication was difficult to bear, but it was better than their real identities becoming known, as the political repercussions could have been disastrous, and Blavatsky was fiercely loyal. So she shouldered the blame, took the path of suffering, and protected the secret. Such, in a nutshell, is Johnson's argument.

My own feeling is that HPB's Masters were in many ways what the seventeenth-century Rosicrucian author Johann Valentin Andreae called a *ludibrium*, a Latin word meaning "serious joke." Andreae was the author of *The Chemical Wedding of Christian Rosenkreutz*, a strange alchemical document published in 1616 following the first Rosicrucian manifestos. When word of the Rosicrucians got out, a "Rosicrucian furor," as the historian Frances Yates called it, broke out across half of Europe. If the tabloid press had been around then, stories about the mysterious Rosicrucians would be turning up there, and they would be "trending" heavily on the Internet and filling tweets on Twitter—as would Blavatsky's Masters. As Olcott did when he met a Master, Europe went crazy for the strange, secret Brotherhood. Yet, soon this furor turned sour, and "the Invisibles" became the target of ridicule and calumny.

In order to protect the *ideals* that the Rosicrucians stood for, Andreae admitted that, yes, the *Chemical Wedding*—and, by inference, the earlier manifestos—were a kind of fiction. There were no *literal* Rosicrucians, but this wasn't important. The *fiction* of a literal Brotherhood was a useful device to convey the ideas of a "general reformation" at the heart of the manifestos. It also provided a model for how individuals, eager to help that "reformation" along, would act. They were the "true lies," which enabled Nietzsche's "great men" to be "play actors of their own ideal." The Rosicrucians of the manifestos may have never existed, but the people who were moved by the manifestos and inspired by their values, *became Rosicrucians themselves*. Two very important self-made Rosicrucians were the English Hermeticist and physician Robert Fludd, and the Bohemian philosopher and educator Jan Comenius, "father of general education" whose pedagogical ideals are recognized by UNESCO in the Comenius Medal it awards for outstanding achievements in education.[20] I write of both elsewhere.[21]

Andreae and his colleagues didn't imagine their manifestos would generate the tumult they did, nor that they would lead to the rancor against the Rosicrucians that quickly followed. Alarmed at this, he thought it better to say the Rosicrucians were a kind of joke that got out of hand, and so diffuse the situation. In this way, the ideas and beliefs informing the Rosicrucian experiment could be salvaged, and put to use elsewhere, which is exactly what Andreae did.[22]

I think HPB's Masters were a *ludibrium* that got out of hand, a serious joke that went wrong, or at least caused as much trouble as good. After the Hodgson affair, HPB realized this and, as Johnson notes, began to soft-pedal both the Masters and phenomena. They had, in any case, served their purpose, and introduced many people to a much needed alternative to a reductive, materialist science, and a sclerotic, dogmatic religion. Sadly, in many ways, the Masters themselves soon became the source of a new dogmatism—or at least the ideas about them that HPB had no control over did. Olcott wasn't the only one to "go crazy" over the Masters, nor was he the only one besides HPB to have seen them "in the flesh." Daniel Caldwell's excellent collection, *The Esoteric World of Madame Blavatsky*, includes many eyewitness accounts of meetings with the Masters by a wide range of people. I can only leave it to the reader to judge their authenticity.

In one case it is possible that a too strong belief in the Masters may even have led to tragedy. In February 1885, Damodar Mavalankar, having received permission to join the Masters at their ashram—or so he believed—left Adyar en route for Tibet. HPB later spoke of Mavalankar as someone who had "fully benefited" by Theosophy, and that he alone proved that the move from New York to India wasn't in vain. Mavalankar held a unique position in the Coulomb-Hodgson scandal, being singled out by Emma Coulomb as one of HPB's dupes and accused by Hodgson of being one of her accomplices. Like many around HPB, his earnestness often outshone his good sense, and some Theosophists, like Franz Hartmann, thought little of him. But he was undeniably dedicated, and he stood by HPB when other Hindus, like T. Subba Row, abandoned her. By April 1 he had reached Darjeeling, and on April 19, he met with a Tibetan lama who was to guide him to KH and M's monastery. On April 23, he made his last note in his diary, saying that he was heading on alone from Kabi—a district in Sikkim—and that he had sent his things back with the coolies.

That was the last official word from Damodar, and some months later there were unconfirmed reports that his frozen body had been found in the snow. Colonel Olcott suggested that the "body" was really a *maya*, an illusion, created to leave a false trail, that is, a "blind," an idea HPB agreed with. As with practically everything else in this story, there is much debate about the fate of Damodar. In a letter of 1886, KH himself said Damodar had arrived but had undergone severe trials, a necessary preparation for the work ahead, and was recovering. In a letter published in *Lucifer* in 1889, a *sannyasin*, Sriman Swamy, said that he had seen Damodar in Lhasa, where he was convalescing. Although HPB was pleased to hear word of her *chela*, she denied he ever was in Lhasa, saying that this was another "blind," thrown out to obscure his true location. She also said that she had already received letters from him previously, acknowledging his arrival, but these have not survived. By the 1930s, Gottfried de Purucker, Katherine Tingley's second-in-command, was stating that Damodar was in Shambhala working with the other Masters in their secret sacred sanctuary. If this was the case, it would be a terrific endorsement for "play acting one's own ideal." Here, Damodar not only reached the Masters, he became one himself, something in fact that HPB believed was, fate willing, in the cards.[23]

The rest of us no doubt will have to settle for something less fantastic, and with the amount of spiritual tourism in the Himalayas these days, the Masters and their troupe have more than likely headed for less popular locations. In Chapter 5, I spoke of C. G. Harrison's strange idea—later repeated by Rudolf Steiner—that for a time Blavatsky was held captive in "occult imprisonment," and that she was only set free by some Hindu mystics, to whom she was then indebted. Johnson makes the point that with the Coulomb-Hodgson scandal, HPB was in a way set free from a different kind of "occult imprisonment," and was then able to follow her own path, no longer in thrall to her particular Masters at the time. Inarguably, her most creative periods were the times prior to and after her years in India, when she produced *Isis Unveiled*, *The Secret Doctrine*, *The Voice of the Silence*, and *The Key to Theosophy*, works by which, with the absence of Masters today, her reputation must either stand or fall. With all due respect to those who argue for its authenticity, how important it is that *The Secret Doctrine* is really based on the mysterious *Book of Dzyan*, and that this really exists, is debatable, a situation followers of Gurdjieff also find themselves in when they anchor the importance of his work in the "real" existence of the Sarmoung Brotherhood. As someone who devoted some years to the Gurdjieff "work," it never made a difference to me whether the ideas and disciplines I was struggling with came from a secret fraternity in Central Asia, or Gurdjieff's own fertile and inventive mind. They were exciting and compelling, and that was enough. In the end, I opted for Gurdjieff's fertile mind rather than the Sarmoung Brotherhood as their source. Others, I know, disagree.

While questions about whether or not HPB was ever in Tibet, ever met "real" Masters, ever learned Senzar, and dozens of others will no doubt trouble all who take her seriously, in the end what is important now are the writings she left behind, and what we can understand about her life. My own belief is that HPB was one of the most creative synthesizers in modern thought, and that she pulled together an enormous wealth of ideas, observations, and speculations about ourselves and the cosmos from a dizzying range of sources, and out of this produced at least two undeniable classics. If she did only this, it would be enough for us to owe her a debt of gratitude. Being one of the most adventurous, fearless, and indomitable women of the nineteenth century in the bargain makes what we owe her almost an embarrassment. Those around her had the benefit of being exposed to her electric character, and many profited by the shocks—it was with some accuracy that Rudolf Steiner described her as an "electrically charged Leyden jar," from whom "electric sparks—occult truths—could be produced."[24] I seriously doubt if Countess Wachtmeister, G. R. S. Mead, or even Colonel Olcott thought getting the "secret doctrine" down correctly was as important as being open to her teaching by example. And, as most accounts show, at this she was surely a Master. If we go in search of her own Masters, more than likely we will not find them. But we may discover someone even more remarkable along the way: that "old lady," "chum," and tireless scourge of flapdoodle, the incomparable HPB.

Acknowledgments

No one familiar with Madame Blavatsky will be surprised if I say this was a difficult book to write. My efforts were aided immeasurably by many helpers, not all of whom I can mention here individually. Special thanks, though, goes to Joscelyn Godwin and Peter Lamont, for answering questions about HPB's relationship with D. D. Home. Lou Lou Belle was instrumental in securing research material, as was, as usual, the staff of the British Library. My friends John, Lisa, and Greta were once again very generous in the use of their home in Munich, where some of this book was written. James Hamilton gracefully endured repeated monologues about Blavatsky's importance. Mike Jay's encyclopedic knowledge of the history of drug use helped clarify some issues, and John Harrison's friendly concern was a welcome support. My editor, Mitch Horowitz, supplied some crucial information. And once again, my sons, Max and Joshua, and their mother, Ruth, were, as usual, a special help.

Notes

INTRODUCTION: WHO WAS MADAME BLAVATSKY?

1. Kurt Vonnegut, "The Mysterious Madame Blavatsky," *McCall's*, March 1970.
2. Christopher Bamford, Introduction to C. G. Harrison, *The Transcendental Universe* (London: Temple Lodge, 1993), p. 8.
3. Sylvia Cranston, *HPB: The Extraordinary Life and Influence of Helena Blavatsky* (New York: Tarcher/Putnam, 1993), pp. 195–96.
4. She appears as "Madame Sosostris," the "famous clairvoyant" who "had a bad cold" but was "nevertheless the wisest woman in Europe, with a wicked pack of cards." Yet Blavatsky didn't read tarot cards (although she was a dab hand at solitaire) nor did she, as Eliot suggests, do horoscopes. And while on occasion she practiced clairvoyance, it was not one of her specialties.
5. On Kandinsky and Theosophy, see my article, "Kandinsky's Thought Forms: The Occult Roots of Modern Art" at www.theosophical.org/publications/quest-magazine/1405.
6. www.teosofiskakompaniet.net/LFrankBaumTheosophist.htm.
7. Cranston, 1993, pp. 195–96.
8. http://theosnet.ning.com/profiles/blogs/meanderings-september-19-2010.also http://theosnet.ning.com/profiles/blogs/what-everyone-should-know?xg_source=activity.
9. Peter Washington, *Madame Blavatsky's Baboon* (London: Secker & Warburg, 1993), p. 32.
10. Rudolf Steiner, *The Occult Movement in the Nineteenth Century* (London: Rudolf Steiner Press, 1973), p. 31.
11. K. Paul Johnson, *Initiates of Theosophical Masters* (Albany: SUNY Press, 1995), p. 140.
12. Maria Carlson, *No Religion Higher Than Truth: A History of the Theosophical Movement in Russia, 1875–1922* (Princeton, N.J.: Princeton University Press, 1993), p. 43.
13. James Santucci, "Does Theosophy Exist in the Theosophical Society?," in *Ésotérisme, Gnoses & Imaginaire Symbolique: Mélanges Offerts À Antoine Faivre,* eds., Richard Caron, Joscelyn Godwin, Wouter J. Hanegraaff and Jean-Louis Viellard-Baron (Leuven, Belgium: Peeters, 2001), p. 473.

14. Johnson, 1995, pp. 140, 158.

15. Cranston, p. 41.

16. Nicholas Goodrick-Clarke, *Helena Blavatsky* (Berkeley: North Atlantic Books, 2004), pp. 6, 5.

17. Helena Petrovna Blavatsky, *The Letters of H. P. Blavatsky to A. P. Sinnett* (Pasadena, Calif.: Theosophical University Press, 1973), p. 154.

18. Quoted in Cranston, p. 64.

19. Helena Petrovna Blavatsky, *The Voice of the Silence* (Adyar, India: Theosophical Publishing House, 1959), p. 137.

20. See my article "Don Carlos and the Witches," in *Fortean Times*, vol. 238, July 2008.

21. Although in its time it was panned by writers as disparate as P. D. Ouspensky and Sax Rohmer, the creator of Dr. Fu Manchu—who mentions Blavatsky and the Mahatmas in one of his thrillers (*The Devil Doctor*, in *The Fu Manchu Omnibus* [London: Alison & Busby, 2000, p. 365]), Solovyov's *A Modern Priestess of Isis* remains a source of "information" about HPB. For Ouspensky, the work "brims over with petty spite and consists of detective-like descriptions of spying, eavesdropping, questioning housemaids, in short, endless trivial details the reader cannot verify" (quoted in Cranston, p. 299). And for Sax Rohmer, "the contrast between this giant soul and the deceptions and pusillanimity attributed to her was not worth a moment's hesitation" (*The Romance of Sorcery* [London: Kegan Paul, 2002, p. 262]). Yet the English translation of this gossipy fabrication appeared in 1895 under the auspices of the Society for Psychical Research as a "psychological study of extraordinary interest."

22. Joscelyn Godwin, *The Beginnings of Theosophy in France* (London: Theosophical History Center, 1989), p. 6.

23. Countess Constance Wachtmeister, *Reminiscence of H. P. Blavatsky and the Secret Doctrine* (Wheaton, Ill.: Theosophical Publishing House, 1976), pp. 135–36.

24. Colin Wilson, *The Occult* (New York: Random House, 1971), p. 379.

25. John Gray, *The Immortalization Commission: Science and the Strange Quest to Cheat Death* (New York: Farrar, Straus and Giroux, 2011), pp. 52–53. Gray draws on Washington's *Madame Blavatsky's Baboon* and the dubious memoirs of Count Witte, Blavatsky's cousin. See Chapter Two: Around the World in Eighty Ways, pp. 26–7.

26. Washington, 1993, p. 45.

27. Jacques Barzun, *A Jacques Barzun Reader* (New York: HarperCollins, 2002), p. 217.

28. Ibid., p. xix.

CHAPTER ONE: FROM RUSSIA WITH LOVE

1. Wilson, 1971, p. 337.

2. Colin Wilson, *The Devil's Party: A History of Charlatan Messiahs* (London: Virgin, 2000), p. 85.

3. "(I'm Always Touched by Your) Presence, Dear" can be found on Blondie's *Greatest Hits* and other Blondie compilations.

4. Although Madame Blavatsky did not become "HPB" until much later—and did not even become Madame Blavatsky until she married—for convenience's sake I will refer to her by these titles in her early years.

5. Cranston, p. 4.

6. Quoted in Cranston, p. 13.

7. Vera Zhelihovsky [in Daniel H. Caldwell, *The Esoteric World of Madame Blavatsky* (Wheaton, Ill.: Quest Books, 2000), p. 5.

8. Cranston, p. 18.
9. Ibid., p. 27.
10. Quoted in Caldwell, p. 3.
11. Ibid., p. 9.
12. Jean Overton Fuller, *Blavatsky and Her Teachers* (London/The Hague: East-West Publications, 1988), p. 2.
13. Ibid.
14. Helena Petrovna Blavatsky, *H.P.B. Speaks*, vol. II, ed. C. Jinarajadasa (Adyar: Theosophical Publishing House, 1951), p. 62.
15. Marion Meade, *Madame Blavatsky: The Woman Behind the Myth* (Lincoln, Neb.: iUniverse, 2000) pp. 43–44.
16. Cranston, p. 43.
17. Blavatsky, 1951, p. 63. It should be noted that Jean Overton Fuller believes the Dondoukov-Korsakov letters to be forgeries, or at least unreliable, and that "there is no warrant for supposing Prince Dolgourouky possessed an alchemical library" or that HPB "would have been so silly" as to suggest that she had read it all by the age of fifteen (Fuller, pp. 236–37). Others disagree, and the research by K. Paul Johnson, Nicholas Goodrick-Clarke, and other scholars into the history of Russian Freemasonry, which Fuller may not have been aware of, is, to me, persuasive.
18. Goodrick-Clarke, pp. 2–3.
19. For more on Baron von Hund, the Knights Templar, and the "unknown superiors," see my *Politics and the Occult* (Wheaton, Ill.: Quest Books, 2008), pp. 40–52.
20. The Russian philosopher Nikolai Berdyaev claimed that Novikov was chiefly concerned with the moral and social side of Freemasonry and that "the passion for alchemy and magic and the occult sciences was alien to his mind." See *The Russian Idea* (Hudson, N.Y.: Lindisfarne Press, 1992), p. 36. Berdyaev does, however, agree that mystical Masonry was an enormous influence on the Russian mind in the late eighteenth century.
21. K. Paul Johnson, 1994, pp. 20–21. I have drawn on Johnson's important work for this section.

CHAPTER TWO: AROUND THE WORLD IN EIGHTY WAYS

1. Wilson, 1971, p. 379.
2. Berdyaev, p. 24.
3. For more on this time in Russia's history, see my *A Dark Muse* (New York: Thunder's Mouth Press, 2005), pp. 212–18.
4. Hesse's thoughts on "Russian Man" can be found in his essay "The Brothers Karamazov, or The Decline of Europe," collected in Hermann Hesse, *My Belief*, ed. Theodore Ziolkowski (London: Jonathan Cape, 1976), pp. 70–85. T. S. Eliot was so impressed by this essay that in 1922 he traveled to Montagnola, Switzerland, to see Hesse, and references to the work appear in the notes to *The Waste Land*, the same poem in which Eliot depicts Madame Blavatsky as "Madame Sosotris." On the idea of "holy sinning," see my *Politics and the Occult*, pp. 57–59; on "Russian Man" and the occult revival of the 1960s, see my *Turn Off Your Mind* (New York: Disinformation Company, 2003).
5. Berdyaev, p. 23.
6. www.archive.org/stream/memoirsofcountwi00wittuoft#page/8/mode/2up, pp. 4–10.
7. Blavatsky, 1951, p. 63.

8. Crowley read the book after seeing a reference to it in A. E. Waite's *Book of Black Magic and Pacts*, and Eckhartshausen's hints about a secret society of adepts led to Crowley's joining the Hermetic Order of the Golden Dawn.

9. Carlson, p. 17.

10. www.fuller.mit.edu/personal/war_peace/alexander_i.htm.

11. Berdyaev, p. 70.

12. Fuller, p. 4.

13. Blavatsky, 1951, p. 63.

14. www.casebook.org/dissertations/collected-donston.8.html.

15. Although all Sufi and dervish groups were banned by Kemal Atatürk in 1925, the Pera *tekke* survived as a museum. In 1996, I had the good fortune to visit it during a stay in Istanbul. At the time, I had no idea that Blavatsky had visited it as well, although I did know that I was following in the footsteps of P. D. Ouspensky, who met with the dervishes there in 1920 before his move to England.

16. Fuller, p. 5.

17. Ibid., p. 34.

18. Meade, 2000, p. 86.

19. O. V. de Lubicz Milosz, *The Noble Traveller*, ed. Czeslaw Milosz (West Stockbridge, Mass.: Inner Traditions/Lindisfarne, 1985), p. 339.

20. Joscelyn Godwin, *The Theosophical Enlightenment* (Albany, N.Y.: SUNY Press, 1994), p. 278.

21. K. Paul Johnson, p. 26; Cranston, p. 43.

22. Quoted in Caldwell, 2000, pp. 44–47.

23. Thanks go to my friend Mike Jay, the historian of drug use, for this information.

24. Helena Petrovna Blavatsky, *The Key to Theosophy* (London: Theosophical Publishing House, 1948), p. 88.

25. René Guénon, *Le Théosophisme, histoire d'une pseudo-religion* (Paris: Editions Traditionnelles, 1921).

26. Godwin, 1994, p. 289.

27. Cranston, p. 44.

28. Jean Overton Fuller, however, argues that London was the "blind," and that Ramsgate was the true site of the meeting. See Fuller, pp. 8–9.

29. Ibid., p. 52.

30. Blavatsky, *Collected Writings,* vol. I, p. xlii, note 85.

31. Fuller, p. 17; Cranston, p. 105.

32. Quoted in Caldwell, 2000, p. 24.

CHAPTER THREE: SEVEN YEARS IN TIBET?

1. See my *Politics and the Occult*, pp. 124–25.

2. Curiously, Alexandra David-Neel's life in many ways parallels HPB's. She first became interested in Tibet after attending lectures on Eastern religions at the Paris Theosophical Society, and she herself became a leading Theosophist. Like HPB, she worked and traveled as both a musician and journalist, was a strongwilled young girl who came from badly matched parents, escaped from a precipitous marriage only days after the wedding ceremony, and remained single for the rest of her long life. She died in 1969, just short of her 101st birthday. Again like HPB, although separated and leading totally independent lives, her husband supported her throughout his life and financed her travels. Like HPB, she was deeply devoted to Tibetan Buddhism, wrote much about it, and embraced its belief in magic and mysticism, a philosophy in evidence in her classic *Magic and Mystery in*

Tibet (1931). And like HPB, she had detractors who claimed that she was never in Lhasa or Tibet, and that her accounts of her travels were pure fiction. Also like HPB, her travels were motivated by a quest for "the unknown." See Alexandra David-Neel, *My Journey to Lhasa* (London: Virago Press, 1988), the introduction by Peter Hopkirk, pp. ix–xvi, and David-Neel's own introduction, p. xvii.

3. David-Neel, *Magic and Mystery*, p. 87.
4. There is also some controversy among pro-HPB biographers over the exact number and dates of her Tibetan sojourns. Cranston reports three attempts, in 1853, 1856, and 1868; Fuller denies the 1853 date and suggests somewhere between 1854 and 1855. Blavatsky herself says her first attempt was in 1856, but then, as we know, she was never good with dates.
5. Quoted in Cranston, p. 51.
6. Washington, p. 33.
7. Cranston, pp. 50–51; Fuller, pp. 13–14.
8. Gertrude Marvin Williams, *Priestess of the Occult: Madame Blavatsky* (New York: Alfred A. Knopf, 1946), p. 28; Arthur Lillie, *Madame Blavatsky and Her "Theosophy"* (London: Swan Sonnenschein & Co., 1985), pp. 12–13. Fuller points out that Arthur Lillie, a spiritualist, was one of HPB's "oldest enemies"; Fuller, p. 14.
9. Fuller, p. 15.
10. Colonel Olcott, "Traces of Blavatsky," quoted in Cranston, pp. 57–58.
11. Fuller, p. 24.
12. Lama Anagarika Govinda, *The Way of the White Clouds* (London: Rider, 1984), p. 203.
13. Cranston, p. 82.
14. See, for example, *Discipleship in the New Age, A Treatise on White Magic*, and *The Externalization of the Hierarchy*, all published by the Lucis Publishing Company.
15. Major Cross's remarks as well as those of Major-General Murray can be found in Walter A. Carrithers, Jr.'s pamphlet, *The Truth about Madame Blavatsky: An Open Letter to the Author of "Priestess of the Occult"* at www.blavatskyfoundation .org/carrith1.htm. The author in question is Gertrude Marvin Williams, whose biography, like that of Marion Meade, depicts HPB's life as one of "scandalous conduct" and a "riot of lust and ignominy." According to Carrithers, Williams's book is "built of the debris that seventy years of slander have cast up on the sands of time."
16. Blavatsky, *Voice of the Silence*, p. ii.
17. See my *Politics and the Occult*, pp. 100–101. For more on Hermes Trismegistus and the *prisca theologia*, see my *The Quest for Hermes Trismegistus* (Edinburgh: Floris Books, 2011).
18. Fuller, p. 1.
19. The classic work on elementals in the Western tradition is the mysterious *Comte de Gabalis*, published anonymously in 1670. The work was later ascribed to the Abbé N. de Montfaucon de Villars. The text is available at www .archive.org/details/cu31924028957467.
20. David-Neel, 1977, p. 168.
21. Govinda, p. 70.
22. Ibid., p. 38.
23. Ibid., pp. 94, 101–02. On hypnagogia, see my *A Secret History of Consciousness* (Great Barrington, Mass.: Lindisfarne, 2003), pp. 85–94. Also see my *Fortean Times* article "Waking Sleep" www.mindpowernews.com/Hypnagogic.htm.
24. David-Neel, 1977, p. 210.
25. Ibid., p. 94.

26. Ibid., p. 221.

27. Ibid., p. 93.

28. Heinrich Zimmer, *Philosophies of India* (New York: Meridian Books, 1957), p. 517; Alexandra David-Neel, 1977, p. 203.

29. Helena Petrovna Blavatsky, "Mr. A. Lillie's Delusions," *Light* 1884, collected in *A Modern Panarion: A Collection of Fugitive Fragments From the Pen of H. P. Blavatsky, A Facsimile of the Original Edition of 1895, Scanned and Edited 2003* (Los Angeles: The Theosophy Company, 1981), pp. 255–57, at www.theosophy.org/Blavatsky/ Modern%20Panarion/Panarion.htm.

CHAPTER FOUR: A HAUNTING IN CHITTENDEN

1. Cranston, pp. 102–03; Fuller, p. 27; Caldwell, 2000, pp. 30–31.

2. John Symonds, *In the Astral Light* (London: Panther Books, 1965), p. 36.

3. Fuller, p. 28.

4. Quoted in Caldwell, 2000, p. 36.

5. According to some accounts, the *société spirite* continued on for a time following HPB's departure. See Joscelyn Godwin, *The Theosopical Enlightenment* (Albany: SUNY Press, 1994), p. 279.

6. Caldwell, 2000, p. 34.

7. Godwin, 1994, p. 280.

8. Johnson, 1994, p. 57.

9. Cranston, p. 107; Fuller, p. 30.

10. Caldwell, 2000, p. 47.

11. Symonds, p. 28.

12. Washington, p. 31.

13. Poe's story "The Balloon Hoax" appeared in the April 13, 1844, issue of *The Sun*.

14. A century later, I would have been one of HPB's neighbors. In 1975, I lived at 266 Bowery. At that time, Elizabeth Street was a predominantly Hispanic neighborhood.

15. Jean Overton Fuller estimates that the one thousand roubles she received would have been worth around £23,000 in 1984 value, the time when Fuller was writing her book. Today this would be around £80,000, roughly $130,000 at the time of writing.

16. Caldwell, 2000, p. 45.

17. See my *Turn Off Your Mind*.

18. Colin Wilson, *Afterlife* (New York: Doubleday & Co., 1985), pp. 84–89.

19. See my *Politics and the Occult*, pp. 111–15.

20. Henry Steel Olcott, *Old Diary Leaves* (New York: G. P. Putnam's Sons, 1895), available online at http://archive.org/details/cu31924029168008.

21. Michael Gomes, *Colonel Olcott and the Healing Arts* (Brentwood, Essex: Doppler Press, 2007), p. 3.

22. P. D. Ouspensky, *A New Model of the Universe* (New York: Alfred A. Knopf, 1969), p. 4.

23. Washington, p. 41.

24. Michael Gomes, *The Dawning of the Theosophical Movement* (Wheaton: Quest Books, 1987), pp. 95–96.

25. Symonds, p. 36. Fuller, p. 56, argues that HPB's remarks about Home were mistakes made by the interviewer—either innocently or consciously. She points out several others in the same interview.

26. See www.spiritualismlink.forumoption.com/t389-blavatsky-versus-dd-home and www.katinkahesselink.net/blavatsky/articles/v1/y1876_008.htm.

27. Fuller, p. 54.
28. My own contribution to this murky business came about after reading two books by the skeptical parapsychologist Peter Lamont. In *The Rise of the Indian Rope Trick* (London: Abacus, 2004), Lamont remarks that "Madame Blavatsky's introduction to the spirit world was as a result of meeting the famous medium D. D. Home" (p. 61). He then refers to the letter from Home in which he laments HPB's power over his poor friend the baron. Yet in a later book, *The First Psychic* (London: Abacus, 2006), a biography of Home, Lamont makes no mention of this. In fact he makes no mention of HPB at all. One would think that, HPB being good copy, Lamont would include at least a brief mention of her in his book on Home who, according to his earlier book, was so concerned about the illicit relation between HPB and his friend. But he doesn't. Why not?

Lamont's source for his remarks about Home and HPB is a pamphlet, "The Fraud of Modern Theosophy Exposed: A Brief History of the Greatest Imposture ever perpetrated under the Cloak of Religion," published in 1913. The title alone should tell us that its author, the stage magician and virulent anti-spiritualist J. N. Maskelyne, was not one of Blavatsky's friends, and Lamont himself—also a stage magician—refers to the work as "vicious." In 1894, three years after HPB's death, Maskelyne filled his Egyptian Hall in London with audiences happy to pay to see a burlesque of Blavatsky and the famous Mahatma Letters. Maskelyne himself got Home's remarks about HPB from the arsenal of William Emmette Coleman, an equally vehement anti-HPB polemicist. A close reading of Home's letter suggests that a meeting between Home and Blavatsky is doubtful—at no point does Home unequivocally say that he either met or saw her—and argues that Home was, at best, criticizing her at second hand. But if he did not actually see HPB in Paris with his friend the baron, then the "evidence" for their supposed liaison is suspect, and Home may unknowingly be referring to the affair between the baron and Nathalie Blavatsky, or perhaps purposefully confusing the two.

When I wrote to Peter Lamont and asked why he left this very good story—or any mention of HPB at all—out of his book on Home, he replied very briefly that he didn't "recall any good evidence of them [HPB and Home] meeting," and that he "probably took the Maskelyne source at face value." Yet one might think that after repeating remarks about HPB in one book that he later discovered were incorrect, he might make a note of this in the later book, which is specifically about the source of some of the earlier incorrect remarks. A footnote relating that he found no evidence that HPB and Home ever met, and that the story of Home's concern over Blavatsky's lascivious designs on his friend was at best doubtful, would have done much to help unravel this knotted tale.

CHAPTER FIVE: ANCIENT WISDOM FOR A MODERN WORLD

1. Symonds, p. 24.
2. Ibid., p. 34.
3. www.katinkahesselink.net/blavatsky/articles/vi/y1874_002.htm.
4. Cranston, p. 130.
5. See especially his relationship to the work of the once popular but today virtually unknown "evolutionist" Ernst Haeckel in my *Rudolf Steiner* (New York: Tarcher/Penguin, 2007), pp. 79–81, 111.
6. Washington, p. 41.
7. Blavatsky, 1948, p. 88.
8. Cranston, pp. 131–32.

9. Fuller, p. 39; Wilson, 1987, p. 73.
10. Symonds, p. 53.
11. You might think the U.S. Civil War had a hand in it, but the phenomena at Hydesville predated this, and the "spiritualist epidemic" occurred in Europe too.
12. For a full account of the "hidden hand" behind Spiritualism, the reader is directed to Joscelyn Godwin's original articles in *Theosophical History*, N.S. III 2/5 (1990–91): 35–43, 66–76, 107–117, 137–148. See also Godwin, 1994. A good summary and interpretation can be found in Christopher Bamford's Introduction to C. G. Harrison, *The Transcendental Universe* (London: Temple Lodge, 1993).
13. See Dingwall's Introduction to Emma Hardinge Britten, *Modern American Spiritualism* (New Hyde Park, N.Y.: University Books, 1970), p. xvi.
14. An online text of *Ghost Land* is available at www.scribd.com/doc/29505505/Ghost-Land-Emma-Hardinge-Britten.
15. For more on Bulwer-Lytton, see my *A Dark Muse* (New York: Thunder's Mouth Press, 2005), pp. 99–105.
16. Godwin, 1994, pp. 206–12.
17. Harrison, 1993, p. 47.
18. Ibid., p. 46.
19. See, for example, the case of Antoine-Joseph Pernety and "the Thing," and the "unknown agent" of Jean-Baptiste Willermoz in my *Politics and the Occult*, pp. 83, 88.
20. Harrison, p. 86.
21. As HPB claimed to have been studying with her Master in Tibet in 1868, the chronology here doesn't quite fit.
22. Steiner, 1973, pp. 61–62.
23. Harrison, pp. 51–55. Annie Besant, *Letters from the Masters of the Wisdom* (Adyar, India: Theosophical Publishing House, 1925), p. 10.
24. In *Historia Vitae et Mortis*, Bacon argued that one can renew one's health by cuddling a puppy, which, as a "hot animal," has an abundance of vitality. The "white dog" has become local legend in Philadelphia, where a café now occupies 3420 Sansom Street, where Blavatsky lived. See www.articles.philly.com/1988-05-07/news/26260563_1_writings-theosophists-hindu.
25. Brian Inglis, *Natural and Supernatural* (Dorset: Prism Press, 1992), p. 267.
26. One of the authors, William Ivins, was HPB's lawyer for her suit against Countess Gerebko. Another, William S. Fales, was Ivins's colleague. During the proceedings, HPB was questioned about occultism and her answers prompted Ivins, Fales, and three friends to write their article.
27. Helena Petrovna Blavatsky, "A Few Questions to Hiraf," in Goodrick-Clarke, pp. 35–48.
28. Godwin, 1994, p. 292.
29. Blavatsky, 1948, pp. 137–38.
30. Washington, p. 54.

CHAPTER SIX: UNVEILING ISIS

1. Quoted in Cranston, p. 145.
2. Washington, p. 55.
3. Helena Petrovna Blavatsky, *Studies in Occultism* (Pasadena, Calif.: Theosophical University Press, 1980), p. 1.
4. Cranston, pp. 149–50.
5. It may be significant that in his adolescence, the psychologist C. G. Jung experienced a similar second consciousness, which, as Blavatsky did, he referred to as "No. 2." See my *Jung the Mystic* (New York: Tarcher/Penguin, 2010), pp. 29–31.

6. Cranston, p. 169.

7. Beatrice Hastings, *Defence of Madame Blavatsky*, vol. 1 (Worthing, Sussex: The Hastings Press, n.d.), pp. 8–11. Beatrice Hastings was for many years the lover of A. R. Orage (see Chapter 1) and was a central contributor to Orage's influential journal, *The New Age*. Unfortunately, she wrote under a number of pseudonyms and her contribution to this important organ of thought has often gone uncredited. She was later the lover of the painter Modigliani, for whom she also modeled. In failing health and despairing of her literary carer, she committed suicide in 1943. For more on Hastings, see John Carswell, *Lives and Letters* (New York: New Directions, 1978).

8. Adam Crabtree, *Multiple Man* (London: Holt, Rinehart, and Winston, 1985), p. 1.

9. Caldwell, 2000, p. 329.

10. It may be worthwhile to note that in *The Journey to the East*, Hermann Hesse remarks that "A long time devoted to small details exalts us and increases our strength." We might also note that the playwright August Strindberg used a similar method to tap the creative forces of the unconscious. Writing to a friend, Strindberg remarked that, in order to get into the creative mood, he had to "trick" himself into it by "distractions, games, cards, sleep . . . without bothering about results." See my *A Dark Muse*, p. 203. Like Blavatsky, Strindberg believed in higher intelligences that were guiding him, what he called "the Powers."

11. Crabtree, pp. 120–34.

12. Symonds, p. 66.

13. Cranston, p. 154.

14. Olcott, *Old Diary Leaves*, vol. I , pp. 99–109; Cranston, p. 159.

15. Ibid., p. 169.

16. Ibid., p. 175.

17. See my *Rudolf Steiner: An Introduction to His Life and Work* (New York: Tarcher/ Penguin, 2007), pp. 148–51.

18. In his account of his time with Gurdjieff, P. D. Ouspensky records a strange incident in which Gurdjieff transformed his appearance from an "ordinary man" into "a man of quite a different order." P. D. Ouspensky, *In Search of the Miraculous* (New York: Harcourt, Brace, 1949), pp. 324–26.

19. Caldwell, 2000, p. 95.

20. Hastings, vol. 1, p. 10.

21. Fuller, p. 50.

22. Blavatsky, 2004, ed. Goodrick-Clarke, p. 52; Hastings, vol.1, p. 28.

23. A list can be found in Goodrick-Clarke, pp. 50–52.

24. See my *The Quest for Hermes Trismegistus, from Ancient Egypt to the Modern World* (Edinburgh: Floris Books, 2011).

25. Deborah Blum, *Ghosthunters* (London: Century, 2007), p. 43.

26. Helena Petrovna Blavatsky, *Isis Unveiled*, vol. 1 (Pasadena: Theosophical Publishing House, 1972), p. 428.

27. Theodore Roszak, *Unfinished Animal: The Aquarian Frontier and the Evolution of Consciousness* (London: Faber and Faber, 1976), pp. 118–19.

28. Blavatsky, 1972, p. 428.

29. Ibid., p. xviii. Blavatsky's comment seems a remarkable pre-echo of Alfred North Whitehead's remark in *Science and the Modern World* (New York: Macmillan, 1925) that the materialist picture of the universe reveals a Nature that is "a dull affair, soundless, scentless, colourless; merely the hurrying of material, endlessly, meaninglessly," p. 77.

30. Blavatsky, 1972, p. 425.

31. In his famous letter to his Polish translator, Witold von Hulewicz, Rilke suggested that by interiorizing the physical world through what he called *Herzwerk* ("the work of the heart"), we create an "invisible" world, an interior microcosm of the external macrocosm. Through this interiorizing, Rilke believed that we may even be creating energies that can produce *new* worlds, "new substances, metals, nebulae and stars." In *The Quest for Hermes Trismegistus,* I relate Rilke's remarkable idea to both the Hermetic notion of the microcosm—ourselves—housing the macrocosm—the universe—and the astronomical conception of a "white gusher," the *other end* of a black hole, that some astrophysicists suggest may be emitting *new* stellar material in some far-flung patch of the universe. I also link these notions to Rudolf Steiner's belief that the actual physical body of the earth is a result of human consciousness. See *The Quest for Hermes Trismegistus,* pp. 197–99.

32. Caldwell, 2000, p. 102.

33. Blavatsky, 1972, pp. 136–37.

34. Ibid., p. 239.

35. Ibid.

36. Ibid., p. 235.

37. G. I. Gurdjieff, *Beelzebub's Tales to His Grandson, First Book* (New York: E. P. Dutton, 1978), p. 134.

38. Blavatsky, 1972, pp. 270–71.

39. Ibid., p. 274.

40. Ibid. Ouspensky, 1949, p. 24.

41. Blavatsky, 1972, p. 274.

42. Gary Lachman, "The Fate of the Earth According to Rudolf Steiner," *Gnosis* 33 (Fall 1994):22–27.

43. Blavatsky, 1972, p. 330.

44. Ibid., p. 284.

45. The "luminiferous ether" remained a staple of physics until the Michelson–Morley experiments of 1887 produced strong evidence against it. With the rise of Einstein's theory of relativity, it was discarded.

46. Blavatsky, 1972, p. 178.

47. Ibid., p. 179.

48. See my *A Secret History of Consciousness,* pp. 58–67.

49. Blavatsky, 1972, p. 179.

50. Ibid., p. 180.

51. Colin Wison, *Beyond the Occult: Twenty Years' Research into the Paranormal* (London: Bantam Press, 1987), p. 110.

52. Again, see *The Quest for Hermes Trismegistus,* chapters 2 and 7, where I relate the Astral Light to the "art of memory," Henry Corbin's "Imaginal World," the experience of hypnagogia, "cosmic consciousness," and Wilson's "Faculty X."

Chapter Seven: A Passage to India

1. Cranston, p. 162.

2. Blavatsky, 1980, p. 99.

3. Cranston, p. 182.

4. Godwin, 1994, p. 298.

5. Ibid., p. 279.

6. Cranston, p. 182.

7. Godwin, 1994, p. 322.

8. Ibid., p. 298.

9. Ibid., p. 300.
10. Josephine Ransom, *A Short History of the Theosophical Society* (Adyar: Theosophical Publishing House, 1938), p. 98.
11. Cranston, pp. 179–80.
12. Whatever we make of Olcott's account, two items do seem to remind us of what we know about the Orphic Circle and the strange occult group that the mysterious Chevalier Louis B encounters in *Ghost Land*. In Chapter 5, we saw that the Orphic Circle employed crystals and "magic mirrors," among other occult devices, and that when Louis B was brought into "mesmeric lucidity," he felt that he could see an "almost illimitable area of space," and that a "vast realm of perception" opened up before him (pp. 134–35). Olcott's visitors have him look into a crystal that, in a word, "mesmerized" him. And in his earlier visit by Liatto, the Master made the walls of Olcott's room disappear, to reveal a strange landscape.
13. Caldwell, 2000, pp. 73–76.
14. Symonds, p. 83.
15. Caldwell, 2000, p. 107.
16. Ibid., p. 109.
17. Ibid., pp. 111–12.
18. www.nytimes.com/1997/01/21/science/physicists-confirm-power-of-nothing-measuring-force-of-universal-flux.html?pagewanted=all&src=pm.
19. See my *Politics and the Occult*, pp. 126–30, for the Theosophical Society's role in this.
20. Carrie Nation (1846–1911) was a temperance movement leader known for vandalizing saloons with a hatchet. She was almost six feet tall, weighed 175 lbs., and had a stern demeanor.

CHAPTER EIGHT: A CRISIS IN ADYAR

1. www.blavatskyarchives.com/muller1.htm.
2. www.blavatskyarchives.com/sinnettesoteric_buddhism.htm.
3. See Donald S. Lopez, *The Tibetan Book of the Dead: A Biography* (Princeton, N.J.: Princeton University Press, 2011). By the time Evans-Wentz's edition of *The Tibetan Book of the Dead* was published in 1927, E. A. Wallis Budge's edition of *The Egyptian Book of the Dead* (1st edition, 1895) had been popular for more than thirty years.
4. http://theosophy.katinkahesselink.net/canadian/Vol-68-4-Theosophist.htm.
5. HPB was known to "precipitate" cigarettes as well, rolling one and then mysteriously "translocating" it to another room; see Caldwell, pp. 155–57. She was also known to change the monogram on a handkerchief, a feat she once performed on board the S.S. *Ellora*, bound for Ceylon; ibid., p. 123.
6. To give one example among many, in July 1881, Sarab J. Padshah reported that he received a letter from Koot Hoomi. "I heard a sound as if a large butterfly had fallen on the table. It was the letter. It fell from some height." Padshah recounts that he then said a silent prayer of thanks. The next morning, HPB remarked that the Masters had been watching him, and then repeated "word for word my unspoken thought" Caldwell, p. 170.
7. Mahatma Letter No. 2, at www.theosociety.org/pasadena/mahatma/ml-2.htm.
8. *The Mahatma Letters to A. P. Sinnett*, ed. A. T. Barker (Adyar: Theosophical Publishing House, 1998), p. 39.
9. C. Jinarajadasa, *Did Madame Blavatsky Forge the Mahatma Letters?* (Adyar: Theosophical Publishing House, 1934), p. 8.

10. Along with the Arya Samaj, for a time HPB was associated with the Sikh Sabha, a Sikh reform movement founded by Sirdar Thakar Singh Sandhawalia. In *The Masters Revealed: Madame Blavatsky and the Myth of the Great White Lodge*, K. Paul Johnson makes a good argument for the influence of Sikhism on the Theosophical Society, and he posits Sirdar Thakar Singh Sandhawalia as a good candidate for a flesh and blood Koot Hoomi (pp. 148–68).

11. Other impressive examples involve other modes of transportation. See the case of William Eglinton's Mahatma Letter while on board the S.S. *Vega* in Caldwell, pp. 174–77. Caldwell's book contains several other examples of either letters from or contact with the Mahatmas, independent of HPB. See also C. Jinarajadasa's accounts of "the precipitation or the mysterious arrival in some phenomenal way of letters at places when Madame Blavatsky was hundreds, if not thousands of miles away," and of "the phenomenal nature of the appearance of the KH script in a folded letter in transit through the post"; C. Jinarajadasa, pp. 5, 24.

12. For a good account of the masses of evidence in support of telepathy and other paranormal abilities, see Brian Inglis's very readable and still relevant *Natural and Supernatural: A History of the Paranormal from Earliest Times to 1914* (Dorset: Prism Press, 1992).

13. Helena Petrovna Blavatsky, "Precipitation," in *The Theosophist*, vol. V, nos. 3–4 (Dec/Jan 1883–84):64, in *Collected Works, 1883–84–85*, vol. VI (Los Angeles: Blavatsky Writings Publication Fund, 1954), p. 120.

14. A. T. Barker, 1998, p. 37.

15. Inglis, p. 286.

16. For what it's worth, Eisenbud's remarks about Serios's character suggest, to some extent, a resonance with HPB: "He does not abide by the laws and customs of our society. He ignores social amenities. . . . He does not exhibit self-control and will blubber, wail and bang his head on the floor when things are not going his way."

17. Colin Wilson, *Mysteries* (London: Watkins Publishing, 2006), p. 380. In *The Occult*, pp. 54–57, Wilson recounts examples of "bi-location" involving the playwright August Strindberg and the novelist John Cowper Powys.

18. Ouspensky, 1949, pp. 262–65.

19. A. T. Barker, 1998, p. 27.

20. See www.esotericbuddhism.net; and www.theosociety.org/pasadena/mahatma/ml-hp.htm.

21. For sheer complexity, this system has few rivals, although the ancient Egyptians spoke of nine components. See my *The Quest for Hermes Trismegistus*, pp. 60–62.

22. Fuller, p. 95; Joscelyn Godwin, *Arktos: The Polar Myth* (Kempton, Ill.: Adventures Unlimited Press, 1996), p. 42.

23. The relation to the musical octave is no coincidence, and readers familiar with the work of Rudolf Steiner and Gurdjieff will again see how both Steiner's notion of the earth "evolving" into its next planetary stage—Jupiter—and Gurdjieff's "Ray of Creation" emerge from this scheme.

24. Alice Leighton Cleather, *H. P. Blavatsky as I Knew Her* (London: Spink & Co., 1923), p. viii.

25. Michael Gomes, *Colonel Olcott and the Healing Arts* (Brentwood, Essex: Doppler Press, 2007), p. 1.

26. I can't resist mentioning a "synchronicity" that occurred while writing this section. Wanting to check some reference to Lafcadio Hearn, I pulled my copy of his *Selected Writings* (New York: Citadel Press, 1991, ed. Henry Goodman) from the shelf. I opened to page 408, and the first sentence I read was, "It is an English copy of Olcott's 'Buddhist Catechism.'"

27. Blavatsky herself evidently had healing powers. In his "Reminiscences of H. P. Blavatsky," Archibald Keightley relates how HPB "cured" him of erysipelas, a bacterial infection also known as "holy fire"; *Theosophical Quarterly* (October 1910):107. Blavatsky did not use her healing powers on herself because, as most "magicians" do, she had taken a vow never to use her "powers" for her own benefit (Wachtmeister, pp. 45–46).

28. William Butler Yeats, "Mohini Chatterjee," in *The Collected Poems of W. B. Yeats* (New York: Collier Books, 1989), p. 247.

29. Godwin, 1994, p. 343.

30. Caldwell, pp. 227–29.

31. Along with writing a biography of the Swiss alchemist Paracelsus, Hartmann was also an early member of the Ordo Templi Orientis, a sex-magic society later led by Aleister Crowley. He was also a supporter of the occult racist and proto-fascist Guido von List.

32. C. Jinarajadasa, *Letters from the Masters of the Wisdom* (Madras: Theosophical Publishing House, 1923), pp. 49–50.

33. See my *In Search of P. D. Ouspensky*, pp. 192–93.

34. Washington, p. 73.

35. Franz Hartmann, *Report of Observations Made During a Nine Months' Stay at the Headquarters of the Theosophical Society at Adyar* (Madras: Scottish Press, 1884), pp. 24–25.

36. Ibid., p. 35.

37. For a concise account of the "Coulomb affair," see Michael Gomes, *The Coulomb Case*, in Theosophical History Occasional Papers, vol. X, 2005.

38. Symonds, p. 149.

39. www.theosophy.org/Blavatsky/Letters%20of%20H.%20P.%20Blavatsky%20to%20A.%20P.%20Sinnett/Letters%20of%20HPB.htm.

40. Blavatsky, 1948, pp. 92–93.

41. Fuller, p. 141.

42. Ibid., pp. 136–38.

43. The vexing question of whether HPB was ever a "Russian spy" remains a subject of intense debate. Maria Carlson argues that a letter supposedly written by Blavatsky in 1872 shows that she offered her services as a spy to the Russian government (Carlson, p. 316), yet more than one researcher has questioned the authenticity of the letter. Blavatsky herself is said to have been more furious over Hodgson's claims that she was a spy than about his supposed "exposure" of her fraud; this could be taken as an admission of guilt or simple anger at a falsehood. As did Gurdjieff, Blavatsky seems to have played fast and loose with her political allegiances, crossing sides, as it were, when it suited her "higher" purposes. For an idea of the complexities involved, see K. Paul Johnson's article "Mikhail Katkov and HPB's Political Loyalties," www.katinkahesselink.net/his/katkov.htm.

44. Fuller, pp. 118, 159.

45. www.blavatskyfoundation.org/obituar2.htm.

46. Gomes, *The Coulomb Case*.

47. www.blavatskyarchives.com/coulomb/coulomb2a3.htm.

Chapter Nine: Secret Doctrines on the Road

1. Cranston, p. 288.

2. In the late 1880s, Countess Wachtmeister, Alfredo Pioda—a member of the Swiss Parliament—Franz Hartmann, and the psychologist, spiritualist, and novelist

Frederik van Eeden—who coined the term "lucid dream"—collaborated on founding a "Theosophical cloister" in Ascona, Switzerland, to be called "Fraternitas." The cloister didn't last, but a few years later, Ascona became the site of the "alternative community" at Monte Verità, the "Mountain of Truth," which attracted the likes of Hermann Hesse, Isadora Duncan, Rudolf Steiner, and Rudolf Laban, among many others. In the 1930s, Ascona also became the site of the legendary Eranos Conferences, held at Casa Gabriella, home of the Dutch socialite and Theosophist Olga Fröbe-Kapteyn, and presided over by C. G. Jung. See my *Politics and the Occult* (pp. 136–38) and *Jung the Mystic* (pp. 73, 165–66).

3. Constance Wachtmeister, *Reminiscences of H. P. B. and the Secret Doctrine* (Wheaton, Ill.: Theosophical Publishing House, 1976), p. 26.

4. Ibid., p. 27.

5. Ibid., pp. 8–9. See also Cleather, p. 3.

6. Wachtmeister, p. 42.

7. Ibid., p. 18.

8. British Library, Additional MSS.45287, *Letters* XLII, XLIII, pp. 95–97.

9. Her relationship with Vsevolod Solovyov, mentioned in the Introduction, is a case in point. Although she claimed that the Master took one look at him and would have nothing to do with him, she allowed him to visit her repeatedly—in Paris and in Würzburg—and importune her with requests to teach him how to do phenomena, and suggestions that she become a Russian spy. It should have been clear early on that Solovyov, a writer of historical fiction, was a sensation seeker out to make a name for himself, unlike his more well-known brother, Vladimir Solovyov, who was a serious spiritual philosopher; see *The Meaning of Love* (West Stockbridge: Lindisfarne, 1985), *War, Progress, and the End of History* (West Stockbridge: Lindisfarne, 1990), and *The Crisis of Western Philosophy* (West Stockbridge: Lindisfarne, 1996). But HPB was either too busy or too focused on her own work to take much notice of him, until she finally realized he was unsuitable material. By this time the damage was done, and her rejection of him as a *chela* led to his scandalous "exposé," published, significantly, only after her death. It may be of some import that Solovyov's companion during his Würzburg visit was Yuliana Glinka, a Russian agent and the person most likely responsible for bringing the forged anti-Semitic tract *The Protocols of the Elders of Zion* from France to Russia. See James Webb, *The Occult Establishment* (La Salle, Ill.: Open Court, 1976), pp. 241–49.

10. The debate over the validity of Hodgson's report is lively and ongoing. See www .blavatskyfoundation.org/obiteruary.htm, www.theosociety.org/pasadena/hpb -spr/hpb-spr1.htm, and www.theosociety.org/pasadena/hpb-spr/hpbspr-h.htm, for starters.

11. Cranston, p. 275.

12. Ibid.

13. www.blavatsky.net/gen/refute/sprpress.htm.

14. Ibid.; and Gomes, *The Coulomb Case*, p 21. For a concise and enlightening history of the criticisms against Hodgson's work, Gomes's book is essential. As early as 1903, Samuel Studd of the Melbourne Theospohical Society investigated Hodgson's work and found it "unconvincing," an assessment reached by Beatrice Hastings, K. F. Vania, Walter Carrithers, John Cutter, Leslie Price, Vernon Harrison, and others. Although K. Paul Johnson argues that Harrison's work does not exonerate HPB completely, it certainly points out flaws and inconsistencies in an investigation that has been accepted as accurate by practically every HPB biographer who was not a Theosophist.

15. Deborah Blum, *Ghost Hunters* (New York: Penguin, 2006), p. 92.

16. Ibid.

17. Inglis, p. 389.

18. Blum, pp. 218–21.

19. Sylvia Cranston makes the observation that like Einstein, Freud, and Darwin, Blavatsky seemed to *need* her illnesses in order to get the best work out of her (Cranston, pp. 312–13). Cranston may also have included in this list the novelist John Cowper Powys, author of the mystical masterpiece *A Glastonbury Romance*, who seemed to derive inspiration from his ulcers, and Friedrich Nietzsche, who made a philosophy out of the experience of convalescence. See Morine Krissdóttir, *Descents of Memory: The Life of John Cowper Powys* (London: Overlook Duckworth, 2007) and Friedrich Nietzsche, *Human, All Too Human*, trans. R. J. Hollingdale (Cambridge, U.K.: Cambridge University Press, 1986), pp. 8–11.

20. See my *Rudolf Steiner*, pp. 66–69.

21. Symonds, p. 183.

22. Cleather, p. viii.

23. *Letters of H. P. Blavatsky to A. P. Sinnett*, p. 205; see "Lethargy in the London Lodge," at www.phx-ult-lodge.org/Letters%20of%20HPB.htm.

24. Wachtmeister, p. 52.

25. Ibid., p. 61. According to some accounts, when the autopsy was performed on Gurdjieff's body, his doctor remarked that "his intestines were in such a state of disintegration and decay that he should have been dead years ago"; Colin Wilson, *The War Against Sleep* (Wellingborough: Aquarian Press, 1980), p. 74.

26. I've already mentioned Aleister Crowley's tongue-in-cheek remark that Blavatsky herself was the Ripper. Oddly, Jack the Ripper turns up in an article HPB wrote for her magazine *Lucifer*, "Psychic and Noetic Action," later reprinted in *Studies in Occultism* and available online at www.theosociety.org/pasadena/hpb-sio/sio-pan.htm. Another odd link between HPB and the Ripper is the relationship between the Theosophist Mabel Collins and Robert D'Onstan Stephenson, who has been pegged as a candidate for the Ripper's true identity. See www.katinkahesselink.net/his/farnell4.html and www.theosnet.ning.com/profiles/blog/show?id=3055387%3ABlogPost%3A76416&commentId=3055387%3AComment%3A77121&xg_source=activity. Oddly enough, Stephenson, who was something of a "black magician," contributed an article on "African Magic" to the November 1890 issue of *Lucifer*.

27. The feud involved an attempt by Elliot Coues to gain control of the Theosophical Society in the U.S.; Cranston, pp. 270–78.

28. See Kim Farnell, *Mystical Vampire: The Life and Works of Mabel Collins* (Oxford: Mandrake Press, 2005).

29. On another occasion, HPB had to apologize to a Miss Leonard after she accused her, in a libelous letter, of seducing Mohini Chatterjee, who had taken a vow of chastity. Mohini, it seems, had provoked the lady's attentions.

30. Cranston, p. 325.

31. Wachtmeister, p. 78.

32. Ibid., p. 30.

33. Ibid., p. 80.

34. Cleather, p. 67.

35. W. B. Yeats, *Autobiographies* (London: Macmillan, 1980), p. 179.

36. Wachtmeister, p. 43.

37. Yeats, 1980, p. 174.

38. Ibid., p. 180.

39. Ibid., p. 177.

40. Cleather, p. 15.
41. Ibid., p. 16.
42. Cranston, p. 365.
43. *Collected Writings*, vol. 12, pp. 488–89.
44. See my *A Dark Muse*, p. 102.
45. www.esotericinstructions.net, pp. 1–2. Readers interested in exploring HPB's "Esoteric Instructions" can find them at this site.
46. www.esotericinstructions.net, pp. 3–4.
47. www.theosociety.org/pasadena/invit-sd/invsd-1.htm.
48. In *The Book of the Law*, we are told that "the lords of the earth are our kin-folk" and that "we have nothing with the outcast and unfit: let them die in their misery." "Compassion is the vice of kings; stamp down the wretched and the weak: this is the law of the strong." "Pity not the fallen . . . strike hard and low and to hell with them." Similar admonitions pepper Crowley's text.
49. The still classic book on the subject is Nicholas Goodrick-Clarke, *The Occult Roots of Nazism* (New York: NYU Press, 1993). For confusion's sake, I'll add that Gurdjieff was also accused of inspiring the Nazi use of the swastika. See Louis Pauwels's highly disinformative *Gurdjieff* (New York: Weiser, 1972). Hyperborea became a central theme in the racially oriented esotericism of the Italian Traditionalist Julius Evola; see his *Revolt Against the Modern World* (Rochester: Inner Traditions, 1995). Evola, like René Guénon and other Traditionalists, is anti-HPB.
50. Interested readers should consult HPB's remarks about "duty" at www.theosociety.org/pasadena/key/key-12.htm.
51. Helena Petrovna Blavatsky, *The Secret Doctrine*, abridged by Michael Gomes (New York: Tarcher/Penguin, 2009).
52. Although all roads to Atlantis start in Plato's *Timaeus* and *Critias*, the central influence on HPB's ideas about the lost continent was Ignatius Donnelly's 1882 bestseller *Atlantis: The Antediluvian World*, which first presented the idea that survivors of Atlantis started civilizations in Egypt and the Americas. Atlantis receives much less attention in *Isis Unveiled* than it does in *The Secret Doctrine*, and one can't help but think that, having read Donnelly's book, HPB thought his ideas too good to leave out of her new work.
53. Gershom Scholem, *Major Trends in Jewish Mysticism* (New York: Schocken, 1961), pp. 398–99.
54. Agehananda Bharati, "Fictitious Tibet: The Origin and Persistence of Rampaism," at www.serendipity.li/baba/rampa.html.
55. Wouter J. Hanegraaf, *New Age Religion and Western Culture* (Leiden: Brill, 1996), p. 453.
56. See their *The Books of Kiu-Te or the Tibetan Buddhist Tantras: A Preliminary Analysis* (San Diego: Wizard's Bookshelf, 1983) and *Blavatsky's Secret Books: Twenty Years' Research* (San Diego: Wizard's Bookshelf, 1999).
57. Annie Besant, *An Autobiography* (Adyar: Theosophical Publishing House, 1939), p. 310.
58. Wilson, 1971, p. 337.
59. See my *Politics and the Occult*, pp. 125–32.
60. Louis Fischer, *The Life of Mahatma Gandhi* (New York: HarperCollins, 1997), p. 437.
61. James Hunt, *Gandhi in London* (New Delhi: Promilla & Company, 1978), p. 34.
62. Mohandas Gandhi, *Autobiography* (New York: Beacon Press, 1993), p. 67.
63. Pyarelal Nair, *Mahatma Gandhi*, vol. 1 of *The Early Years* (Ahmedabad, India: Navajian Publishing House, 1965), p. 259.

64. Gandhi, 1993, p. 321.
65. Tima Vlasto, "Gandhi, Theosophy, and Union Square Park in NYC," July 29, 2009; available at www.examiner.com/holistic-science-spirit-in-national/gandhi-theosophy-and-union-square-park-nyc.
66. Hari Kunzru, "Appreciating Gandhi through His Human Side," *New York Times*, March 29, 2011; available at www.nytimes.com/2011/03/30/books/in-great-soul-joseph-lelyveld-re-examines-gandhi.html?_r=.
67. Blavatsky, 1948, pp. 27, 23 25, 14, 21, 77; the full text is online at www.theo society.org/pasadena/key/key-hp.htm.
68. Blavatsky, 1959, p. 106. The full text is available online at www.theosociety .org/pasadena/voice/voice.htm.
69. *Eastern Buddhist* (old series) 5:377; *The Middle Way*, August 1965, p. 90.
70. Mircea Eliade, *Journal II, 1957–1969* (Chicago: University of Chicago Press, 1989), p. 208.
71. W. Y. Evans-Wentz, *The Tibetan Book of the Dead* (London: Oxford University Press, 1970), p. 7.
72. www.blavatskynews.blogspot.com/2010/05/blavatskiana-voice-of-silence.html.
73. K. Paul Johnson, *Initiates of Theosophical Masters* (Albany: SUNY Press, 1995), p. 4.
74. Blavatsky, 1948, p. 77.
75. Cleather, p. 21.
76. 19 Avenue Road isn't far from where I live in London. I was unable to determine whether the security-gated house that stands on the property now was the same that HPB spent her last days in, nor whether the seven-sided room or lecture hall still exists.
77. G. R. S. Mead, *Concerning HPB: Stray Thoughts on Theosophy* (Adyar: Theosophical Publishing, n.d.), p. 4.
78. Ibid., p. 5.
79. Caldwell, 2000, p. 322.
80. Fuller, p. 230; Cranston, pp. 370–78.
81. Mead, pp. 21–22.

CHAPTER TEN: THE MASTERS REVEALED?

1. Cleather, p. 9.
2. Ibid., p. 27.
3. Among Besant's own "trials" on joining the TS was her public denunciation of birth control, a cause she had previously championed and for which she was arrested in 1877 with her friend and fellow campaigner Charles Bradlaugh.
4. Washington, pp. 102–03.
5. Ibid., p.103.
6. Katherine Tingley, *The Gods Await*, Chapter 4, "My First Meeting with Blavatsky's Teacher" (Pasadena: Theosophical University Press, 1992); available at www.theosociety.org/pasadena/kt-gods/tga4.htm.
7. See en.wikipedia.org/wiki/Lomaland; and also www.sandiegohistory.org/journal/74summer/lomaland.htm.
8. For more on Katherine Tingley, see my *Politics and the Occult*, pp. 133–36.
9. See my article "Kandinsky's Thought Forms and the Occult Roots of Modern Art," available at www.theosophical.org/publications/quest-magazine/1405.
10. Washington, pp. 121–23.
11. See my *Turn Off Your Mind*, pp. 158–59.
12. For more on Jacolliot, d'Alveydre, Guénon, Ossendowski, and Roerich, see my *Politics and the Occult*.

13. Ibid., pp. 63–65.

14. Ouspensky, 1949, pp. 4–5.

15. See my *In Search of P. D. Ouspensky*, p. 245.

16. Fuller, pp. 7–8.

17. K. Paul Johnson, "Blavatsky and Her Masters," in *The Inner West*, ed. Jay Kinney (New York: Tarcher/Penguin, 2004), p. 241.

18. Quoted in Mitch Horowitz, *Occult America* (New York: Bantam Books, 2009), p. 190.

19. Fischer, p. 437.

20. www.ibe.unesco.org/en/areas-of-action/international-conference-on-education-ice/comenius-medal.html.

21. See my *Politics and the Occult*.

22. Ibid.

23. www.davidpratt.info/damodar.htm.

24. Steiner, p. 6. A Leyden jar is a device for storing electrical charges. It was invented in 1745 by Pieter van Musschenbroek.

Index

About the Author

GARY LACHMAN is the author of several books on the links between consciousness, culture, and the Western esoteric tradition, including *Swedenborg*; *Rudolf Steiner: An Introduction to His Life and Work*; *In Search of P. D. Ouspensky*; *A Secret History of Consciousness*; and *Politics and the Occult*. As a critic and journalist, Lachman has written for *The Times Literary Supplement*, *The Independent on Sunday*, *Fortean Times*, *The Guardian*, and other journals in the United States and United Kingdom, and is a frequent guest on BBC Radio Three and Four. A founding member of the rock group Blondie, in 2006 he was inducted into the Rock and Roll Hall of Fame, and his *New York Rocker* (written as Gary Valentine) is an account of his years as a musician. Born in New Jersey, he has lived in London since 1996, where he lectures frequently on his work. Lachman can be reached at www.garylachman.co.uk.